2013:

The End of Days or a New Beginning?

2013:

The End of Days or a New Beginning?

Envisioning the World After the Events of 2012

By Marie D. Jones

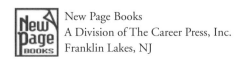

New Page Books
A Division of The Career Press, Inc.
Franklin Lakes, NJ

2013: The End of Days or a New Beginning?
Edited and Typeset by Gina Talucci
Cover design by Ian Shimkoviak
Printed in the U.S.A. by Book-mart Press

To order this title, please call toll-free 1-800-CAREER-1 (NJ and Canada: 201-848-0310) to order using VISA or MasterCard, or for further information on books from Career Press.

The Career Press, Inc., 3 Tice Road, PO Box 687,
Franklin Lakes, NJ 07417
www.careerpress.com
www.newpagebooks.com

Library of Congress Cataloging-in-Publication Data

Jones, Marie D., 1961-
    2013 : the end of days or a new beginning? : envisioning the world after the events of
    2012 / by Marie D. Jones.
        p. cm.
    Includes bibliographical references (p.   ) and index.
    ISBN 978-1-60163-007-0
    1. Maya calendar. 2. Maya astrology. 3. Maya cosmology. 4. Mayas—Prophecies.
    I. Title.

F1435.3.C14J66 2008
133.5089'974--dc22

                                                                                    2008005676

Dedication

For Max.
His eyes are green; his hair is blondish brown...
and his imagination is the key to the future.

Acknowledgments

Writing a book is never easy, so I am grateful for the help and support of so many people. First and foremost, thanks to my agent, Lisa Hagan, who is also my dear, dear friend. To Michael Pye and his amazing staff at New Page Books, thanks for your belief in me and your continued support for my work. To Lisa Collazo of Writewhatyouknow.com, what would I ever achieve without you?

To my mom, Milly, and my dad, John, for their love and continued support for me. One of these days it will pay off, I promise! To my sister Angella, my brother John, their families, and all my family members, of whom there are too many to mention. To my good friends and cheerleaders Andrea S. Glass, Helen "Sparkle" Cooper, Ron Jones, Marit Flowers, Jeeni, Sharon, Ginger, Lucy, John True, and especially to Larry Flaxman for his amazing support and input. I owe you!

To all of you who have read my other books and have taken the time to e-mail me and share your ideas and your friendship, I am grateful.

And thank you to Whitley Strieber for his insightful foreword, and to everyone who contributed an essay. I am so honored to have you all as a part of this book.

Contents

Part III
Ascendance: The Coming Evolution Revolution

Foreword

It's interesting that a non-believer in 2012 would be asked to write a foreword for a book about possible changes expected to happen on or around December 23 of that year. I am confidently expecting that December 24, 2012, will be pretty much the same as December 23. I am also expecting that plenty of people will anticipate the end of the world on that night, and plenty more will expect profound changes in human consciousness, neither of which are going to happen.

With that said, there are reasons why so many people are beginning to pay attention to the date on which the ancient Mayan Long Count calendar ends. To the Maya, this was, literally, the end of reality as they knew it. After that date, there would be another ideation of the universe. Conventional Mayan scholars tell us that the Maya had no idea about the existence of galaxies, let alone the notion that our solar system might be passing across the dead center of the plane of our galaxy on that date. It is obvious, though, that they were able to calculate the solstice correctly, working forward from their own time and using their own mathematical system. This was no mean feat, and suggests that their astronomical skills were, to say the least, extremely sophisticated. Our profoundly Eurocentric scholarship works from the basic assumption that we are, in all and everything, the superior culture—superior in science, knowledge of nature, and wisdom, and far less superstitious than past cultures.

Whether or not that's true, it has an unfortunate tendency to degrade our ability to fully embrace the implications of past ways of thinking, gathering, and using knowledge. So it's quite possible that Native American scholar Jose Arguilles, whose brilliant decoding of the Mayan Calendar has led to the current interest in 2012, is correct when he asserts that they did know about such things as galaxies, and were aware of the position of the Earth.

The idea that they might have known about galaxies is not far-fetched at all. The reason is that the galaxy nearest to the Milky Way, the Andromeda galaxy, can be seen (by a person with exquisite vision) as a disk with a suggestion of tiny stars around its edges. I know this anecdotally, because I know an amateur astronomer with such vision; he can also clearly see the moons of Jupiter with his naked eye.

Given the much clearer atmosphere and the much darker nights of Mayan times, it's easy to understand why their information about the sky might have been surprisingly sophisticated, despite their lack of telescopes. They cared about it deeply and observed it with extraordinary care, keeping records throughout hundreds of years.

Among the things that they and others understood, apparently from quite early times, was the significance of the precession of the equinox, the slow retrograde motion of the Earth's North Pole around an imaginary circle in the sky, caused by the planet being slightly off the horizontal.

The reason I can say this with confidence is that the Zodiac records the precession, and it is at least 2,000 years old. There is evidence from Babylonian and Sumerian writings that it is much older, along with evidence from Stone Age carvings that the constellation Taurus was known more than 10,000 years ago.

The Maya certainly knew about the precession, and there is something extremely strange about the Zodiac that suggests certain people in the past saw and used it as a template for a great plan of human existence, and in some extraordinary ways, emblemized their knowledge of their place in that plan.

The last four signs of the Zodiac that the North Pole has moved through are, in ascending order, Taurus, Aries, and Pisces. We are now in the process of moving into the fourth sign, Aquarius. Extraordinarily enough, there is evidence that our earliest Western civilizations were well aware of their position in the Zodiac. Between 4- and 6,000 years ago, during the Age of Taurus, the Mediterranean world was dominated by a bull cult that is reflected in the art left behind by Cretan and Mycenean civilizations. Remnants of the famous bull dance painted on the walls of the palace at Knossos on the island of Crete can be found today in bullfighting, still a popular sport in Spain.

The next age, Aries, commenced around 4,000 years ago, and is emblemized in the Old Testament, which mentions the ram 72 times, more than any other animal.

The Age of Pisces commenced at the beginning of the Christian era, and Christ, we should not be too surprised to find, is called the fisher of men; he gathered fishermen to his side to spread his gospel of transformation, and became known in poetry and myth as the Fisher King. The earliest Christian symbol was the fish, and it is still commonly used today.

All of this certainly suggests that the ancients at least respected their position on the Zodiac, and perhaps understood on a deeper level the famous teachings of the mythical father of alchemy, Hermes Trismegistus: "As above, so below."

As it happens—and it probably isn't an accident—2012 falls during the period of transition between Pisces and Aquarius. Of course, we have lost the knowledge that caused the ancients to build their worlds around the inner meaning of the Zodiacal signs they were under. However, it's becoming evident that the larger reality in which we live has not followed us into ignorance and the arrogance of ignorance, and we will—and are—being affected by the larger implication of the movement between signs, whether we like it or not.

Pisces is the fish, a creature swimming in the water, which gives it everything it needs: the space for its life to unfold, its food, and even its breath. Aquarius, however, pours out the water, leaving the fish stranded on dry land where it is not equipped to live. No longer will the waters of life support it. Now it must either change or die.

And suddenly we find ourselves standing before the reason this book is so important. We have indeed, as Pisces ends and Aquarius begins, arrived at just such a stark point in our evolutionary history. Earth can no longer support us. We must either change or die.

This book focuses on how to go about changing, because otherwise we are certainly going to die. In any case, we are going to experience the full upheaval of ending up in a situation in which the Earth—our water—is no longer going to be able to support us. And this is not something that's going to happen somewhere down the vasty halls of time. It is upon us right now. It's happening. And I will predict one change by 2012: By then, every human being on this planet is going to know for certain that the water is being poured out—in other words, the environment that has faithfully supported us all these years is collapsing.

As this is being written in January of 2008, the U.S. Department of Agriculture has just announced a further tightening of American wheat supplies, and prices, which have been rising now for a year, will most likely double by 2009. They will never return to present levels, and by 2012 (if not before), there will be many people in presently well-fed areas of the planet who no longer have enough to eat.

Our weather is in a state of upheaval, and there is evidence that this is being caused by a faster-than-anticipated increase in greenhouse gases in the Earth's atmosphere. In addition, spectacular and unprecedented melting of the Greenland ice sheet and the North Polar ice cap are flooding the North Atlantic with fresh water, making the collapse of the North Atlantic Current inevitable. The effects of its weakening could already be seen in the "year without a summer" that the British Isles experienced in 2007, and the extraordinarily brutal winter experienced worldwide in 2007–2008.

In addition, NASA has announced that the next solar max, which will reach its height in 2011–2012, is likely to be among the most powerful on record, meaning that it will have powerful effects on our planet, and its weather, as well.

Economically, mankind stands under a literal Sword of Damocles, as environmental changes work against established patterns of trade, especially in foodstuffs, and there is increasing evidence that both the Kuwaiti and

Saudi oil fields have peaked in production at a time when India and China are generating massive new demands for oil.

In addition, instability in countries possessing nuclear weapons raises the specter that such weapons could end up in the hands of terrorists, and be used to create a stunning reversal of the axis of world power if they were placed in crucial world cities and used as a threat.

Certainly, as Pisces gives way to Aquarius, the world is in a state of profound upheaval and deep change that is consistent with the meaning of the movement between the two signs, and the Maya have placed their marker of the end of the age at the correct time. Not only the Mayan Calendar, but also the world around us, tells us that this age is indeed ending.

As it ends, denial—which is the state we are in now—will give way to confusion, then astonishment, then finally to terror, and, in the end, acceptance of what cannot be changed. Right now, we are still trying to believe that some sort of change in the way we live—taking better care of the environment—will save the situation. However, the situation is already out of control. Just a year ago scientists were confidently predicting that the North Pole wouldn't experience iceless summers until at least 2050. But now it seems inevitable that this will happen in just the next few years—that, in fact, our first iceless summer could be as early as 2012. According to the National Snow and Ice Data Center, 2007 saw a fantastic decline in the amount of sea ice in the north. An area the size of Florida melted in just a few days. The effect of all this fresh water gushing into the North Atlantic is the same as what happened when Lake Agassiz collapsed 8,000 years ago. The flood of fresh water stopped the Gulf Stream in its tracks. The result was a 14-degree Fahrenheit decline in average temperatures that took place throughout the next few years. It was a hundred years before the Gulf Stream started again.

Such a temperature drop now—and it appears to already be underway—will radically reduce crop-growing seasons in what is presently the bread basket of the world—the United States, Canada, and the Ukraine.

So, the New Age hope that some sort of magical change will affect humanity on December 23, 2012, may or may not be true. And the idea that the world will literally end on that day appears far-fetched. However, we are indeed in an era of profound upheaval that will lead to fundamental changes in human life and human society. There is no question of this. The die is already cast.

This, also, then, is true: Somewhere in the deep past, beyond the mists of history, somebody created a vast scale that is measured in different ways by the Mayan Long Count calendar and the Zodiac, but with the same conclusion. This period is going to be a time of great change.

Whoever they were, their knowledge and their skills have been buried in the depths of forgetfulness, but their accomplishments have not. Look to the record, and you can see it. All those ages ago, some people saw so deeply into the nature of experience and the unfolding of time that they were able to point to a figure thousands of years into their own future, and make a calendar that would predict events. And it appears that they have called it exactly.

—Whitley Strieber,
author of *Warday*, *Communion*, *The Coming Global Superstorm* (which was made into the movie *The Day After Tomorrow*), and *2012: The War for Souls*, as well as many other books

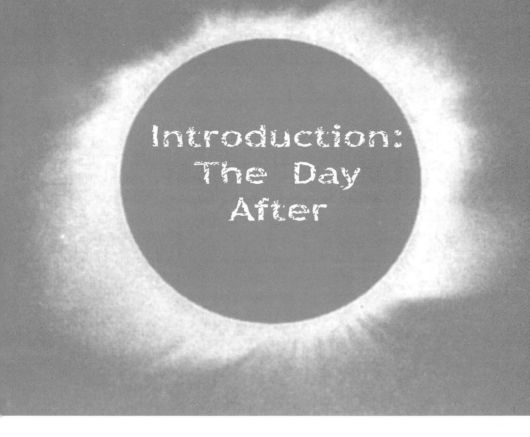

Introduction: The Day After

This is not a dress rehearsal for the apocalypse. This is not a pseudo-millennium. This is the real thing folks. This is not a test. This is the last chance before things become so dissipated that there is no chance for cohesiveness.
—Terence McKenna

Things alter for the worse spontaneously, if they be not altered for the better designedly.
—Sir Francis Bacon

It ain't over 'til it's over.
—Yogi Berra

The year 2012—everyone is talking about it. Some dread it, thinking it is the beginning of the end. Others await it with delicious anticipation, believing it to be the catalyst for a transformational period that will bring about a whole new way of being…a whole new world. The dawning of a new age.

Others wonder if anything, indeed, will happen at all (remember Y2K?), or if this whole "2012 enigma" is the invention of imaginative minds eager for something to live for, to look forward to, or even...to fear.

As metaphysicians and New Agers talk animatedly about the lining-up of cosmic forces, historians ponder the meaning behind the Mayan Long Count calendar and why it ends when it does (a few years from now), and biologists, scientists, and geneticists wonder at the increasing rate of information and technology and how it might save us from ourselves (or destroy us outright), the world continues to turn, heading toward a future some believe will be as dark as eternal night. Others believe it will bring about the return of the light. Either way, there is something in the air, and it must be talked about, discussed, and debated—maybe even be prepared for individually and collectively.

2013 will examine all of these beliefs, mythologies, and prophecies, and lay out all of the forces in play right now, today, that will shift and shape the future, as well as the many paradigms just waiting to stand, or fall, as we move toward "the year everyone is talking about." It will also present predictions by today's leading scientists, philosophers, and thinkers about just what might be in store for humanity throughout the next few years: earth changes, natural disasters, threats from the sea and from beyond the stars, political strife, survival issues, and a planet crying out for attention as its resources are used and abused. All of these will play a role in how this mystery will unfold, perhaps culminating in a wake-up call for every man, woman, and child alive today.

The winds of change are blowing. On that we can all agree. But whether those winds will obliterate us , or carry us with them into a new tomorrow, only time will tell for sure.

And while most everyone is asking what will happen that year, in 2012, this book will attempt to go one bold and daring step further and ask, what will it all look like in 2013?

Will it be the Apocalypse that so many feared—or the rebirth of the world and the transformation of humanity?

1

Prophesies
and
Predictions

1

Tales of the Quickening

For everything there is a season, and a time for every matter under heaven.
—Ecclesiastes 3:1–8

Time discovers Truth.
—Seneca

Time is speeding up.

There are still 24 hours in each day, and a fixed number of days in each month, with 365 days in each year. Or so it seems.

But for many, time is speeding up. There is a quickening afoot, a mutating perception of time moving faster and faster, with more and more information filling each hour, each day, each month...each year.

The 2012 enigma begins with such tales of quickening. The Maya civilization has long been associated with coming changes revolving around this mysterious year. To the Maya, the year marked the end of their Long Count calendar at a time when, some speculate, the world would end one phase and begin anew—a transformation of consciousness and a shift in the common perception of humanity, and its place in the grand cosmic landscape.

The story of 2012 must begin with the Mayan calendar, for this is where the mythology of mass transformation and an end to our known world originates most fully. The Maya civilization was a Mesoamerican civilization that spanned from southern Mexico to the Central American countries of Honduras, Belize, Guatemala, and El Salvador. The Mesoamerican civilizations of the Maya, Aztec, Toltec, Zapata, Mixtecs, and Teotihuanacos varied in some traits, most notably political leanings, but culturally they embraced common goals and pursuits, the influence of which can be seen today in art, language, and religious tradition.

The Rising of the Maya

The first Mayan settlements were established approximately 1800–1900 BCE, during the Early Preclassic Period, although historians state that the entire region was inhabited much earlier.

During the first millennium after the death of Christ, the Maya rose to eminence as a culture with an advanced understanding of astronomy and mathematical knowledge, as well as high art and ceremonial architecture, made visible in the stunning pyramids of Palenque, Tikal, and Chichen Itza. More than 5 million people embraced the Mayan culture at the height of the Classical Period, which most historians place at 250–900 CE, and today, the Maya and their descendants continue to populate the region, and hold on to their pre-Columbian ideologies and traditions, despite subsequent Spanish colonization and a more recent embrace of Roman Catholicism, as well as the merging of other cultural beliefs rising to prominence at the time.

During the height of the Mayan civilization, the people traded cacao, spices, jade, and obsidian with other Mesoamerican cultures, and even extended their reach to include what is currently Panama. The art of the Classical Period is considered to be some of the most intricate and sophisticated in the ancient New World, and Mayan architecture rivaled that of ancient Greece and Rome, with palatial royal homes and cultural monuments, such as the famed "stepped pyramids" and important religious "cave sites" that are still being used today in modern Mayan rituals.

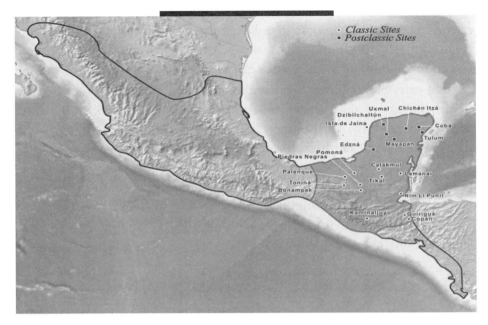

Figure 1.1: The Maya civilization was focused around these cultural mainsteads and major cities. Image courtesy of Wikimedia Commons.

Figure 1.2: The Palenque Ruins. Image courtesy of Wikimedia Commons.

The Codices

Most of what we know about true Mayan belief and culture comes to us from four pre-Columbian codices, all of them calendars that survived mass book burnings by the invading Spanish missionaries and priests that conquered the entire Yucatan region during the 16th century CE:

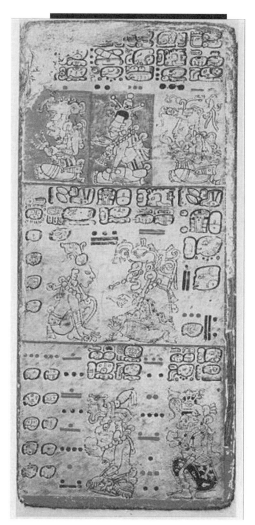

Figure 1.3: An image from the Dresden Codex.

∞ **The Dresden Codex**—considered the most critical of the surviving Mayan calendrical texts, this highly artistic combination of ritualistic works, almanacs, and astrological calculations involving the planet Venus is currently displayed at the state library in Dresden, Germany.

∞ **The Madrid Codex**—the product of eight different writers, currently in the Museo de America in Madrid, Spain.

∞ **The Paris Codex**—a prophetic codex that includes a Mayan Zodiacal system, which is in poor condition and currently at the Bibliotheque Nationale in Paris, France.

∞ **The Grolier Codex**—a more recent codex, discovered in a cave in the 1970s, its authenticity is questionable. Currently held in a Mexican museum, but not on display to the public (although several scanned pages are said to be available on the Internet).

These codices were written in Mayan hieroglyphics on paper made from tree bark known as huun. The codices took the shape of folding books, and were among possibly hundreds of such books in existence before the conquest by the Conquistadors. Other than these four codices, what we know of Mayan belief comes to us from sources written after the arrival of the Spaniards. Among these, the *Popol Vuh* has most notably taken the place of a true "bible" of the Mayan people, containing much information about Mayan mythology, cosmology, and creation.

The Sacred Calendar

There have been many excellent, detailed books written about the Maya, some of which are mentioned in the Bibliography of this book. But our main concern, in terms of the 2012 phenomenon, focuses primarily on the Sacred Calendar, a 260-day calendar used by the Maya and other Mesoamerican cultures until the rise of the Gregorian calendar in 1582.

The Sacred Calendar, also known as the "tzolkin," or "count of days," is an intricate measuring of time characterized by the usage of a 13-day count and a 20-day cycle that parallels it, with a different sign ascribed to each day, collectively known as a "uinal." The 13-day count and the uinal work together to give each day its own unique number (kon) and corresponding sign. The total number of possible number/sign combinations is 260, with each number and corresponding sign recurring every 260 days.

The Aztecs also used a similar day-sign calendar, which corresponded to the Mayan day signs; though the signs themselves varied in imagery, the meanings are said to be the same. Each day, with its own sign, is ruled by a different deity, which has its own distinct energy, called a Day Lord.

The Mayan Long Count Calendar

The Sacred Calendar is only part of the 2012 equation. The Mayan Long Count, most associated with the coming changes predicted for 2012, is the actual chronology used to track time throughout the millennia. Carl Johan Calleman, a physical biologist and expert on Mayan calendrical systems, and author of *The Mayan Calendar and the Transformation of Consciousness*, best describes the structure of the Long Count, which he states is inscribed

Figure 1.4A: The Mayan Calendar and day signs.

on almost all of the ancient pyramid and stelae sites throughout the Mesoamerican region.

"The Long Count consisted of 13 baktuns, which are periods of 400 tuns (360-day periods). One baktun is thus 400×360=144,000 days, amounting to 3,94.3 solar years." Calleman goes on to state that most archeologists agree that "the beginning date of the 13 baktuns of the Long Count was the day we would now call August 11, 3114 BCE." Thus, by adding that magical number of 13 baktuns to this start date, we end up with the date most 2012 "experts" call the end of the Mayan Calendar: December 21, 2012 CE. But this date may not be as accurate as originally thought.

Figure 1.4B: This Aztec Calendar shares many similarities with the Mayan Calendar. Image courtesy of Wikimedia Commons.

First, let's take a more detailed look at the Long Count.

The Long Count is essentially a vigesimal system (base-20) as opposed to our own base-10 decimal system. In a vigesimal system, each unit of a given position represents 20 times the unit of the preceding position. Interestingly, the Maya made an exception for the second-place value, which represented 18×20 for a total of 360 days, which closely approximates the solar year. However, the Long Count cycles are not dependent upon the accepted solar year system.

The Maya used the vigesimal system and counted by dots and bars, to represent zero and multiples of 20. The concept of zero was not even understood in Europe until the Muslims introduced it in Spain around 1000.

The Long Count system consists of five place values:

1. Baktuns—144,000 days (interestingly, the same number of those who will be raptured and saved in the New Testament book of Revelation).
2. Katuns—7,200 days.
3. Tuns—360 days.
4. Uinals—20 days.
5. Kins—1 day.

So, for example, the Long Count date of 10.15.5.1.2 would translate to 10 baktuns, 15 katuns, 5 tuns, 1 uinal, and 2 kins.

A period of 13 baktuns, totaling 5,125.36 years, is called a World Age. Four World Ages equal a precession cycle of approximately 25,627 years. Therefore, the most widely accepted end date is the last day of the 13-baktun cycle: December 21, 2012.

This end date coincides with a major astronomical event when a rare alignment of the December solstice sun and the Galactic Center of the Milky Way is going to occur. According to John Major Jenkins, author of *Galactic Alignment: The Transformation of Consciousness According to Mayan, Egyptian and Vedic Traditions*, this critical cosmological event may be behind why the Maya chose December 21, 2012, as their "end date." They even pinpointed a time, or so experts say, of 11:11 UT (Universal Time) when this moment of alignment would occur.

The Awareness of Time

That the Maya would even be aware of the precession of the equinoxes, which many historians and archeologists suggest was "discovered" by the Greek astronomer Hipparchus around 120 BCE, is an example of their advanced knowledge of such an intricate cosmic event, which was later refined and expanded upon by Newtonian physics in 1687.

The precession, as described by the American Heritage Dictionary, is "a slow westward shift of the equinoxes along the plane of the ecliptic, resulting

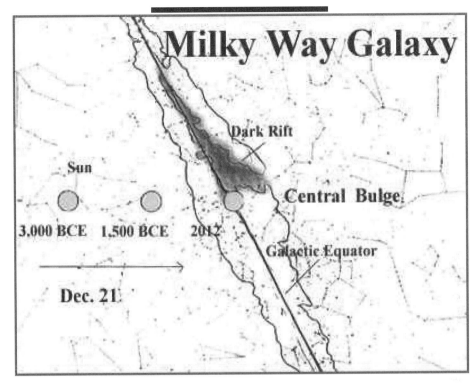

Figure 1.5: The Galactic Center of the Milky Way.

from the precession of the Earth's axis of rotation, and causing the equinoxes to occur earlier each sidereal year. The precession of the equinoxes occurs at a rate of 50.27 of arc a year, with a complete precession requiring 25,800 years." This precession is caused by the gravity of the sun and moon acting on the Earth's equatorial bulge, creating a wobbling in the orientation of the axis of the Earth at cycles of approximately 26,000–27,000 years.

Hipparchus's discovery of the sun's movement in relation to the Zodiac affected astrological beliefs. Western astrologers typically mark the beginning of the year at the spring equinox, when the sun is located in the constellation Aries. As the sun progresses through the Zodiac signs, the precession is complete, although the beginning of the year does change slightly each spring equinox, due to a slight alteration in the positioning of Aries.

An astrological age is defined as one movement of the sun from one Zodiac sign to another, and is approximately 2,150 years, with a total precession taking close to 27,000 years to complete. Astrologers point to each astrological age as having its own effects, influences, and impacts on the galaxy, and on us. The Maya were no stranger to "ages," having their own World Ages, which will be fully explored in Chapter 3.

The Galactic Alignment predicted for the winter solstice of December 21, 2012, is the one event most associated with the belief that the Mayan calendar was a profound indicator of "the shape of things to come." But there are varying theories about this actual end date itself.

In John Major Jenkins' book *Maya Cosmogenesis 2012*, he identified this rare astronomical alignment as the key behind the December 21, 2012, end date, and many experts in the study of the 2012 phenomenon join him in that belief. Jenkins points to the correlation of the Mayan, and more recently adopted Gregorian, calendar in determining this end date, with the beginning date of August 13, 3114 BCE as the most widely accepted beginning date of the Mayan Long Count calendar. Jenkins uses to his own vast research when pinpointing this date, which included trying to determine (with the help of other scholars), "what day it is, today, in the 260-day Mayan Calendar." By determining that, he could then work backward to clarify the beginning date, as well as forward to clarify the end date.

Many correlation problems arose for Jenkins, and other 2012 researchers, including trying to determine how the modern Gregorian calendar fit into the measurement of Mayan time, and how to properly reconstruct the Mayan Venus calendar. Jenkins also looked at surviving Mayan beliefs about the day-count among the Quiche Maya of the highlands (Jenkins lived and worked among the highland Maya when he began his research into Mayan cosmology in the 1980s), which claim to have an unbroken calendar tradition tracing back approximately 3,000 years.

In his book *Galactic Alignment*, Jenkins discusses the massive research he put into his end-date determination, as well as how it put him at odds with Jose Arguelles, a "planetary whole systems anthropologist," as described on his own Website, who, with his wife Lloydine, founded the Planet Art Network. Arguelles has studied the Mayan calendar and its prophecies for decades, and was instrumental in founding both Earth Day in 1970, and the Harmonic Convergence, which he initiated in August of 1987.

Arguelles promotes an interpretation of the Mayan calendar that is at odds with most Mayan scholars, and many other writers and researchers. His interpretation involves the influence of non-Mayan sources, and has more of a New Age take on the ancient calendrical tradition. He uses a different day-count, resulting in his own Dreamspell calendar, which is a 13-moon/28-day calendar. This 13-moon calendar does not take leap years into account, resulting in what mathematician Michael Finley stated as an inaccurate synchronization. Finley noted that the 365-day Mayan haab (the Mayan version of the 365-day calendar known to many of the pre-Columbian cultures of Mesoamerica, which approximated the solar year, comprising 18 "months" of 20 days each, plus an additional period of five days ["nameless days"] at the end of the year) didn't account for leap years, so its starting date, in Gregorian calendrical time, would advance by one day every four years. Thus, Arguelles's calendar, with its fixed start date of July 26, simply departed from the haab, and did not align with the day signs observed by the Maya themselves.

But Arguelles defended his own calendar as being "correct and biologically accurate" in terms of the whole planet, and he and his wife offer their extensive research into the "scientific and mathematic investigations of the timing frequency underlying the Mayan Calendar" through their Website and published works.

Thus, most 2012 experts work with the start date to the Long Count of August 13, 3114 BCE, or in Mayan terms, 0.0.0.0.1 (Day One), thus making the end date of December 21, 2012 (13.0.0.0.0. Day Last), the most agreed-upon as well. But two scholars, Linda Schele and Michael Coe, placed the end date two days later, at December 23. Schele, a noted expert in Mayan epigraphy and iconography, and founder of the Maya Hieroglyphic Workshop in Texas, authored many impressive texts relating to the Maya, including *A Forest of Kings* with David Friedel in 1990, and *Hidden Faces of the Maya* with Jorge Perez de Lara in 1997. Michael Coe is an anthropologist and archeologist, and is considered one of the foremost Mayan scholars. His books include *Breaking the Maya Code*.

Schele and Coe utilized the earlier works of Schele's mentor, Dr. Floyd Glenn Lounsbury, the American linguist, anthropologist, and Mayanist scholar, epigrapher, and developer of the Mesoamerican Long Count calendar correlation, a method that allows translation of a given Long Count date into its comparable Western calendar date. But the two-day discrepancy, according to Jenkins, was nothing but a misconception furthered by other researchers, and Jenkins continues to focus on the 21st of December as the correct end date.

But although Jenkins's start and end dates find great support in the 2012 research community, as fully documented in his books *Maya Cosmogenesis 2012* and *Tzolkin: Visionary Perspectives and Calendar Studies*, there is another end date that deserves equal attention and support, signifying that indeed, when it comes to the end of the world, timing is everything.

The End?

Carl Johan Calleman, mentioned earlier, believes the focus should instead be placed upon a date one year earlier: October 28, 2011. In his book *The Mayan Calendar and the Transformation of Consciousness*, Calleman points to the fact that this date in particular has the energy of 13 Ahau, which is the last day of a tzolkin round. He believes this to be a time when "the light will pass through all Underworlds without any obscuring filtering of darkness blocking the contact between humankind and the Divine."

Calleman places the start date of the Long Count one year later than many of his peers, at August 11, 3115 BCE. His extensive research is documented in *The Mayan Calendar and the Transformation of Consciousness* and *Solving the Greatest Mystery of Our Time: The Mayan Calendar*. He posits that the end date of December 21, 2012, is "indeed correct as far as archeology goes," but that the discrepancy occurs when we look at the beginning date, which Calleman claims is based upon a tradition in Izapa, where the Long Count itself was invented. This tradition, he goes on, states that time began on the day of the year that corresponds to August 11, "when the sun was at its zenith in this location." This day in the solar year, Calleman explains, had become a holy day in the region, one that, similar to our own Christmas, could never be changed.

"If the exact beginning date of the Long Count was based on a very local tradition in Izapa, it has no relevance as we apply the Mayan calendar on a global scale," Calleman states. He believes that the ancient Maya didn't have as much of an interest in the end date, no matter what it might be, as they did in the beginning, and to the people of Izapa, where the Mayan Long Count most likey first came into use, the origin date was really one of significance to their traditions alone. That the sun would be in its zenith in Izapa would have tremendous impact on the people of Izapa. But what about the rest of the world?

Instead, Calleman focuses on the origin date as part of a creation cycle that begins with the First Father erecting the World Tree. The end of this cycle, which will be explored more fully in Chapter 3, falls on the day of 13 Ahau and has great prophetic relevance. That day is October 28, 2011.

But no matter the actual end date (most 2012 experts agree that a year discrepancy is to be expected when looking at a calendrical system that covers billions of years), we have to ask: What does this have to do with time itself?

Time

Is time speeding up? Is there a quickening afoot? According to the Mayan calendar, or at least to the most popular interpretations of it, yes. Time is speeding up.

The calendar is associated with creation cycles, nine in total, that correspond to different levels of consciousness. These levels are called Underworlds. According to Calleman:

"Time, in fact, is speeding up as we transition from the materialistic Planetary Underworld that still governs us to a new and higher frequency of consciousness, the Galactic Underworld, in preparation for the final Universal level of conscious enlightenment."

This sense of time acceleration may not be a figment of the imagination. Mayan experts all agree that the Mayan calendar points to a system of Nine Underworlds, spanning from approximately 16.4 billion years ago to the end date of 2011/12.

The Nine Underworlds of the Mayan Long Count

Underworld	Start Date/Event	Duration
Cellular	16 billion years ago/big bang	1.26 billion years
Mammalian	850 million years ago/first animals	63.1 million years
Familial	40 million years ago/first primates	3.1 million years
Tribal	2 million years ago/first humans	180,000 years
Cultural	102,000 years ago/spoken language	7,900 years
National	3100 BCE/written language	396 years
Planetary	1755–1759 CE/Industrial Age	19.7 years
Galactic	January 4, 1999/Internet-global economy	360 days
Universal	February 10, 2111/conscious revolution	20 days

(Adapted from Calleman's *The Mayan Calendar* and 360-day Mayan Tun calendar, as per Ian Xel Lungold, *www.mayanmajix.com*.)

———

    The obvious timespans between Underworlds get shorter as the final end date approaches, which creates the theory that time itself is accelerating consciousness as we approach the final Universal Underworld, which has the duration of less than one year. Both Carl Johan Calleman and Barbara Hand Clow, author of *The Mayan Code: Time Acceleration and Awakening the World Mind*, point to the meaning of the Mayan calendar as a literal description or chronology of the divine process of creation, as evolving throughout the nine spans of time, each one moving the human species faster and faster toward a revolutionary transformation of consciousness. Although the emphasis is on the "Great Year" of the last 5,125 years of the Long Count, the entire spectrum of evolution can be seen in the Underworlds, culminating in the premier event of the Galactic Alignment in December of 2012. Barbara Hand Clow believes that the two conflicting end dates come together here, because "from my point of view, time and evolutionary acceleration will be completed on October 28, 2011, yet the Maya actually had the foresight to see that the Long Count will be completed on December 21, 2012, under the influence of critical astrological cycles."

The speeding-up of time, as it corresponds to the awakening of human consciousness, is a shared concept, as we will see in future chapters discussing information theory, singularity, and living systems. For the ancients, however, it mainly referred to awareness and evolution, in terms of human potential and development, which we will discuss in Chapter 3.

But the Mayan concept of time acceleration has a modern counterpart in the more modern Novelty Theory, Timewave Theory, and even the Jumping Jesus Phenomenon of Robert Anton Wilson. In a later chapter, we will look at another time acceleration theory called Technological Singularity along with accelerating change in cultural development. But for now, let's focus on a novel concept of time.

Novelty Theory

Novelty Theory, in brief, seeks to calculate the rate of novelty, or newness, in the universe as it relates to time. Novelty Theory has some basic tenets, among them (adapted from Wikipedia):

1. The Universe is a living system with a teleological attractor at the end of time that drives the increase and conservation of complexity in material forms. The word *teleological* is derived from the Greek word *telos*, meaning "end" or "purpose."

Teleology is the supposition that there is purpose or directive principle in the works and processes of nature.

2. Novelty and complexity increase through time, in a snowball effect, despite repeated setbacks.

3. The human brain represents the pinnacle of complex organization in the known universe.

4. As complexity and sophistication of human thought and culture increase, universal novelty approaches a Koch curve (a non-differentiable curve that is continuous and does not have a tangent at any of its points) of infinite, exponential growth.

5. In the time immediately prior to and during this omega point (singularity) of infinite novelty, anything and everything the human mind can conceive will occur simultaneously.

6. This historical endpoint date is December 21, 2012, coinciding with the end of the Mayan Long Count.

Timewave Zero Theory

The strange attractor toward which universal evolution plunges is called the Eschaton. In the early 1970s, Terence McKenna, along with his brother Dennis conceived of the Timewave Zero Theory that graphs novelty over time to reveal a fractal waveform, known as timewave zero, or, simply, the timewave. This graph indicates the time novelty is actually increasing and decreasing, and combines both numerology and mathematics to create a sequence that, when graphed according to a set of mathematical ratios, reveals a fractal nature and resonances in waveform.

Because the McKennas based some of their ideas on entheogenic experiences documented in their book *True Hallucinations*, and because the theory never received the peer review of scientific sources necessary to give credence and recognition, the Timewave Theory has taken off in more metaphysical circles, especially after the theory was revised by nuclear physicist John Sheliak, who found an error in the basic formulation and corrected it, thus strengthening McKenna's theoretical basis. He re-released the revised version as Timewave One. Timewave One is said to give a better picture of the ebb and flow of novelty during the specified times of World War II and the century that gave birth to Islam, two events McKenna considered critical for Novelty Theory.

Timewave software allows anyone to demonstrate the fractal timewave concept, which combines mathematical and philosophical elements of the I Ching and a mathematical fractal operation that results in a "timewave" mapping out novelty throughout the course of the big bang to the predicted Eschaton of 2012. McKenna himself describes this end date, or the Omega Point, as a time when we humans will encounter a trans-dimensional object that could include hyperspatial breakthrough, planetesimal impact, alien contact, historical metamorphosis, solar explosion, and quasar ignition at the galactic core.

John Sheliak stated on his Website (*www.levity.com/eschaton/sheliak*) that the I Ching, from which McKenna derived the timewave using the King Wen Sequence of Hexagrams, finds considerable correspondence in science, philosophy, and even quantum mechanics. When viewed as a system that reflects a process of flow, motion, or change in natural or human experience, Sheliak commented, "If correct, Novelty Theory is then a description of the form in which this information expresses itself—i.e. the TimeWave."

People interested in trying out the timewave software can visit *www.timewave2012.com* or google Fractal Time 7.1.

Jumping Jesus Phenomena

A more intriguing time acceleration theory comes to us via author Robert Anton Wilson, who coined the term *Jumping Jesus Phenomena* to describe the exponentially, or even logarithmically, shorter periods of time between information-processing-systems invention and development; that is, the time between the library at Alexandria, Jesus, and Gutenberg's Printing Press; and between Gutenberg's Bible to the first commercially published book, going on and on until a critical mass or singularity is achieved. Again, this snowball effect of accelerating information corresponds to accelerating perception of time, and, to the Maya, accelerating evolutionary development of human consciousness. Anton Wilson is stated to have first discussed this Jumping

Jesus Phenomena during a seminar he gave in 1988, "The Acceleration of Knowledge," during which he theorized that information has doubled throughout history, with each doubling coming faster and faster.

$$\infty$$

So, if time is hurtling our species and our universe toward a point of singular exponential growth, development, and transformation, what is there to fear about the end of days the Mayan calendar hints at? Before we examine the more transformative aspects of time acceleration, let's stop and take a look at exactly what many believers think we should fear.

2
End of Days

Don't worry about the world coming to an end today. It is already tomorrow in Australia.
—Charles M. Schulz

It's the end of the world as we know it, and I feel fine...
—R.E.M.

We are all going to die. Well, not all of us; according to the most prevalent end-of-the-world prophecies associated with 2012 is the Judeo-Christian concept of a coming Apocalypse that will cleanse the Earth of wicked unbelievers, and ascend the righteous to the heights of heaven during the Rapture. Either way, none of us will get out of this alive.

In Chapter 1, we discussed the various prophecies and predictions associated with the Mayan Long Count calendar and the various time acceleration theories that speak of a great quickening, a period of rapid spiritual and physical evolution that will lead to a spectacular transformation on or around December 21, 2012.

But the Maya, modern theorists, and philosophers, such as Terence McKenna, are not the only ones shouting from the rooftops about the significance of the year 2012. Religions based upon Western fundamentalist Abrahamic thought, or the Big Three of Judaism, Christianity, and Islam, are all moving toward a final scenario that is anything but transformative and positive, anything but joyful—except to those righteous few who believe they alone will cross the threshold of a final judgment to reign with God forever in heaven.

Revelations and Speculations

Eschatology is the study or doctrine of what various religions believe will occur at the end of the world. Based upon the Greek term for "last discourse," Judeo-Christian eschatology specifically concerns itself with "the four last things" that will happen when the lights go out for good. There is also individual eschatology, which deals with what happens to humans after they die, but we are concerned more with general eschatology, which indicates four specific events that will coincide with the Apocalypse:

1. The Second Coming of Christ.
2. The resurrection of the dead.
3. The Last Judgment of the dead and the living.
4. The final separation of the damned and the saved.

Throughout the Bible's Old and New Testaments are predictions about this end time. In Mark 9:1, we are told that Jesus prophesized the coming Kingdom of God. "Verily I say unto you, that there shall be some of them that stand here, which shall not taste of death, till they have seen the Kingdom of God come with power." Yet more than 2,000 years later, Christians still await this event and the four last things…none of which have yet come to pass.

Much of the rising interest in the Christian apocalyptic vision of a world that ends in fiery and bloody battles between good and evil comes as we inch toward the year 2012, a year already rampant with mythological and spiritual connotations. Yet we forget that throughout the last 2,000 years, the Apocalypse has been expected, including just seven years ago during the rather anticlimactic turn of the millennium. But the belief that the end days are near is once again at the forefront of fundamentalist Christian thought, and on the lips of those hoping to be among the lucky raptured who will not be "left behind," to quote the name of a hugely popular series of End Times novels selling like hotcakes.

But why? What is it about end-of-the-world scenarios, especially those of a more violent bent, that turn us on so much? Could it be because these visions of doom and gloom offer us a chance to think about what the world might be like if we were to start all over from scratch? Clean the slate? Get it right this time? Those of us who survived, anyway...

In the year 1033, 1,000 years after the death of Christ, believers looked toward the heavens for signs of the return of Jesus and the beginning of the end. It happened again in 1666 when believers combined the millennium with the number of the Beast described in the Apocalypse of St. John the Divine. And, as stated previously, it became the number-one hot topic just prior to Y2K, a year that turned out to be about as anticlimactic as 1975 or 1983 or 2004…years like any other.

The Apocalypse of St. John the Divine, also known as the Revelation, or book of Revelation, is basically a bizarre and imaginative vision of John of Patmos, a man who eats a strange little book and has a powerful and profound vision of the future. In fact, many scholars and philosophers, including George Bernard Shaw, have suggested John ingested a psychedelic substance, perhaps mushrooms, and was simply conveying the images of his "trip."

Regardless of the source of John's wild imaginings, he does refer throughout Revelation to the prior prophecies of both Daniel and Ezekiel in the Hebrew Old Testament, and many of his predictions match theirs. Scholars who have objectively studied Revelation point to the lack of consistency, and the lack of images that even remotely resemble Christ in the way he is depicted in other New Testament sources. But most readers, and believers, concern themselves with the apocalyptic content that begins in the third chapter, when John enters into the spirit and goes out of his body. From this point on, John's vision closely matches that of Ezekiel (who came before him), with images of the flying throne of Jehovah and the same four beasts Ezekiel once saw surrounding Jehovah: the lion, calf, man, and eagle.

The entire book of Revelation could be a retelling of the prophecies with which John must have been familiar from his own religious upbringing, with some of his own interpretation added in for good measure. Little of John's vision of seven trumpets signaling the coming of plagues, death, wrath, hellfire, and damnation make any sense in conjunction with other New Testament teachings of a loving and forgiving God. This holds little weight with those obsessed with the idea of the righteous being uplifted and raptured away from the wicked and sinful, left on earth to suffer a brutal punishment from a vengeful deity.

John reports that "the Word of God" will return in the end on a white horse and wear many crowns as he and his heavenly troops vanquish the Beast, or Antichrist, (who over the years has been associated with Nero, Hitler, and George W. Bush/Dick Cheney), and his minions and all of the worldly kings. As religious fundamentalism has been in the news, thanks to the terrorist acts of extremists on all sides of the fence, many believers pointed to the coming of the second millennium as "the time at hand" of which John warned. As the battle cry went up between fundamentalist Judeo-Christianity on one side, and fundamentalist Islam on the other, many look at this newfound antagonism as the final sign of the End Times. Yet few remember the Crusades and wars of past centuries, when these same armies raged and battled, never resolving conflicts that persist to the present day. When it comes to the end of the world, we could say that those who seem to welcome it have selective historical memory.

Take the many books by author Hal Lindsey, whose *Late Great Planet Earth* sold millions of copies when it hit the market in the 1970s and introduced believers and non-believers alike to a whole chronology of End Times predictions. Followed by books such as *Satan Is Alive and Well On Planet Earth* and *Planet Earth: The Final Chapter*, these books made bold predictions of events, including the general year in which they would occur. And just as boldly, when those events failed to happen, the author went on to write more books explaining why the event dates were now different, bumped up a few years for whatever reason made the most sense.

Other authors did likewise, selling tons of books and making tons of money predicting world events that never quite happened, then writing new best-selling books to explain why the time line for Armageddon kept moving up. To this day, Lindsey and his counterparts, such as John Hagee, author of *Jerusalem Countdown* and *From Daniel to Doomsday: The Countdown Has Begun*, and Tim LaHaye and Jerry B. Jenkins of the famed, hot-selling fictional "Left Behind" book series continue predictioning the End Times, while promoting the personal participation of believers in bringing about the End Times as God's faithful warriors.

This form of Dispensational Premillennialism, as promoted by the "Left Behind" books, incorporates the four events of Christian eschatology: the millennium interval of 1,000 years of Christ's rule; the Tribulation seven-year interval when the Antichrist rises to power; the war of Armageddon in which most people on Earth will die; and the Rapture of born-again believers. Dispensational Premillennialism (DP) itself is one of several End Times eschatological theories of various Protestant denominations and other Christian sects, mainly fundamentalist and evangelical churches. DP was once considered a heresy, and found rebirth in the work of John N. Darby, minister of the Church of Ireland in the 1830s. Similar to an earlier theory called Historical Premillennialism, DP promoted the belief that the Tribulation would precede the Second Coming of Christ and the subsequent establishment of his Kingdom on Earth for 1,000 years. Then the Final Judgment would occur.

Interestingly, there is a war among DP believers because its advocates, who believe that moral decay will bring about the return of Christ, are actually delaying that return by speaking out against such immoralities as gay marriage, adultery, premarital sex, and abortion. By opposing these immoralities, hardliner DPers state, they are in fact delaying the end of the world and the Rapture itself!

The Rapture

The Rapture has become a sore spot for varying Premillennialist theories. Competing Rapture theories include:

∞ **Pre-Tribulation Rapture**—it happens just before the Tribulation, thus freeing "believers" from the horrors of the Tribulation.

∞ **Mid-Tribulation Rapture**—it happens 42 months into the Tribulation. Beforehand, the Antichrist brings world peace, but at the 42-month point, all hell, so to speak, breaks loose.

- ∞ **Post-Tribulation Rapture**—it happens after the Tribulation, and the faithful will experience the horrors right alongside the sinners.
- ∞ **Pre-Wrath Rapture**—a new theory that claims the Church must experience most of the Tribulation before being raptured.
- ∞ **Partial Rapture**—has the faithful born-agains raptured quickly, the newly born-again later on in the Tribulation.

Intriguingingly, the word *rapture* never appears in the Bible. The word is of Latin origin, meaning "having been seized." Its Greek equivalent, as found in the Greek version of 1 Thessalonians 4:17 is *harpazo*, which, when translated to English, means, "to be caught up, snatched away." The actual word Paul uses in this biblical excerpt is translated to mean, "raised from the ground."

The word *rapture* became a popular term in Christian eschatology much later in the 1830s by the same John Nelson Darby who helped bring about the rise of both Premillennialism and Dispensationalism at the end of the 19th century.

Aside from the actual origin of the word itself, the concept of rapture remains a prominent part of modern fundamentalist and evangelical belief that the good and holy will be removed from the hell on earth we are soon to face. Or some think we should have already faced the Rapture, for predictions about the actual date of the entire process leading to rapture and beyond have run the gamut from:

- ∞ 47 CE and the fall of Jerusalem.
- ∞ 1000 CE as the first millennium.
- ∞ 1992 as predicted by the Korean group "Mission for the Coming Days."
- ∞ 1994 as predicted by Pastor John Hinkle of Christ Church Los Angeles.
- ∞ 1998 as predicted by Marilyn Hagee in *The End of the Age*.
- ∞ 2000 as the Y2K.
- ∞ 2012 as the Mayan calendar end date.

Keep in mind, this is only a handful of the hundreds, if not thousands, of predictions made for the End Times, which one can easily access online at

Websites such as The Doomsday List and *www.surfingtheapocalypse.com* that actually track and list predictions from various sources. Luckily, none of them have yet come to pass!

Conflict Over the Final Conflict

Although all Premillennialist beliefs teach that the Tribulation will be followed by 1,000 years of blissful peace under Christ's rule until the final battle with Satan is won, there are varying theories as to some of the specifics:

∞ *Amillennialism—A belief system present in early Christianity that posits that the Kingdom of Heaven is here today and now, and that good and evil will exist side by side until Christ returns and the good ones are raptured, the bad ones taken to hell, and history will end.*

∞ *Postmillennialism—Arose during the early 19th century, and says that the Kingdom of God is now being extended over the earth through preaching and evangelizing, and that the entire human race, including Jews, will become Christians right before Jesus returns, resurrects the dead, and conducts the last judgment.*

∞ *Preterism—Suggests events prophesized in Revelation and the New Testament have already occurred in the late 60s CE and into the 70s CE, when the Temple of Jerusalem was destroyed. Many scholars agree that when Jesus talked about the end of the world, and when John had his Revelation, they both were referring to events in their own "time."*

∞ *No Millennialism—Skeptics and liberal Christians believe that the books of Daniel and Revelation are visions, hallucinations, or nightmares, not future predictions, and hold little value for today's Christians. Many also believe Revelation was written to help the early Christian movement hold up to Roman prosecution, bolstering a sense of avenged righteousness against a powerful wicked enemy.*

Roman Catholics in general follow Amillennialism, but do not use the term *Rapture*. Mormons, or members of The Church of Jesus Christ of Latter-Day Saints, believe that Jesus will appear at the beginning of the millennial era and follow the usual time line of End Times, although they differ in their belief that even the unsaved will be resurrected at the end of the millennium.

Interpretations of the End

Christians are not the only religious group with eschatology. In fact, all major religions, and a few minor ones, have their own version of how it will all end—the ultimate destiny of humanity. Mystical sects suggest more of a transformational experience, which will be discussed in the next chapter, but for many religions, and certainly all Western monotheistic religions, doctrines include that there will be "chosen" people saved even as the unworthy are punished, and that one true religion will be delivered from the wrathful judgment of God and ushered into heaven.

Judaism refers to the end of the world as "Acharit hayamim," during which catastrophic events will destroy the old world and create a new world. God will ultimately be recognized as the one true ruler of everyone. There will be great conflict and suffering, according to the Talmud Avodah Zarah, page 9A, which states that our world will exist for only 6,000 years. Using the Jewish calendar with time beginning at the creation of the first man, Adam, we can posit that the end of days will occur at or before the year 2240 CE, which is the year 6000 in the Hebrew Calendar.

In order for this to come about, as in any eschatology, certain conditions must be met. Jewish tradition suggests that all Jews will return to Israel; all of Israel's enemies will be defeated; a third Jewish temple will be constructed in Jerusalem; the dead will be revived/resurrected; and a Jewish Messiah will be the anointed King of Israel, who will divide the land into the original tribes, then be attacked by Gog, King of Magog, in the final battle of Armageddon.

The other major Western religion, Islam, also believes in an end time called *Qiyamah*, which is translated to mean "Last Judgment." This will also be a time of challenges and judgment, with such concepts as the resurrection of the dead, the punishment of the sinful, and the salvation of the righteous in Jannah, or Heaven. The three Western religious traditions share this basic Abrahamic eschatology, even as they share the basic concept of the God of Abraham at the core of their doctrinal beliefs.

Eastern traditions also predict an end time. Buddha predicted that his own teachings would vanish within 500 years of his death, but that was later expanded to a period of 5,000 years; actual events or steps were laid out to measure these stages, but many scholars wonder at these concepts, which were added during the Middle Ages. Modern Buddhists, such as Hindus, believe in a general cycle of creation and destruction, but there is no end of the world in fire and brimstone, only a personal advancement to Nirvana.

Hindus have prophecies described in the Puranas and Bhagavad-Gita texts pointing to a world that tumbles into chaos and conflict, and that wherever this chaos exists, an avatar will arise to bring back purity and righteousness. Hindus do not believe in eternal damnation of souls, or any specific end time. Time is cyclical, with different "yugas," or ages, and their counterpart avatars, appearing accordingly. Interestingly, similar to the Mayan calendar, the cycle of yugas is directly related to the amount of chaos and evil in the world, with the current yuga being the most evil, and therefore bringing about a cycle that is specifically devastating and requiring of a "bottoming out" of humanity before the avatar can restore order and purity. The Hindu understanding of the cycle or "Kalpa" (in which both external event and internal spirit move through a pattern of decline) does actually have an end date, according to the Brahma Kumaris World Spiritual University of orthodox Hindus, putting the final over and out in the year 2039 CE, when the final avatar will incarnate as Kali, and bring about the destruction of all wicked people.

The oldest eschatology in recorded history is that of Zoroastrianism. A fully developed eschatology was established by 500 BC, and many scholars point to the similarities with Christian, Judaic, and Islamic End Times prophecies, suggesting that the three great Western traditions were all influenced by the earlier ideas expounded in Zoroastrianism, including the concepts of a world ending in a devouring divine fire, the Final Judgment of souls, and the final perfection of the world, or Heaven on Earth.

The oldest mythologies contain stories of both creation and destruction, and a cosmic cycle that would continue, despite the interference of humans. These myths, stories, and legends have permeated religious and spiritual traditions, including many Native American traditions. Because much of these traditions speak of a positive transformation, they will be discussed further in the next chapter, but here are a few basic End Time beliefs.

The Hopi tribal leaders such as Dan Evehema and Thomas Banyaca have long prophesized the coming of the End Times, coinciding with the coming of the white man, in which the earth would suffer degradation and even potential seismic and cosmic chaos, until the return of the Pahana or True White Brother, who would restore wisdom and usher in the Fifth World. They call this the "Day of Purification."

The Lakota believe that this savior will come in the form of a "White Buffalo Calf Woman" who will purify and restore the world's harmony and balance. White buffalo have been spotted throughout the last 10 years, leading many tribal elders to suggest this prophecy is at hand.

Even Rastafarians have an end time, which they believe began with the crowning of Haile Selassie as the Emperor of Ethiopia in 1930. Closely following Ethiopian history, Rastafarians suggest Selassie will soon reveal himself as God, and call for the day of judgment against the wicked, which will be followed by an exodus of the righteous back to Africa at Mount Zion.

The commonalities of End Times theories strongly suggest a shared belief in the cycle of birth, death, and rebirth, and the promise of righteousness and judgment. These elements are present even in the End Times predictions of individual prophets and seers, many of whom obviously speak from their religious backgrounds and the influences of the doctrine to which they have been exposed.

The Old and New Testaments, the Torah, Koran, and other major religious texts all speak of the words and visions of the prophets, from Daniel to Ezekiel to Mohammed to Jesus. But more modern voices have also seen the future, scrying similar visions of massive destruction, trials and tribulations, upheavals of both geological and political natures, and the great judgment of humankind.

There have been sorcerers, scryers, and seers through the ages, but most of us know the names of only a select few. Most, such as the Abbot Johannes

Trithemius, who spoke with angels and predicted the end of the world in 2233 CE, and St. Malachy, who stated that the final pope before world's end would be named Peter, follow the usual pattern of end time events already discussed at length. Though Malachy mainly focuses on the role of pontiffs in the coming of the End Times, the prophets of the past have been heavily marked by preexisting eschatology, offering little new information about the general plan of what will happen when.

Nostradamus

Most added details to the End Times story have come in more modern times, with the likes of Nostradamus, the Prince of Prophets. Born in Provence, France, in 1503, Michel de Nostredame (Latinized later to Nostradamus) was the son of Jewish converts, and a highly educated student of the classics, Hebrew, astrology, the Kabbalah, and ancient Greek prophecy. He even studied magic and esoteric arts, and later focused on philosophy and medicine.

In 1555, he published *Les Propheties*, the book for which he is most widely known. Between 1555 and 1568, he composed "Centuries," which is made up of 10 groups of approximately 100

Figure 2.1: Michel de Nostredame. Portrait painted by his son Cesar de Nostredame.

quatrains or verses that prophesized about events from 1555 to the end of the world in 3797 CE. Nostradamus practiced his prophesies at night, seeing the events as if he were looking into a mirror, recording them, and then using his knowledge of astrology and astronomy to calculate precise dates for each vision.

Many scholars have poked and prodded these quatrains, interpreting them to fit historical and political events of the past and present, but our only concern here is with the Apocalypse, and Nostradamus used a planetary "clock" of 60 years to date his prophecies, based upon the knowledge of planetary influence at the time. This Nostradamus Code, if you will, uses periods of 60 years, or "normae," to date the events he predicted. Sixty is also the magic number used by Chinese astrology to denote a complete astrological cycle.

Scholars have argued about this orbital period and its flaws at dating the quatrains, but Nostradamus mentioned significantly specific clues as to when we might expect the final curtain. Again, much of it follows Christian eschatology, and all of it is open to interpretation, but the seer focuses on the appearance of three Antichrists, major wars, and a final Apocalypse that will, again, happen a long way off from 2012.

Yet others argue that Nostradamus's prophecies may be happening much quicker than he even expected, with the appearance of the first two Antichrists—Napoleon and Hitler—having already occurred. And according to modern American psychic Jean Dixon, the third Antichrist was born on February 5, 1962. He would be now in his mid-40s, coming into power at age 37 in 1999 during a solar eclipse both Dixon and Nostradamus predicted. Nostradamus also predicts that the one who would deliver us from the third Antichrist would come from somewhere near Vienna, or Orleans, and would also be alive now, in our time. After a predicted 25 years of rule under the third Antichrist, we are told of a Golden Age around the year 2024 CE, which coincides with the popular calculation of the Age of Aquarius (2023 CE).

This means, according to Nostradamus the seer, we will still be alive and kicking in 2013—in the midst of hell under the rule of the Third Antichrist, mind you, but we will be alive and kicking.

Nostradamus believed that the earth was created in 4137 BCE, and that there were seven millenniums. If his prophecies, and their popular interpretations are correct, we are living at the end of the sixth millennium, and the seventh holds nothing but the promise of chaos and strife. He mentions a "year of the great seventh number," which must coincide with the arrival of the seventh millennium in 2000 CE. Nostradamus believed that this would mark a time of apocalyptic events, but that the earth itself would last until

3797 CE, for a total planetary life span of approximately 7,970 years. Interestingly, some scholars claim he also predicted a future nuclear holocaust when he stated, "the rains will be so diminished and such abundance of fire and fiery missiles shall fall from the heavens that nothing shall escape the holocaust." This could also be interpreted as a supervolcanic eruption, or even an asteroid attack from on high!

It's hard to point the finger of blame on Nostradamus (or any other prophet) for failed predictions. Nostradamus, according to author Rene Noorbergen's *Nostradamus Predicts the End of the World,* prophesized that before the year 2000 CE, the Arab world would wipe Israel off the map, New York City would be obliterated by a massive earthquake, and that the U.S. would align with Russia against China in a Third World War. None of which has yet to happen, begging the question, when predictions and prophecies fail to materialize, is it the fault of the prophet, or of those interpreting the prophecy? In Chapter 4, we will discuss a third stunning possibility for failed predictions.

Helena Petrovna Blavatsky

Another intriguing seer was Helena Petrovna Blavatsky, the founder of the theosophy movement. In 1888, Blavatsky claimed that the lost continent of Lemuria, a sister to Atlantis, was the home of a "third root race" that was destroyed by a violent volcanic eruption. Blavatsky, the daughter of a Russian army officer, believed there were seven root races, and that life on earth would end with the appearance of the seventh, at which point the survivors would all move to the planet Mercury to begin anew. Students of theosophy believe that the sixth root race exists now, and will develop throughout thousands of years, eventually replacing the current populace. Thus, the year 2012 as an end date seems way too soon for such an evolutionary leap and a one-way trip to Mercury.

A peer of Blavatsky's, often called the Prophet of the New Age, Aleister Crowley claimed to have been visited in the spring of 1904 by an Egyptian entity called Aiwass, who foretold to Crowley the end of Christianity. In Stephen Skinner's *Millennium Prophecies*, he writes of Crowley's prediction that the end time period would be rife with violence, war, and devastation (including the end of Christianity), to be followed by a golden new age.

Crowley wrote "The Book of the Law," or "Liber Al vel Legis," a three-chapter prose/poem that made the author a modern prophet to his many followers, who claim his channeled writings predicted the Balkan War of 1912 and World War I. But as far as an actual End Times date, Crowley's writings were vague at most, and poetic at best, referring to a war in Europe around 1997 that never manifested, and a conflict spreading throughout Eastern Europe, with the end of the century as a time of "direful judgments." Crowley has since fallen out of favor, except for the small and loyal following of magickal practitioners and those still trying to figure out if he was really the Beast 666 of Revelation, as he claimed to be.

Edgar Cayce

The most well-known modern prophet who "saw" End Times events is no doubt Edgar Cayce, the so-called sleeping prophet. Born in 1877 in Hopkinsville, Kentucky, Cayce was poorly educated, but at a very early age, he showed evidence of a talent for mastering his school studies by sleeping on his books. By age 21, he had developed a throat paralysis, which threatened to permanently disable his vocal chords. When doctors were unable to reverse the situation, Cayce took it upon himself to cure it by going into the same hypnotic sleep state he had during his studying, and in this trance state, he was able to recommend a cure that eventually fully restored his voice and throat muscle ability.

Figure 2.2: Edgar Cayce in 1910.

For more than 40 years, Cayce demonstrated this incredible ability to put himself into a self-induced sleep state and tap into the vast knowledge of the universe to cure the illnesses of others, including his own son, who almost lost his eyesight, but was cured at the advice of a reading Cayce did. Cayce wrote more than 300 books that covered things like meditation, auras, the Akashic Records (the theosophical concept of a mystical log book that stored every thought and action of each human's many incarnations), soul mates, and reincarnation, as well as a vast history of the lost continent of Atlantis, which he believed would one day rise again.

Cayce was also a loving husband, father of two, a photographer, a Sunday school teacher, and he loved to garden. But it was as the sleeping prophet that he would be remembered, amassing a cult-like following of devoted "fans" who believe he was directly in tune with the most fundamental source of life, which allowed him to gain access to knowledge no ordinary man or woman could have. As a devout member of the Disciples of Christ, his work and readings hold a strong Christian theme, especially his End Times predictions, but many Christian conservatives cringe at his claim of psychic and healing abilities, and his belief in reincarnation, astrology, and Atlantis.

On file today at the Association for Research and Enlightenment, Inc. (A.R.E.) in Virginia Beach, Virginia, are copies of more than 14,000 of Cayce's readings from a 43-year period spanning from 1901 to 1944, available to the public along with follow-up reports from individuals who had originally asked for the readings. Cayce's track record as a seer who can heal is impressive, but his predictions of future events, of which this book is more concerned, failed to live up to expectations.

In 1934, Cayce went into a trance and gave a reading of future events he claimed would occur before the end of the century. Among these events were:

∞ A shift in the planets' axis in or around the year 2000 CE, leading to the flooding of coastal regions and the loss of much of Japan, Greenland, and some of northern Europe.

∞ New land appearing off the East Coast of the United States.

∞ Massive destruction of Los Angeles, San Francisco, and the disappearance of New York.

∞ Volcanic eruptions of increasing intensity along the Pacific Rim, most damaging to Japan and China, Eastern Australia, and the Pacific coast of South America.

∞ The appearance of a land bridge between South America and Antarctica (which surprisingly used to appear on the ancient Piri Reis maps!).

∞ Global warming in cool regions, and cooling in warm regions.

In other readings, Cayce also predicted geopolitical changes, such as the coming Holocaust and Nazi rule; the end of Communism and rebirth of Russia; the "downward movement of long duration" of the stock market (which he gave just before the Wall Street crash in 1929); the establishment of China as the new "cradle of Christianity"; and the arrival of World War III in 1999, to be followed by a New Age and the Second Coming of Christ. Cayce even saw himself being reincarnated somewhere in Nebraska in 2100 CE.

Although he did get it quite wrong in regard to China and the starting date of World War III, he was, according to some interpreters, able to predict the coming of World Wars I and II, and also, in 1939, the deaths of two presidents in office:

"Ye are to have turmoils…ye are to have strife between capital and labor. Ye are to have division in thy own land, before ye have the second of the Presidents that next will not live through his office…a mob rule!"

Presidents Franklin D. Roosevelt and John F. Kennedy both died in office when racial tensions were high, and many associate Kennedy's death with the real mob rule: the Mafia.

Cayce's End Times predictions also mention a major global change in 1998, along with the rediscovery of the Hall of Records, once buried in a huge chamber beneath the Sphinx in Egypt by the survivors of the destruction of Atlantis. This revelation was to occur between 1996 and 1998, but to date no such records of the entire wisdom and knowledge of humanity have been unearthed. Perhaps they still exist deep beneath the Egyptian desert. Cayce believed that once these records were revealed, Christ would return to earth.

According to the *Fortean Times* story "The Sleeping Prophet," a recent poll showed that three quarters of history students at American universities believe that Atlantis will one day resurface. Cayce spent many trances pondering the rise and fall of the strange and mysterious lost continent. His own son, Edgar Evans Cayce, wrote a book about his father's predictions titled *Edgar Cayce on Atlantis*, documenting startling information taken from Cayce's life readings such as:

∞ Atlantis was the first place on Earth where spiritual man became physically human.

∞ People alive today have experienced previous incarnations on Atlantis.

∞ Atlantis reached an astounding level of technology before it sank into the ocean around 10,000 BCE, including TV, lasers, atomic energy, and cybernetics.

∞ Atlantis will rise again.

Cayce believed that the story of Atlantis was a lesson for any rising empire that becomes too heavily burdened by its own technological capability, which hits home with us today, and future chapters in this book will prove that we are indeed on the cusp of reaching far beyond our grasp when it comes to technology. The warning for all prophets has always been: if you get too technologically savvy at the expense of spiritual awakening, your empire will sink, crumble, burn, or drown beneath the sea. Cayce believed this imbalance, along with greed and self-gratification, led to the downfall of the Atlantean empire.

But it is his prediction that Atlantis will once again make an appearance that most interests those concerned with the coming changes surrounding 2012, and the dawn of a new day in 2013, should we survive. Cayce directly tied the resurfacing of Atlantis with the discovery of the Hall of Records (sometimes referred to as the Atlantean Library), and some scholars have wondered if this new rising of Atlantis is more about the knowledge being brought up to the light, rather than an actual reappearance of a lost continent now lurking somewhere beneath the deep waters of the Atlantic.

Some of the predictions associated with an actual appearance of land, such as the reading Cayce made in which he states, "In the next few years, lands will appear in the Atlantic as well as the Pacific. And what is the coastline now of many a land will be bed of the ocean," sound more like the effects of global warming, which we are now seeing, and which Cayce did indeed predict (the warming of cool lands, and cooling of warm lands). If this is what he was invisioning, we may very well see the rise of a piece of land with evidence of a once-great civilization, although Cayce's predictions that these changes would occur before the year 2000 CE is inaccurate. The rediscovery of the Atlantean Library would, he believed, usher in a golden New Age—the Age of Aquarius—and as we shall see in a later chapter, this metaphysical era of enlightenment is ripe with its own controversy and conflicts concerning exact timing.

To Cayce, the end of the world would be more of a beginning, marked by the reappearance of the lost continent that, to many, symbolizes a golden era of spirituality and technology, albeit one that fell under the weight of its own imbalance. Still, the desire to see a new golden age, in which spiritual transformation trumps technology, is the lesson of Atlantis, and the hope of its return. Atlantis, or evidence of it, may still be out there, ready to rise again and show us proof that progress without spirit is never a good thing. Empires always fall.

Cayce also predicted that the Third World War, to commence in 1999 CE, would involve strife and unrest in the Middle East, involving Libya, Syria, and surrounding nations, and we are now watching smaller wars being fought in Afghanistan, Iraq, and possibly Iran. Islamic terrorism and expansionism has worried some scholars, now suggesting that perhaps the End Times date that Cayce predicted may indeed be underway. In the cases of other prophets who predicted the End Times further along in the 21st century, perhaps the dates they foresaw can now be moved up due to new threats of terrorist nations getting nuclear weapons capabilities, and a rebirth of aggressive American hegemony prompting enemy nations to step up their own defenses. Additionally, the Doomsday Clock has been moved closer to midnight since the 2001 terrorist attacks on New York City. Perhaps the prophets see the coming reality, but just get the dates a bit wrong?

Zecharia Sitchin

In Zecharia Sitchin's book *The End of Days: Armageddon and Prophecies of the Return*, he refers to Ezekiel, chapters 38–39, as part of an End Times scenario that involves a final annihilating battle between the Kings of the

East and Kings of the West. This battle involves "Gog and Magog" as the principle instigators of a war that will be fought in the valley of Megiddo, at the foot of Mt. Megiddo, from which the word *Armageddon* gets its origin. Sitchin points out the references in the Dead Sea Scrolls, found in 1945, of a coming battle between the "War of the Sons of Light Against the Sons of Darkness," and also refers to the terrifying fact that one of the first nations to strike up the drumbeat of this final war will be Persia (today's Iran), a country now involved in attempts to develop nuclear power and potential weapons.

Yet one could also say that these battles could have been any of the wars throughout the course of human history between Christians and Muslims, from the death of Christ to the Crusades, to the rise of the Moors, and the repeated Middle East crises of 20th century. Why now should the same signs seen then finally signal the end of the End Times debate?

Could the year 2012 have anything to do with this rising call toward redemption before the first trumpet of Revelation sounds? Or is it just another misinterpretation, more bad timing, or, in the case of Rapture Christians eagerly waiting for it all to begin, wishful thinking?

Sitchin pinpoints 2012 as the most popular end time of choice, claiming that the biblical prophecies of the Return operate on a cyclical element similar to the Mayan calendar, which predicts the return of Quetzalcoatl. The Mayan calendar, he states, operates on a cycle that ends, as we saw in Chapter 1, in the year 2012.

But Sitchin goes on to point out other prophetic end time dates. If one applies the fact that the source of "millennium" as eschatological time has its origins in Jewish apocryphal writings, Sitchin claims the search for meaning must begin there. By examining the Old Testament predictions along with applications of numbers and lengths of years, then applying that information to the Hebrew calendar of Nippur, which began on 3760 BCE, End Times should occur in 2240 CE. He also suggests the end could come in 2087 CE, Thoth's magical year of the Return, or, as Sir Isaac Newton configured, either 2060 CE or 2090 CE. Or, it could end in 2900 CE when we are due for a visit from (and a potential collision with) the comet Nibiru.

Sitchin then shifts the focus from an actual end of times to the more probable end of astrological eras. We are now moving out of the Age of Pisces and into the Age of Aquarius. The Age of Pisces is the age of Christianity, thus the association of Jesus with the symbol of the fish, and the "fisher of men." Perhaps the End Times concept is really more about the end of one astrologically divided Age and the dawn of a new Age. This would explain the apocalyptic stories and eschatology of Christianity—the dominant force of the Age of Pisces—as it struggles with the loss of its power as we enter an Age of spiritual transformation that will not, according to prophets, be marked by any one religion. Could the End Times stories of ancient religious texts, and the prophetic cries of modern preachers and prophets, be the death cry of a great religious triad—Judaism, Christianity, and Islam—as a higher level of consciousness threatens to undermine, if not undo, their very existence?

The Bible Code

The year 2012 does figure into several other End Times predictions. In 1997, the best-selling book *The Bible Code* predicted that a meteor, asteroid, or comet would strike Earth that fateful year. Another book written in 1998, *The Nostradamus Code*, also warns of a potential headbutt with a comet or asteroid, which will allow the Antichrist the opportunity to disperse troops around the globe to aid in the preparation of nuclear war; in *The Orion Prophecy*, written in 2002, we are warned that in 2012 the Earth's magnetic field will reverse. Later chapters will show how the year 2012 fits into many scenarios of a coming major shift, involving positive transcendence, earth changes, or geopolitical trends.

The Bible Code was published in 1997 and became a huge best-seller worldwide. Author Michael Drosnin, an American journalist, spent years researching an alleged mathematically encoded system of predictions and prophecies. His book caused huge controversy, with believers and skeptics going head to head in an all-out war to determine if the Torah (Hebrew Bible), truly contained hidden glimpses into the future.

Though many religious scholars and historians do believe that the Torah contains words, phrases, and clusters of words that can, depending on inter-pretation, hold meaning, they disagree on whether this is proof of divine intervention. Drosnin, who went on to author a sequel, *The Bible Code II*, and had a third installment published in 2007 titled *The Bible Code III: The Quest*, suggests the code is extraterrestrial in origin, and that it does not make actual predictions, but rather speaks of probabilities.

Some of Drosnin's "probabilities" he found in the Bible Code include:

∞ Proof Lee Harvey Oswald was going to kill JFK (interestingly, a recent headline news story suggested more evidence *against* the lone gunman theory).

∞ World war and atomic holocaust in 2006 CE.

∞ The 1995 assassination of Israeli Prime Minister Yitzhak Rabin.

∞ The assassinations of the Kennedy brothers.

∞ The assassination of Anwar Sadat.

Of these, Drosnin was only able to exactly pinpoint the Rabin assassination *beforehand*, and many critics believe that this was only because of the political turmoil at the time the book was being written, and not some great insight. Furthermore, the technique employed by Drosnin, described more fully in the paper "Equidistant Letter Sequences in the Book of Genesis" by Eliyahu Rips of Israel's Hebrew University, and colleagues Doron Witztum and Yoav Rosenberg, has been employed in other books with equally impressive results.

For example, one image shows how Equidistant Letter Sequences, or ELS, is used in the *Bible Code* to predict the Apocalypse, which Drosnin placed as beginning in 2006. (There is even a bottom reference to 2012, which is to be the final end date!) Could the end be just around the corner indeed? That might depend on when the end actually begins…

In June of 1997, Drosnin was quoted in a *Newsweek* article responding to criticism that this ELS could be used to find messages in just about any text, saying, "When my critics find a message about the assassination of a prime minister encrypted in *Moby Dick*, I'll believe them."

Up for the challenge, Australian mathematician Brendan McKay found many ELS arrays in *Moby Dick* that predicted the assassination of Rabin, including the Prime Minister's first and last names and the university he attended! and McKay also found assassinations of other major figures to be included, including Prime Minister Indira Gandhi, the assassin Sirhan Sirhan, Leon Trotsky, JFK, MLK, Princess Diana, and Abraham Lincoln.

United States physicist Dave Thomas looked at other texts and used ELS to find a variety of intriguing codes. Believe it or not, in his TV series *John Safran vs. God*, Australian celebrity John Safran actually found references about the September 11 terrorist attacks encoded in one-hit-wonder rapper Vanilla Ice's lyrics!

Many *Bible Code* critics point to the flexibility of the Hebrew language as Drosnin's (and others') means of toying with factual data and rearranging, or perhaps just misinterpreting, Hebrew words for modern English. No matter what, we are only interested in knowing if *The Bible Code*, or any other book (*Moby Dick* included), can predict the beginning of the end of the world. Drosnin claimed 2006 as the year, which we know for a fact is not correct. Now if he is just a few years off, we still could see that end date of 2012 as being accurate.

It's not hard to imagine that every book ever published might possibly hold a code to an entirely different End Times date, if someone had the time and extreme level of patience required to look for it. Both Margaret Mitchell's *Gone With the Wind* and Stephen King's *The Stand* could possibly contain encoded evidence of every president ever elected, or every product now on sale at a Wal-Mart near you!

The end of the world seems to be as elusive as the key to the *Bible Code* that author Drosnin claims is buried in a steel obelisk near the Dead Sea. Should that key ever be found, if it does indeed exist, we might then get a real idea of what will happen, and when. Until then, it's all open to human interpretation, and error.

Nibiru

I would be remiss to discuss the End Times scenarios without mentioning Planet X, or Nibiru. Made "famous" in 1976 by Zecharia Sitchin with his book *The Twelfth Planet*, the story of Nibiru was fashioned from Sitchin's translation of ancient Sumerian texts that tell the tale of a 12th planet in our solar system. This mythical planet was supposedly the home world of an ancient race of sentient beings called the Anunnaki. To get the full story, read Sitchin's book; suffice it to say, the supposition is that Nibiru is not just part of a mythic creationist tale, but a real planet. Many believe that Nibiru is on a collision course with Earth…in 2012.

Although some mainstream astronomers and scientists will admit to the possibility of its existence, fewer still admit that there are some signs of a yet undiscovered celestial body beyond Pluto, which could theoretically affect Earth with its gravitational force, should it venture too close. To the vast majority of astronomers, Planet X remains more in the realm of fringe science. Sitchin and others claim that the Bible itself predicts the return of Nibiru—possibly to coincide with Armageddon itself. However, in his latest book, *The End of Days: Armageddon and Prophecies of the Return*, Sitchin identifies several potential dates when Nibiru, or Planet X, could make its presence known again. If one follows the Mayan calendar, the dates for End Times range from 2012 CE, to 2087 CE, based upon a challenge to the 2012 date by scholar Fritz Buck, all the way to the year 2240 CE, if we consider the Hebrew calendar of Nippur.

The legend of Nibiru may be just that—legend and myth. One of the wondrous things about our race is the need to combine fact and fiction to spin tales of the human experience—creation, birth, death, and everything in between. We like to expound upon who we are, where we came from, and ultimately, how we die.

Even being relegated to the legend and myth category does not emphatically mean that Planet X is not out there, traveling stealthily toward the sun and Earth.

A handful of researchers have been tracking potential Planet X's for years, and continue to do so. In an October 7, 1999 article on MSNBC.com titled "A Mystery Revolves Around the Sun," we learn that two teams of researchers proposed the existence of "an unseen planet or failed star" with a solar orbit of some 2 trillion miles. Numerous other articles abound, including the July 2001 Discovery News story, "Large Object Discovered Orbiting the Sun," which has served to compel even more scientists to take seriously the potential existence of this mythological planet.

What might happen if Nibiru did happen to fly by the Earth in the near future? Would increased gravitational effects lead to potential flooding, tidal waves, earthquakes, and even increased volcanic activity? Might the Earth's rotation even be manipulated in such a manner as to cause day to turn to night? Is it possible that this event may well be the wormwood of revelations that will decimate the planet of most of its life?

Ultimately, only time will tell of the existence of Planet X. One thing is certain, however. If a huge planet truly is approaching our world, it is hopeful that we will get enough advance notice to put our houses in order, tie up our loose ends, and pray.

∞

But for the gloom and doom crowd awaiting a specific pattern of End Times events leading to the return of Christ (or a similar purity figure), to restore order, punish the wicked, and judge the living and the dead, the story, and the song, remains the same. As political and planetary events increase, leading some to become more anxious, and others to become more hopeful, depending on your eschatological viewpoint, the sense of something big around the bend thickens…and quickens.

Though hundreds of books and movies (and now video games) about the end of the world continue to sell and proliferate, and modern day seers continue to predict a rapid progression toward hell on earth followed by heaven for the chosen ones, do they really indicate a coming inevitable change we cannot avoid, or maybe, just maybe, a collective desire for our own downfall, our own mass catastrophic end? End Times prophecies are abundant, but as the next chapter shows, so too are those who speak of a powerful and positive transformation of the human species, an evolutionary leap of consciousness that will bring light back to a planet immersed in darkness.

3

New Dawn Rising

All things change; nothing perishes.
—Ovid, *Metamorphoses*

Once you stop clinging and let things be, you'll be free, even of birth and death. You'll transform everything.
—Bodhidharma (440 CE–528 CE), *The Zen Teaching of Bodhidharma: A Bilingual Edition*

Regardless of the persistence of violent and deadly End-Times scenarios, many 2012 experts agree that whatever this final countdown may be leading up to is not at all negative, but rather a profound transformation of human consciousness…a shifting of paradigms. An archetypal revolution.

Heavens and Underworlds

Yes, they say, the world will end. But only the world *as we know it.*

The Maya believed in spiritual transformation and the acceleration of conscious evolution, as described in their vision of the Thirteen Heavens and the Nine Underworlds. The number 13 played a significant role in ancient cultures, as it did in the Christian religion with Jesus and the 12 disciples. The Zodiac has 12 symbols, with its entirety as the 13th. To the Maya, and to all of the civilizations of Mesoamerica specifically, the Thirteen Heavens corresponded to a process of evolutionary growth through time, and each Heaven had its own ruling deity, and stage or step in the growth process.

Thirteen Heavens

The Thirteen Heavens also corresponded to birds that, as each evolutionary cycle progressed, became bigger in size, from the blue hummingbird of the first Heaven, to the parrot of the thirteenth. The Thirteen Heavens takes on great significance when we understand that the 13-day Tzolkin count was considered a symbol of the entire creation process. The Thirteen Heavens, according to Carl Johan Calleman, actually manifests in the creation process of the Long Count's 13 baktuns, albeit on a grander scale. Calleman points to the construction of seven-story pyramids, such as the Pyramid of the High Priest in Chichen Itza, with the progression through the heavens symbolized by the 13-step climb up and down each side of the pyramid.

The odd-numbered years ushered in stages of progress, and, intriguingly, represented a more "feminine" energy cycle; the even years were represented by deities more associated with masculine energies of death, destruction, and war. We see this cyclical aspect in the even-numbered heavens as times of rest, and the odd-numbered times of novelty and activity.

Therefore, as Calleman proposes, "The Thirteen Heavens of the Great Cycle constitute a cyclical wave movement of history."

This Thirteen Heaven cycle, according to his "Calleman Matrix," repeats itself in each of the Nine Underworlds, in a sort of microcosmic/macrocosmic blueprint of history, with the seven-day/six-night cycle embedded within.

Though the Thirteen Heavens are critical to understanding the Mayan calendar, along with the beliefs of Mesoamerican civilizations in a progression of both biological and conscious evolution, we are most concerned, in terms of "what might happen" in 2013, with the Nine Underworlds themselves, for the Nine Underworlds tell a more detailed story of where we've been, where we are now, and where we are headed.

Thirteen Heavens

Heaven	Ruling Deity	Stages of Growth
1.	Xiuhtecuhtli: God of Fire and Time	Sowing
2.	Tlaltecuhtli: God of Earth	
3.	Chalchiuhtlicue: Goddess of Water	Germination
4.	Tonatiuh: God of Sun and the Warriors	
5.	Tlacoteotl: Goddess of Love/Childbirth	Sprouting
6.	Miclantechutli: God of Death	
7.	Cinteotl: God of Maize/Sustenance	Proliferation
8.	Tlaloc: God of Rain and Water	
9.	Quetzalcoatl: God of Light	Budding
10.	Tezcatlipoca: God of Darkness	
11.	Yohualticitl: Goddess of Birth	Flowering
12.	Tlahuizcalpantecuhtli: God Before Dawn	
13.	Ometeotl/Omecinatl: Dual/Creator God	Fruition

Nine Underworlds

Each of the Nine Underworlds signals a shift in consciousness as evolution progresses. The duration of each Underworld is also of great significance, because this is where the acceleration of time is most apparent. In the following chart, adapted from Carl Johan Calleman's *The Mayan Calendar and the Transformation of Consciousness*, we can see this profound acceleration at play.

Underworld	Duration	Level of Consciousness	Evolution
Universal	13 uinals	Cosmic	Ninth
Galactic	13 tuns	Galactic	Eighth
Planetary	13 katuns	Global	Seventh
National	13 baktuns	Civilized	Sixth
Regional	13 pictuns	Human	Fifth
Tribal	13 kalabtuns	Hominid	Fourth
Familial	13 kinchiltuns	Anthropoid	Third
Mammalian	13 alautuns	Mammalian	Second
Cellular	13 hablatuns	Cellular	First

The forward progression from cellular forms of life and consciousness to a higher level of existence that banishes all boundaries of form is what the Mayan calendar seems to be documenting. The First Underworld begins at the moment of the big bang, some 16.4 billion years ago, and moves through 13 hablatuns, each of which is 1.26 billion years long. As both physical and conscious evolution escalates, the duration of each Underworld shortens, with the Planetary through Universal Underworlds propelling life forward at exponentially faster and faster rates.

In her book *The Mayan Code: Time Acceleration and Awakening the World Mind*, author and International Mayan Elder Barbara Hand Clow describes it this way:

"When a new Underworld begins, higher forms of life organize with more complex brains to receive greater information from the universe. Although the evolution of the previous Underworld continues, the new Underworld brings in changes because the time acceleration is so intense." As we learned before, each Underworld accelerates 20 times faster than the previous one.

She continues in direct reference to the final Underworld that leads into the 2011–2012 time window: "During the 260-day Universal Underworld in 2011, unitized, whole-brained consciousness will return to Earth for the third time, while we are aligned with the Galaxy. This period arrives while we retain all the knowledge we've attained during the National and Planetary Underworlds; at this point we will seek to integrate this knowledge to achieve enlightenment in 2011. This 'brain integration' will transpire in a period whose length of time is less than one year, as we experience another acceleration times 20."

Hand Clow goes into great depth describing each Underworld in detail, which we won't do here, but suffice it to say that the leaps life has made along the evolutionary scale appear to have been predicted with great accuracy by the Mesoamericans and their calendrical systems. They had a vast and profound understanding of the snowball effect of increasing information, and how, in a sense, the more we humans evolve, the more Godlike we become (at least potentially Godlike).

To make matters more confusing, each Underworld is divided into seven days and six nights, each with its own meaning and intention. The Long

Count calendar, with its 5,125-year span, concerns itself with the four final Underworlds—the National through the Universal, so that is where we will focus. At the time of the writing of this book, we are in the Galactic Underworld. Mesoamericans, including the Maya, Aztec, and Toltec, also believed in the five worlds, another sub-pattern of the Tzolkin. Each Underworld can also be divided into Five Worlds of its own, even as the entire Long Count has its own Five World system of measurement.

By the time this book is released, we will be entering the Fourth World of the Galactic Underworld, which is set to last from August 15, 2008, to October 28, 2011, according to Calleman, and December 21, 2012, according to Jenkins and others. We can also say that we are now in Night Five of the Galactic Underworld, which will last from November 19, 2007 to November 12, 2008. Day Six will follow, from November 13, 2008 to November 7, 2009. Night Six follows, from November 8, 2009 to November 10, 2010. Finally, Day Seven will begin on November 11, 2010, and end, of course, on October 28, 2011/December 21, 2012. (Please note that the day spans may vary according to which end date theory you are looking at, but for simplicity purposes, we focus here on Calleman's.)

The Four Worlds

The Four Worlds, or World Ages, each composed of 13 baktuns (5,125.36-year span) combine to equal one precession cycle of approximately 25,627 years. The World Ages of the Mesoamericans have a counterpart in the Hindu Vedic Yugas, which are a part of the vast mythology of the Hindu, and describe the evolution of life and time on Earth. Each successive Yuga is one quarter shorter in duration then the one before it, unlike the more fixed Worlds of the Mayan Calendar.

We are currently in the Kali Yuga, a period of darkness and despair, when the more materialistic and greed-based goals of humanity threaten to push the species to the brink of extinction. The Kali Yuga is considered the final World Age, a time of negativity and destruction.

Yuga	Age	Duration	Key Events
Satya Yuga	Golden Age	1,728,000 years	Peace, longevity, harmony
Treta Yuga	Silver Age	1,296,000 years	Introduction to evil
Dvapara Yuga	Bronze Age	864,000 years	Fall of humanity, disharmony, and chaos
Kali Yuga	Iron Age	432,000 years	Evil prevails, war, greed, and famine

64-World Cycle

The ancient Greeks also had a system of world ages or races. They traced humanity throughout a period of five successive ages that correlate with the Golden Age through the Iron Age of modern days. The Theravada Buddhist commentary, "Visuddhimagga," mentions a 64-world cycle that periodically cleanses the planet and destroys humanity. The 64-world cycle is divided into eight cycles of destruction—seven by fire and one by water—which repeat seven times. The eighth cycle is a final Apocalypse of devastating winds. Then, the entire 64-cycle begins again.

Life Cycles

The concept of birth, death, and renewal, along with the parallel evolution of physical life and consciousness, runs throughout many major spiritual traditions, as we have seen. The theory that time equals transcendence permeates world mythologies, religions, and traditions, and serves as the foundational backbone for the New Age beliefs of modern times. Plato and the ancient Greeks believed in the Great Year that charged the precessional cycle,

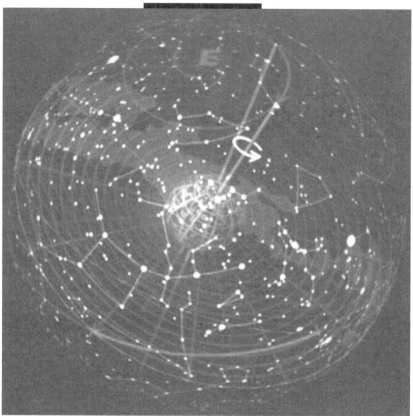

Figure 3.1: The precession of the equinoxes as seen from outside the celestial dome. Image courtesy of Wikimedia Commons/Tau'olunga.

as did the Chinese, and believed that just as the planet followed seasonal cycles, it also had a long period of transformation from darkness to enlightenment, and then back again. The Binary Research Institute in Southern California describes this ancient Great Year as divided into two parts of 12,000 years each. The first 12,000 years are ascending years, followed by 12,000 descending years, when darker days prevail. This precessional period is further broken down into the Four Ages of Golden, Silver, Bronze, and Iron, each age with its own particular characteristics.

The Four Ages that divide the precessional Great Year also correspond with the Zodiac when broken into four periods of three sign durations each.

The Hindu Vedic culture most notably utilized this cycle to describe the rise and fall and rise again of humanity, with higher ages of harmony and enlightenment constantly giving way to dark ages of misery and evil, only to give way again to a "new age" of enlightenment. But even the Western traditions posit a rise and fall from grace, one that occurs in cycles, from Adam and Eve being cast out of the Garden, to the coming of the Kingdom of Heaven on Earth, to a time after the end days of great peace, only to be once again presented with a direct threat of evil.

The cycle of life itself mirrors the cycle of ascension of consciousness. New Age followers point to the writings of channeled masters such as St. Germain and Ascended Ones, the archangel Michael and Ramtha, and even a teenager named Matthew, who is channeled through his mother and provides some astonishing insight into world affairs (although whether that information is really coming from the other side, or from the mother's own ability to tap into a field of information herself could be debated).

All of these alleged spiritual masters who speak from the other realms of reality talk about coming destruction, to be followed by enlightenment and ascension for those who remain fully awake. But these cycles are obvious not only to people who have researched the cultural beliefs and traditions of the Mayan and other ancient peoples, but also to anyone with a fundamentally basic background in science. The Earth moves through cycles of creation, destruction, and creation again, even as it moves through the cycles of seasons in its motion around the sun. Life—existence itself—is cyclical.

The Trinity

To me, the most intriguing aspect of transformation being discussed in relation to the 2012 end date involves a subject near and dear to my heart—the Trinity. While studying for my ministerial ordination, I wrote a detailed thesis on the Trinity symbolism in religion, science, and psychology after finding some stunning correlations in those fields that spoke of a triune nature to reality, to consciousness…even to the Divine itself. My paper took everyone by surprise, because most people only know of the Trinity as a tenet of Catholicism that became a major influence throughout Christianity after the Council of Nice in 300 CE.

My studies led me to discover that the Trinity is not a three-faced image of God, but rather a process of enlightenment—a direct path to the Divine that requires no priest or cardinal or human go-between. This three-step process is mirrored throughout nature, science, and even psychology as a format for the evolution of human consciousness and physical growth. Turns out, I was not alone in that assumption.

Neuroscientist Paul MacLean describes the human brain as being triune in nature. He suggests the brain is composed of three structures, each of which evolved at different times. The first brain is the ancient reptilian brain that drives us toward survival. The second brain is the more recently developed and more advanced limbic brain. The third is the most recently evolved neo-cortex. He uses the term *schizophysiology* to describe our current lack of integration of the three brains.

To further complicate matters, the two "older" parts of the brain continue to influence human behavior, despite their more "crude" abilities and their total inability to process the power of speech. We are, in a sense, new brains trapped by old brains.

So what might happen when the three brains fully integrate?

Perhaps the answer is a shift in consciousness, a wholeness of perception and awareness, or, as Rupert Sheldrake puts it in *The Evolutionary Mind: Conversations of Science, Imagination and Spirit*:

> Theological attempts to deal with this problem have led to a variety of models where you have the idea that the ultimate is not an undifferentiated unity, but rather a pattern of relationships. In the Taoist model you have the yin and the yang with a kind of fractal boundary between them. The circle containing the two is the whole that unifies them. In the model of the Holy Trinity, the Father is the source of the Word and the Spirit.

Sheldrake goes on to describe the underlying metaphor as spoken word, that the spirit is the breath on which the "word can happen," as a pattern of vibrations and harmonics that is also possibly a fractal pattern in time.

This model suggests that unity is actually more about the sense of inter-relationship within a common source. All these models of an ultimate unity are models of a relationship which something holds together.

The Trinity concept lends itself to a metaphysical understanding of the enlightenment process, in which the Father is the Divine Source, or God; the Son is humanity, or man/woman; and the Holy Spirit is the connective link between the two, yet is also the activating agent necessary for Divine union. Yet it also shows up in the natural world as the cycle of birth, death, and renewal, which, according to Ralph Abraham, also describes the Utopian Structure of good followed by the abyss of deep despair followed by a period of renewal and even greater good than that which preceded the despair. Physicist David Bohm presented a triune nature of reality with his three orders of existence: the explicate, the implicate, and the all-encompassing super-implicate. It's easy to see here the correlation with body, mind, and spirit; or man, the Divine, and a connecting agent.

Perhaps 2012 will be the year when the triune brain finally achieves unification, as well as our own triune nature of being, and a permanent connection to the Divine will be fully established when the Eschaton, or end point, is reached. Reality will take on a wholeness that we currently do not see, experience, or in many cases, even imagine. Truly, as St. Paul suggested, we will stop seeing through the dark glass and set aside childish ways. Our eyes, minds, hearts, and souls will be opened, all at the same time; we will finally grow up and get a real life.

Leaps of Consciousness

This is not a time of fear and dread; it is simply a time of change. Some believe that the leaps we make will be between levels of consciousness as follows:

∞ **Tribal consciousness**—the lowest form of consciousness that responds to mass thought, or groupthink, and reacts in a lemming-like fashion. Usually motivated by fear and anxiety.

∞ **Individual consciousness**—a stronger-developed sense of self, more ego-driven, but focused less on groupthink and more on individual awareness of place in the scheme of things.

∞ **Group consciousness**—the reverse of tribal consciousness, in that this time, the motivation is for the good of all people, with positive intention at the forefront of action and change.

∞ **Soul consciousness**—the ultimate, highest level of awareness, where all matter and form is left behind and a true union with the Source, and with all others, is achieved.

If we take a good look at what is going on in the world today, it becomes clear to this author that we are desperately trying to move from tribal consciousness into soul consciousness in an accelerated fashion, leaving many people feeling breathless and overwhelmed. Perhaps this speeding-up of transformation is necessary, but it leaves many without the advantages of first having worked through the process of individual growth. This is why many believers in 2012 warn others who *are* awake and aware to help the nonbelievers through such trying times.

Leaders will be made, and followers will have a choice: to change, or not to change, with the times.

Those who anticipate the coming great date of 2012 wonder if there is anything we can do to stop or change what will happen. Is this our fate? Destiny? Or do we have free will?

In the next chapter, we take a look at how both destiny and free will play a huge role in the outcome of 2012.

4
Who's Behind the Curtain?

Note: For simplicity purposes, 2012 will be the end date for the rest of the book, having already presented the compelling arguments in previous chapters for varying end dates. Because 2012 is the more widely known date, from this point on it will represent the end date in general; however, this does not mean it is the most accurate.

> Whoever wills the end, wills also...the means in his power
> which are indispensably necessary thereto.
> —Immanuel Kant, *Fundamental Principles of the Metaphysics of Ethics*

In a recent e-mail message to subscribers and followers of the ascended master known as St. Germain, we are told:

We consistently tell you that you have great power of thought, and that you are great Beings. We do so because we wish to emphasize these facts about you, and to be fully aware of them. Much of the progress you are making is down to your ability to mold your own future within the framework we have given you. We refer to the end times known by many as the time of Ascension that is tied in with the Winter Solstice of 2012.

It is important for your understanding, that everyone realizes that they have the power to manifest their vision of the future. It then becomes a collective energy that connects with those of a like vibration, as a massive thought form. At present there is sufficient energy of Light to ensure that it is victorious, and it is causing opposition to it to by the dark to fall away. Not completely, but sufficient to allow the changes you seek to come into being.

Bear in mind that we greatly influence those who are aligned with the Light, but in no measure do we force it upon people. We help direct your efforts into suitable channels, so that the plan for Man unfolds as intended by the higher forces of Light. We stand alongside each soul that supports and assists the goals that are laid out before you, and together we wield the power of the Light for the good of all. Also know that many of you have entered this time specifically to work with the Light, and it is a key factor in your life plan.

The Power of Intention

Whether or not you personally buy into these channeled messages from alleged Ascended Ones matters not, because the message itself raises a critical question on the lips of everyone talking, thinking, and worrying about 2012. The question is: How much of what happens to us is predestined, as fate, and how much of it is free will or choice?

Mass transformation simply cannot take place without a collective paradigm shift, and 2012 may just have been, to the Maya, one of those very shifts (but by no means the last shift). It is hard to go anywhere nowadays and not hear someone talking about "The Secret" or the power of "intention," using focused thought to manifest outer reality.

But could intention have a direct affect on 2012? We may only have to look back at major historical events to see that, indeed, collective thought not only influences history, but also shapes it.

Philosopher Jean Gebser, author of *The Ever-Present Origin*, posits that human development mirrors the quantum-based model of consciousness—unfolding and evolving through sudden leaps and shifts into new consciousness structures. In each new structure, humans perceive time and space in a newly aware state that is successively more able to create new and emergent brain capacities. "Every consciousness mutation," he states, "is apparently a sudden and acute of latent possibilities present since origin."

In a move from tribal or group consciousness, which presents a very crude awareness of individuality, to a more modern "unity" consciousness, such that individuals realize their alignment with everything and their "higher" creative source, Gebser points to an unfolding origin that, when progressive, leads humanity to higher states of being and transcendence. But he also points to how, when regressive, the return to the earlier, deindividuated structure leads to things such as mass hysteria, mob rule-type behavior, fundamentalism, and fanaticism.

The power of collective human intention has two paths. One leads to such events such as the Spanish Inquisition, the witch burnings, inner city riots, and even terrorism. The other path leads to social trends, tipping points, and paradigm shifts that progressively move humanity forward, including raised levels of charitable awareness resulting from a natural disaster or crisis, movements toward civil rights, and even global awareness of pending crises such as climate change, poverty, and diminishing resources.

The key, however, is in the power of collective intention to create a collective future, and 2012 could possibly be the ultimate proving ground. We all remember (well, we Baby Boomers do!) coming up on the year 1984 with some dread, yet also some sense of dismay that George Orwell's dystopic view never manifested. In fact, some might say that things weren't too good, but they really weren't so bad at all, and we woke up in 1985 to find that life was pretty much status quo.

Then came Y2K, and a wave of fear swept over the nation. Rumors of technological ruin and economic collapse sent millions into a tailspin of survivalism, stocking up on food and water and making sure their family members all knew who the contact person was on the eve of destruction. Yet, very little happened, and what did was dealt with swiftly and accordingly.

The question must be asked—if so many people feared the worst, why did the worst not happen?

Are we simply not as powerful as we think?

Waiting for the World to End

Yet we did manifest exactly what we set out to. Intention is not surface fear or passing thought. It is a deep focus of will, and the will was to survive and come through Y2K, which we did. In fact, many people attended celebratory New Year's Eve parties to welcome in the new millennium. No fear to be found in a glass or two of bubbly.

We intended Y2K to be a nonevent even more than we intended it to destroy our bank records and wipe out our hard drives.

We also need to look at the motivation behind wanting the world to end, whether in a bang, a whimper, or otherwise. Psychologists have long suggested that the obsession with the "end of the world" comes from a real desire for righteous justice, one that manifests or projects itself almost in reverse. People of certain religious backgrounds might drool over the coming Rapture and judgment against non-believers, even going to the extreme of welcoming violence in the name of said judgment. But in reality, what these extremists really want is righteous justice; not to die, but to be proven right. Not to see others burning in hellfire, but to see others admit they were wrong.

Being right means you matter, and that your life matters. Thus, the cry for End Times is really a wail for purpose, a mourning for meaning. There is a pervasive and potent underlying desire for salvation and life renewed buried under proclamations of End Times, in a type of reverse psychology. People who say they want the world to end really want it to go on forever, just differently.

Millenniums and 2012 and 1984…these dates hold a dark appeal to many, but it is a false darkness, buoyed instead by the intense inner hunger for light and transformation. And perhaps people are bored and tired of the rat race of life and long for something outside of themselves to wipe the whole slate clean. They want to put an end to banality and bring about a fiery cleansing from which a phoenix can rise from the ashes.

But in terms of intention, what you see is not what you get; what you believe is. If people want to make something happen, they can, but what they make happen will not really be based upon what they want. It will be based upon what they believe—deep inside in their heart of hearts and the dark place in their soul of which they may not even be aware. The shadowy subconscious rules intention. Lip service need not apply.

If I had to choose the single-most powerful and profound book I've read in the last 20 years, it would no doubt be the seminal work of David R. Hawkins, MD, PhD, *Power vs. Force: The Hidden Determinants of Human Behavior*. Hawkins is a world-renowned lecturer, expert on mental processes, lifetime member of the American Psychiatric Association, coauthor with Nobel Prize-winner Linus Pauling of *Orthomolecular Psychiatry*, and is the current director of The Institute for Advanced Theoretical Research.

In *Power vs. Force*, Hawkins details the various levels of human consciousness, from the most basic "bottom" level of shame, which he considers "perilously proximate to death," to the highest level of enlightenment as exemplified by the Great Ones throughout history, such as Lord Krishna, Buddha, and Christ. In between are the levels at which most of us exist. Each level is assigned an Energy Level range, and Hawkins suggests that leaps to rising levels require a constant striving toward being awake, and awareness.

===

Levels of Human Consciousness

From David. R. Hawkings's Power vs. Force

Throughout many years of study, Hawkins determined his levels of human consciousness involving millions of calibrations in kinesiological testing, in order to define a range of values accurately corresponding to well-recognized sets of attitudes and emotions localized by specific attractor energy fields. This classification is the result of the research. Note that the calibration figures are a logarithmic progression; for example, the level of 300 is not twice the amplitude of the 150 level, but rather is 10 to the 300th power. This denotes just how little an increase in power is needed to result in a enormous jump in consciousness. Also note, there is no level before 20, as Hawkins considers anything below totally destructive to humanity.

Energy Level 20	Shame
Energy Level 30	Guilt
Energy Level 50	Apathy
Energy Level 75	Grief
Energy Level 100	Fear
Energy Level 125	Desire
Energy Level 150	Anger
Energy Level 175	Pride
Energy Level 200	Courage
Energy Level 250	Neutrality
Energy Level 310	Willingness
Energy Level 350	Acceptance
Energy Level 400	Reason
Energy Level 500	Love
Energy Level 540	Joy
Energy Level 600	Peace
Energy Level 700–1,000	Enlightenment

Enlightenment and Energy

Naturally, the highest level of enlightenment, according to Hawkins, sets in place "attractor energy fields that influence all of mankind." This highest level may be where we end up in 2012, but we must realize just how much work it will take to get there.

For example, Hawkins posits that the collective consciousness of humankind has been hovering at 190 for centuries, and only at the end of the 20th century did we leap to the current level of 207. Looking at the scale, things are not very encouraging. The level of 207, which is the level encompassing courage moving toward neutrality, is when "power first appears." We are finding our inner courage, trying new things, and showing a willingness to face fears and character defects that do not serve us. The trend is away from the lower stages of evolution, and toward productivity. At this stage, we begin to put back into the world just as much as we take, and we collectively move toward a more positive state of neutrality, which is "epitomized by release from the positionality that typifies lower levels." In other words, we are striving to get to a point of acceptance and inner confidence, a sense of well-being, and the ability to be relatively unattached to outcome.

As a collective body, humanity may not have had the power to affect Y2K events. If we are operating in the low 200s, that would explain the apparent inability to shift an entire paradigm, even a fear-based one.

Let's look at how much actual work it takes to move to the levels of powerful intention, based upon Hawkins's research.

Hawkins posits that only 4 percent of the world population calibrates at an energy field of 500 or above. Only 0.4 percent will reach 540, and, worse still, only one person in 10 million will reach 600 or above. Much of the world's peoples live in subsurvival states of existence, with most others living at sustainable levels, but in fear. "The majority of humans spend their lives in a quest for one form of security or another," Hawkins suggests, which doesn't leave much time for enlightenment.

Hawkins finds that, at energy level 200, a critical change in consciousness takes place, moving humanity out of fear and into a more courageous awakening. At level 500, another huge leap takes place, where the motivation of love and creativity come into full expression, and "excellence is common in every field of human endeavor." But just getting to that level requires tremendous energy and intention on the part of millions of people.

So how could we possibly ever hope to achieve the rise in consciousness needed to propel us into the 2012 transformation? Hawkins's research points to a way.

Hawkins states that it is "uncommon for people to move from one level to another during their lifetimes," and that the energy field calibrated at the birth of a person only increases, on average, by five points. Although this looks and sounds utterly depressing, Hawkins points out that this statistical figure must take into account the cumulative life choices that may actually lower a person's energy level. But depressingly, he admits that his research indicates that it only takes 2.6 percent of the human population to account for 72 percent of humanity's problems!

It's not impossible to move up a level in a lifetime, and even a percentage point of a percentage point rise means greater awareness and progress. With so many people living at these lower, weaker levels of existence, struggling to rise even a hair's breadth in a lifetime, we could posit that any resultant event of mass intention we might see in 2012 would be *just as negative and weak as we are as a species*. Or, even more realistically, it would prove our incapacity to truly affect our collective outcome, for if our negative intention was so strong, we would have already brought about the Apocalypse, for which so many millions of Christians long.

So we are back to square one, with the power of intention a reality, but not enough of one to truly shape the future…unless…

As a final kudos to Hawkins's amazing research, we need to look at the potential impact of higher-level people upon those below them. Two very intriguing statistics Hawkins puts forth suggest that:

1. One single avatar operating at the 700-plus level or above would counterbalance the collective negative energy levels of humanity today.
2. Growth, either individually or collectively, can take place slowly or suddenly.

Lest you fret that it will take an avatar to change the world, Hawkins also found that even one person actualizing at the energy level of 500 (love) would counterbalance the negativity of 750,000 lower-calibrating individuals. Someone operating at the level of peace (600) would offset 10 million lower-vibrating people. And even if you only calibrate at the measly level of 310 (willingness), you can be sure you are counterbalancing perhaps 90,000 lower-level individuals simply by being willing to experience the rapid growth indicative of this "gateway" level that leads to bigger leaps of transformation.

Global Consciousness Project

Intention experiments are going on all over the world, under the auspices of such organization as the Global Consciousness Project (*http://noosphere.princeton.edu/*), and the Intention Experiments of Lynne McTaggart's *Living the Field*.

The Global Consciousness Project (GCP), as described on their Website:

...is an international effort involving researchers from several institutions and countries, designed to explore whether the construct of interconnected consciousness can be scientifically validated through objective measurement. The project builds on excellent experiments conducted throughout the past 35 years at a number of laboratories, demonstrating that human consciousness interacts with random event generators (REGs), apparently "causing" them to produce non-random patterns. The experimental results clearly show that a broader examination of this phenomenon is warranted. In recent work, prior to the Global Consciousness Project, an array of REG devices in Europe and the United States showed non-random activity during widely shared experiences of deeply engaging events. For example, the funeral ceremonies for Princess Diana, and the Winter Olympics in Nagano, Japan, created shared emotions and a coherence of consciousness that appeared to be correlated with structure in the otherwise random data. In the fully developed project, a world-spanning array of labile REG detectors is connected to computers that are running software to collect data, and sending it to a central server via the

Internet. This network is designed to document and display any subtle, but direct effects of our collective consciousness reacting to global events. The research hypothesis predicts the appearance of coherence and structure in the globally distributed data collected during major events that engage the world population.

The GCP is run by Project Director Roger Nelson, and has been collecting data from their global REGs since 1998, with 65 host sites running custom software that reads output from REGs, recording a 200-bit trial once each second. The data then goes to a server in Princeton, New Jersey, for analysis.

Other Ways of Consciousness

Nelson and his colleagues state on the Website that "when millions of us share intentions and emotions the GCP/EEG network shows correlations." They interpret these correlations as evidence of a growing global consciousness, one that puts the responsibility of conscious evolution in human hands…and minds.

In England, Lynne McTaggart, author of *The Field* and *The Intention Experiment* is conducting what she calls "the largest mind-over-matter experiment in history," involving several specific experiments designed as a series of scientifically controlled, Web-based experiments. These experiments include everything from working with Russian physicist Dr. Konstantin Korotkov to study whether human intention can affect the "cluster structure" of water simply by sending focused, loving thoughts to it, to attempting to lower certain measurable biodynamic processes in a group of 16 meditators. Future experiments, which can be tracked on *www.theintention experiment.com*, will attempt to influence the temperature of the ecosphere, help barley seeds germinate early and grow more healthily, and even lower mortality at a specific hospital.

With some evidence to speak of, yet perhaps not enough to solidify our position as powerful co-creators of future events, these intention experiments do suggest that we have a collective influence that, with practice, can be amplified. But as Hawkins points out in *Power vs. Force*, we are fighting against great odds in terms of human numbers, and time. At the writing of this book, there are only a handful of years left before 2012. Unless a major spiritual leader appears, one operating at the avatar level, or humanity makes a surprise sudden collective leap, the events of 2012 may be, well, non-events.

In *The Mystery of 2012: Predictions, Prophecies and Possibilities*, Ervin Lazlo looks at the correlations between chaos dynamics in society and what we might expect in 2012. He suggests that, according to chaos and systems theory, societal transformations follow four distinct stages:

1. **The Trigger Phase**, involving hard technology innovations that bring about greater efficiency in utilizing nature for human ends.

2. **The Accumulation Phase**, in which higher technology improves social and environmental relations

3. **The Decision-Window**, in which "changed social and environmental relations put pressure on established order," and call into question values and worldviews.

4. **Chaos Point**, the final stage, where "the system is critically unstable." The status quo "becomes unsustainable, and the system's evolution tips in one direction or another." Lazlo points to two quite different options:

   a. Evolution (devolution) Toward Breakdown: Where the values, worldviews, and ethics of the critical mass don't change, change too slowly, or allow established institutions to negate timely transformation. This leads to a social order that degenerates into violence, conflict, and war.

   b. Evolution to Breakthrough: The mind-set of the critical mass evolves in time, shifts societal development to an adaptable mode, and brings about improved order and a more nonconflictual and sustainable society in terms of economic, political, and ecological dimensions.

Depending upon which path we collectively take out of the Chaos Point, the end result will no doubt make itself known during the next five years, when, in the coming chapters, we will explore the amazing and frightening obstacles, challenges, and opportunities we face. Ultimately, the choice is ours; we can either sit idle and not grow or grow too slowly, or up the ante and be the captains of our own evolutionary ship, so to speak.

It all depends on the power of our intention, and the ability to align mass consciousness for one grand, bold, determined purpose.

11

Gaia's
Revenge

5

Gaia Revolts

Nature, to be commanded, must be obeyed.
—Sir Francis Bacon, *Novum Organum*

We can argue until we are blue in the face about the exact moment in history when nature lost the game: when the Earth became more of a used and abused dumping ground instead of a soft place to fall.

Most might agree that the rise of patriarchal societies and the big three Western religious traditions announced the end game, the two minute warning that we now find ourselves closing in on, with no chance of overtime play in sight.

No matter when it happened, it happened, and as 2012 fast approaches, the planet itself may make the final goal and have the last laugh.

Global Warming and Climate Change

We begin with global warming and climate change, a subject far too vast to examine in one chapter, let alone one book. But if we face any challenge by the year 2012, climate change stands out as the big one. The arctic ice cap is melting at a rate 30 years ahead of predictions made by the Intergovernmental Panel of Climate Change. Because the Arctic is critical in keeping the earth cool, a decrease of ice this soon promises for a much warmer earth, with darker land and seas absorbing more light and heat. But some scientists predict this will happen even sooner. The only ones to benefit from this are oil companies that are now clamoring to secure rights to the newly thawed territories of the Lomonosov Ridge, the Beaufort Sea, and the Chuckchi Sea. Drilling could possibly begin by the year 2010, if not before.

In a December 2007 article titled "Scientist: Arctic is Screaming" for CNN.com's Planet in Peril series, new NASA satellite data points to a situation beyond critical. "The Arctic is screaming," states Mark Serreze, senior scientist at the government's snow and ice data center in Boulder, Colorado, referring to the relentless melting that is occurring at breakneck speed. In this same article, NASA climate scientist Jay Swally stated, "At this rate, the Arctic Ocean could be nearly ice-free at the end of the summer by 2012, much faster than previously thought."

Cooling Down, Heating Up

2012. The end of arctic summer ice.

In the year 2007, records for arctic ice melt were shattered in a variety of ways, including a 15 percent rise in the annual average summer melt for the Greenland ice sheet. Add to this an increase in Alaska's permafrost warming, a record amount of loss for Greenland's surface ice, and a 23-percent decline in the surface area of summer floating sea ice—the signs present a clear and present danger.

As the planet struggles to cool down in an environment of rising greenhouse gases, less reflective ice, and warmer waters, glaciologist Ted Scambos, in a Reuters news story in May 2007, sharply discounted the theory that natural cycles were causing the climate changes on which he and his panel colleagues reported. Scambos had no doubt that greenhouse gases were the culprits. And the only thing he could think of to stop the rush of global warming in the Arctic?

A large volcanic eruption and the "nuclear winter" it would create.

His final warning: "We just barely now, I think, have enough time and enough collective will to be able to get through this century in good shape, but it means we have to start acting now and in a big way."

The same scientific panel, which included the input of hundreds of scientists, released a summary in April 2007 that sent chills through the global warming community (pardon the pun). This summary stated that we are already seeing the effects of global warming in our daily lives, but when (not if) the earth warms a few degrees more, those effects will become deadly.

At the writing of this book, the year 2007 was recorded as the warmest year on record by scientists at NOAA's National Climatic Data Center. As reported to Jennifer C. Kerr, AP writer for Yahoo News on December 13, 2007, Jay Lawrimore, chief of the climate monitoring branch at the center stated, "Within the last 30 years, the rate of warming is about three times greater than the rate of warming since 1900. The annual temperatures continue to be either near-record or at record levels year in and year out."

Some of the statistics cited in the branch's report include:

∞ In the United States, the months of March and August were the second warmest in more than 100 years.

∞ Six states—Kentucky, Tennessee, South Carolina, Georgia, Alabama, and Florida—reported the warmest month of August on record.

∞ All but four states—Maine, Texas, Vermont, and New Hampshire— experienced above-average or significantly above-average temperatures between January and November.

∞ North Carolina had its driest year on record.

∞ Texas had its wettest summer on record.

∞ Globally, seven of the eight warmest years on record occurred since 2001, and the 10 warmest occurred since 1997.

Meanwhile, a World Wide Fund for Nature report released at the U.N. Climate Change Conference in Bali in 2007 warned that global climate change, combined with deforestation, could either wipe out or severely damage almost 60 percent of the Amazon forest by the year 2030. AP environmental writer Michael Casey reported on the conference findings, stating that this wipeout of the Amazon (which in many ways acts as a cooling agent for the world's temperatures, as well as a major source of fresh water) would make it impossible to keep global temperatures from reaching "catastrophic levels."

Because large swaths of the Amazon are valuable "carbon sinks," which absorb carbon dioxide, continued deforestation kills off precious vegetation needed to keep these poisons out of the atmosphere. Excessive logging, livestock expansion, and drought are the three culprits behind the decimation of the Amazon. Casey reports, "Scientists say if global temperatures rise more than 3.6 degrees above preindustrial levels, the risks to the environment and to people will be enormous. It is essentially the 'tipping point' for catastrophic floods and droughts, rising sea levels and heat wave deaths and diseases."

Daniel Nepstad, senior scientist at the Woods Hole Research Center, and author of the report, added, "It will be very difficult to keep the temperatures at 3.6 degrees if we don't conserve the Amazon." Although some scientists argue that the Amazon is too big to ever disrupt irreversibly, most side with Nepstad and call for urgent action to slow the raping of the Amazon.

Lest the powerhouse known as the North American continent think itself immune, the report's executive director of the U.N. Environment Program, Achim Steiner, stated in an AP news story on April 10, 2007, "Canada and the United States are, despite being strong economies with the financial power to cope, facing many of the same impacts that are projected for the rest of the world." Those impacts include: shifts in rainfall patterns, melting glaciers and ice caps, rising temperatures, reduced water supplies and greater global demand for water, and rising geopolitical tensions over diminishing resources.

Because the United States and Canada rely so heavily on water from snowmelt runoff, rising temps leading to less runoff spell coming disaster, and the results are already being felt. In Southern California, the 2007 wildfires that captured the attention of the entire nation opened a new can of worms in the battle over limited water supplies and the growing threat of supersized firestorms. The community of Ramona in San Diego County actually ran out of water, leaving thousands of residents without fresh supplies for weeks. With limited water, firefighters struggled to find other resources for dowsing flames that rage across years of dry brush growth. Experts believe that by 2020 (if not sooner with escalating warming a factor), more than 40 percent of Southern California's water supply will be vulnerable. This in a region still growing and expanding, adding suburban "water traps"—homes with large lawns, and golf courses—as if they were going out of style.

Water diversion is already being argued about in cities that took for granted sources that are now drying up at record rates, and for some cities, the opposite scenario will unfold, with potential superstorms flooding out regions in the tri-state area and the Gulf region. Rising sea levels, accompanied by further rising tides and storm surges, will, by the end of the 21st century, threaten to sink cities such as Boston and New York, if not sooner.

Global warming threatens the very survival of humanity, and can be held at bay, although experts argue whether it can be stopped altogether. Seemingly, we have crossed that end point and are now moving beyond maintenance mode into survival mode. And yet, governments and industry continue to find every excuse in the book to protect the economy instead of the planet.

Healthy Economy or Dying Planet?

One of the world's worst greenhouse polluters is China. With power plant emissions predicted to rise by 60 percent in the next 10 years alone, China, along with India, may outpace even the United States as the current leader in power plant emissions of carbon dioxide by the year 2017. With rising economic clout, these Eastern powerhouse nations do not seem interested in controlling emission rates, most likely looking to the nonchalance of their Western counterparts as role models. The sheer and extraordinary economic influence of the top polluters make up a critical group of CEOs determined not to let a little thing such as climate change alter their bottom line.

According to the Environmental Protection Agency's Website on climate change:

In February 2002, the United States announced a comprehensive strategy to reduce the greenhouse gas intensity of the American economy by 18 percent over the 10-year period from 2002 to 2012. Greenhouse gas intensity is a measurement of greenhouse gas emissions per unit of economic activity. Meeting this commitment will prevent the release of more than 100 million metric tons of carbon-equivalent emissions to the atmosphere (annually) by 2012 and more than 500 million metric tons (cumulatively) between 2002 and 2012.

But the leaders of other nations, as well as environmentalists and concerned citizens, protest the sheer lack of strategy from the United States in meeting these projections. In the year 2012, if we survive, the Kyoto Protocol (the protocol of the International Framework Convention on Climate Change), ratified by more than 137 countries (excluding the United States, which pulled out of the Protocol in 2001, and Australia), will end. Once it does, no nation will feel the pressure to continue to push for the stabilization of dangerous greenhouse gas concentrations in the atmosphere, especially in light of the United States's total lack of support. The current presidential administration not only rejected Kyoto, but also refused to comment to UN scientists on any future involvement beyond 2012.

Interestingly, humans may not be entirely to blame for rising global temps. In a February 26, 2006 article in *India Daily*, the India Daily Technological Team suggested that global warming might also be due to "an exponential rise in underwater volcanoes." The release of hot methane under water, the team predicted, would cause a devastating rise in ocean temperatures if "the trend continues until 2012." An interesting end date indeed.

Storms of the Century

Regardless of who, or what, is behind rises in sea levels and global climate change, the threat intensifies. In 1993, North America experienced a first. In mid-March, a severe winter storm killed more than 300 people and caused more than $10 billion in damages. This "Storm of the Century," as it would become known, was a cyclonic blizzard that stretched from Canada to

Central America during the most intense period of its five-day assault on the eastern part of the continent. Accompanied by freakishly intense snowfall, hurricane-force gusts, and record low barometric pressure, the 1993 storm brought unseasonably cold temps to many states, and snowfall levels unheard of in March. Airports from Nova Scotia to Georgia were shut down, and more than 10 million people would lose electrical power.

What makes this storm so interesting, though, is the fact that it is reportedly the first time the term superstorm became widely used. Attributed to the Weather Channel's coverage of the event, the term is now being used by climatologists and meteorologists alike to describe the growing threat of monster storms, fueled by global warming, resulting in the increase of frequency, and intensity, of extremely severe meteorological events. These extremes include everything from monster blizzards to massive floods; firestorms to deadly frosts; droughts to unrelenting tropical storms.

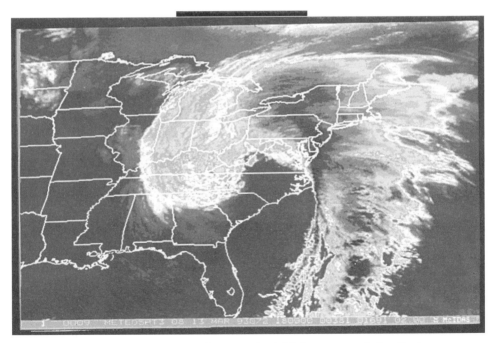

Figure 5.1: The Storm of the Century in 1993 spawned the first usage of the term *superstorm*. Image courtesy of NASA LANDSAT.

A 2007 study by NASA scientists, led by Tony Del Genio, reported in a paper for the September issue of *Geophysical Research Letters*, indicates a rising trend in more severe thunderstorms, deadly lightning, damaging hail, and increasingly deadly tornadoes. Del Genio, the coauthor of the paper, used computer models to show that global warming will produce more strong wind updrafts, thus producing more lightning and bigger hail, as well as stronger and more severe storms and tornadoes of greater frequency.

Increases in lightning, which are predicted for the western United States as the amount of carbon dioxide in the air doubles, will lead to rising firestorm fears, coupled with loss of water resources. Del Genio's research did show one benefit: decreased wind shear that might offset the effects of updrafts. But during specific times of year, wind shear would be predicted to increase throughout certain parts of the country.

In an earlier study by Leo Donner, a climate-modeling scientist with NOAA'S Geophysical Fluid Dynamics Lab in New Jersey, predicted heavier rainfall as temperatures rose, and NOAA's Harold Brooks, of the Severe Storms Lab, found similar results in terms of hail, which is predicted to increase in size and severity.

Perhaps the most obvious evidence of the superstorm threat occurred during the 2005 Atlantic hurricane season, which to date is the most active hurricane season in recorded history. It shattered all records with an unprecedented seven major hurricanes, including five Category 4s and four Category 5s, and a record 28 tropical and sub-tropical storms, 15 of which became full-fledged hurricanes. Of course, Hurricane Katrina is the most memorable of these events, which, along with Wilma, became the costliest and most intense Atlantic hurricane ever recorded. Katrina devastated the Gulf Coast region, causing widespread catastrophic damage and destruction to the coastlines and coastal cities of three states.

This record-breaking hurricane season made many in the climate studies field sit up and demand that more attention be given to global warming. The hurricane season not only began earlier than normal, but also doubled the expected activity level of former and more normal seasons. The sheer economic and political impact of the unusually strong hurricane season brought to light many of the weaknesses in the emergency management systems in place, highlighting a drastic need for greater natural disaster preparedness and planning.

Figure 5.2: Hurricane Katrina devastated the Gulf Coast region and topped off a record hurricane season in 2005. Image courtesy of NASA/Jeff Schmaltz, MODIS Land Rapid Response Team.

And that preparedness and planning is going to be more important than ever, because despite the government's party line of "global warming is not a human-caused phenomenon, and is not a threat," the evidence points to a different outcome. Along with burgeoning populations in threat regions along the vulnerable coastal areas of the United States, South America, Asia, and the Caribbean, even with only a natural climate cycle as the culprit, scientists predict a "baby boom" of Atlantic hurricanes for the next decade. Add human-generated warming to that, and the potential for years of ever-increasing storm activity, paired with increasing populations in coastal regions, promise many "ecodisasters" for which we may not be prepared. Hurricane Katrina, from which many have yet to recover, may only hint at the intensity of storms to come.

Troubles Under the Sea

Storms over the seas are not the only threat we face as we move in on the year 2012. Some experts fear what goes on under the sea even more. Imagine a greenhouse gas 20 times stronger than carbon dioxide. Now imagine mass quantities of said gas trapped beneath the bottom of the oceans, many under the arctic tundra, in a strange kind of ice called "methane clathrate."

Methane

Methane burps are considered a ticking time bomb, and they are directly related to global warming. A temperature increase of just a few degrees could cause these trapped gas reserves to become highly volatile, and release into the atmosphere as a "burp" that would further raise temperatures and heat up the earth and the ocean waters, triggering a chain reaction of runaway global warming. Submarine landslides, sea-level drops, and changes in water temperature can also cause methane burps.

Scientists believe that the most recent methane burp produced catastrophic results. During the Paleocene-Eocene Thermal Maximum (PETM), about 55 million years ago, trillions of tons of methane were released, which caused increased global warming. This spurred massive die-offs on land and sea, and created an altered climate that lasted more than 100,000 years. An even bigger series of burps occurred approximately 250 million years ago at the end of the Permian era, and destroyed more than 94 percent of all marine species. Scientists believe it could happen again, if global temperatures are allowed to continue rising.

Methane is usually released into the atmosphere via swamps and biomass burning, but the methane clathrates stored under ocean-floor sediments pose a threat that could take normal quantities into the out-of-control range. Add to that increased methane release from grazing cattle, as beef production takes over swaths of former rainforest, and that threat is intensified.

But not all scientists agree that we might one day be burped out of existence. Known as the "Clathrate Gun Hypothesis," the idea that all Quaternary global warming events have been associated with increased atmospheric methane, has had its share of controversy. Many marine scientists believe that this is more of an effect, and not a trigger, global climate changes, pointing to evidence of a rise in methane decades after temperatures began to climb.

Despite the controversy, most scientists agree that methane burps will contribute to rising temps if disturbed. It will be up to us not to disturb these sleeping gassy giants, if we so choose. Regardless, global warming signs are appearing with greater and greater frequency, and can no longer be politicized or ignored. Tiny Southern Pacific coral atoll islands such as Tuvalu are already disappearing under rising seas and a new phenomenon called "king tide," which literally brings waves that break across the entire low-lying islands.

Sea Changes

Meanwhile, on the Galapagos Islands, 10 species of local coral are now threatened for the first time in history, and 74 seaweeds have also been added to the threatened list, indicating the increasing acidity of warming waters. And in Greenland, melting glacial ice sheets are revealing islands where none existed before. Across the globe in China, brown pollution clouds are melting Himalayan glaciers, and in Japan, researchers have quantified the greenhouse-gas emissions involved in cattle production that indicate the amounts of carbon dioxide and methane that cattle add to the atmosphere.

There are other threats we face in the coming years; even outer space holds its own dark wonders.

Worries in Space

Scientists have long known that sunspots operate on a roughly 11-year cycle, from peak activity to quieter, calmer periods in between. Researchers at the National Center for Atmospheric Research (NCAR) in Boulder, Colorado, have managed to used new computer models of solar activity to simulate the intensity of the last eight solar cycles with almost 100 percent accuracy. The model examines and analyzes sunspots, which are cool, dark spots on the surface of the sun that result in solar storms capable of slowing satellite orbits, knocking out communications systems, and even creating massive power outages. These sun storms tend to occur near active sunspots, when the twisted magnetic fields in the sun suddenly snap, releasing massive amounts of energy.

The next solar cycle, according to NCAR scientists, is going to be a big one, approximately 30 to 50 percent stronger than the last cycle. Known as Cycle 24, this highly-anticipated time of unprecedented sunspot and solar storm activity is set to begin in late 2007, or early 2008, and will reach its peak in—you guessed it—2012.

Even NASA is jumping into the fray, hoping to offset the damages of this upcoming severe solar weather event. Since 1995, NASA has been observing the sun with SOHO (Solar and Heliospheric Observatory). What was generally only set as a two-year mission, SOHO has received funding through 2009 so they can continue to "watch the sun," this time along with the more sophisticated STEREO (3-D Solar Terrestrial Relations Observatory) and SDO (Solar Dynamics Observatory). The trio will continue to track magnetic storms, which can cause temporary disturbances to Earth's magnetosphere, along with coronal mass ejections, solar flares, and anything else under the sun, so to speak. The idea behind this quest to keep an eye on the sun is geared toward better prediction methods to help prevent solar storm damage, by first examining the peaks and troughs of solar storms and how they affect the Earth.

When the cycle peaks in 2012, many doomsayers predict complete shutdowns of satellite and communications systems, but past sunspot cycles, while they have had effects, have failed to bring humanity to its knees. Even the more drastic solar flares and their associated coronal mass ejections—which heat plasma to tens of millions of kelvins and propel electromagnetic radiation from all ends of the spectrum, from radio waves to the shorter bursts of gamma rays—have failed to cause catastrophic damage. X-rays and UV radiation do affect Earth's ionosphere, and have disrupted radar, long-range radio communications, and any other radio device operating on affected frequencies. But as of yet, we have not experienced the kind of complete "meltdown" that something such as a nearby gamma ray burst might cause.

Figure 5.3: The Earth's magnetosphere interacting with solar flares. Image courtesy of NASA.

Geomagnetic storms of any kind can last for many days, although most have a duration of 24 to 48 hours. During this time, the solar wind shockwave strikes the magnetic field on Earth, causing an interaction of solar particles with the magnetosphere, thus disrupting power grids, satellites, and even the Earth's ionosphere itself, creating the right conditions for auroras in the North and South Pole regions. Severe geomagnetic storms have been blamed for the collapse of the Hydro-Quebec power grid in March 1989, leaving millions without power for hours. The same storm caused auroras as far south as Texas. And a storm in August 1989 halted trading on the Toronto stock market when computers crashed.

Radiation Hazards

Obviously, a geomagnetic superstorm of epic proportions could cripple the economy, render computers useless, and put our defenses in danger by posing hazards to satellite electronic systems; radar, telephone, and communications lines; and even damage flow meters in pipelines. But the biggest threat just might be what they can do to us.

Directly, it appears that radiation hazards from geomagnetic storms only pose a problem for someone not standing upon the earth (for a great chart of hazards and affects, see *www.swpc.noaa.gov/NOAAscales/*). Because our atmosphere and magnetosphere offer humans protection against the penetration of the high-energy particles released during solar flare activity, we can assume we are pretty safe. But for astronauts moving about in space, or onboard the space station, the story is different. Potentially deadly doses of radiation can subject those in space to more than twice the danger of anyone on the ground. Astronauts on the *Mir* space station were subjected to a year's worth of radiation in just three or four hours during a particularly intense solar storm in 1989. This radiation risk is now being discussed as a major concern for future manned missions to Mars or the moon. A major solar flare in January 2005 released the highest concentration of protons on record, and traveled to Earth at a velocity of one-third light speed. This event spurred scientists to come up with a better, and faster way to protect astronauts with some type of magnetic shielding to keep them from getting bombarded with radiation before they can get to shelter. Known as Sunspot 720/Cycle 23, this incredible solar event was the size of the planet Jupiter, and ended up being the largest radiation storm since October 1989. Interestingly, 2005 was considered to be a low-level or "solar minimum" year, climaxing in September with Sunspot 798, which released the second-largest solar flare ever recorded.

Huge X-class flares (the solar flare rating scale is: C for light, M for Middle, X for most intense) were abundant during the year 2005. In September alone, approximately 10 X-class flares bombarded earth with radiation storms and caused a temporary shutdown of CB, ham, and shortwave radio transmissions in the Western Hemisphere.

Biological Effects

Indirectly (yet no less critically), we humans might see the damages of geomagnetic shifts, storms, and disruptions on a more biological level, and one that might reveal itself throughout longer durations of time through genetic mutations. What we do know now is that geomagnetic storms, and any solar activity that produces higher than normal radiation levels, do seem to mess with some "internal compass" of creatures such as whales, pigeons, and dolphins. Homing pigeons and dolphins have an organ containing tiny crystals of "magnetite" that allow them to discern magnetic fields. This also may be the case for whales, especially those that migrate long distances with little visual aids. Similarly, the human brain supposedly contains magnetite.

A May 2005 AFP article titled "Whale Strandings Linked to Solar Activity" suggested that "surges of solar activity may cause whales to run aground, possibly by disrupting the creatures' internal compasses." The same article pointed to research by Klaus Vaneslow and Klaus Ricklefs of the University of Kiel, which examined beached sperm whales in the North Sea from 1712 to 2003. Their records showed that more whale strandings occurred when sunspot activity was high, paralleling the whale beaching data with historical astronomical observations.

Homing pigeons suffer the greatest effects, with degradation of their navigational abilities during geomagnetic storms responsible for "smashes," a term used to indicate when only a small percentage of racing birds return to their home from a release site. Higher geomagnetic storm activity leads to higher smashes, enough so that many homing pigeon handlers insist on geomagnetic alerts as aids in scheduling races!

Acupuncturists have long believed that the human body is surrounded and permeated by a magnetic grid that, when out of balance, creates illness and disease. Charged particles that hit the Eearth from solar storms and flares interact with not only the Earth's magnetic field, but also our own bodily magnetic field. Some in the holistic field wonder if this might be the reason behind record-breaking numbers of mood and personality disorders such as depression, addiction, and anxiety.

The magnetite-bearing organs in dolphins, honeybees, and homing pigeons may correspond to the human inner compass of this inner grid. The British *Sunday Times* reported in September 2005 that research on behalf of a private company called the Health Protection Agency found links between human illness and electromagnetic fluctuations. The illnesses mentioned included headaches, nausea, anxiety, depression, and even muscle pains, and suggested that even things such as EMFs from mobile phones and computer screens could be contributing to a general malaise now known as "electrosensitivity."

Paranormal Changes

GMF (geomagnetic field) activity has also been linked, strangely enough, to increases of ESP and paranormal activity, poltergeist phenomenon, and even bursts of human creativity, as well as increased hallucinations due to possible influences upon the pineal hormone and melatonin (reported in "The Solar Wind and Hallucinations" by Walter and Steffani Randall for the 1991 issue of *Bioelectromagnetics*). Other research reports show correlations between increased GMF activity and the number of admissions to psychiatric hospitals (Raps Avi et al., "Geophysical Variables and Behavior: Solar Activity and Admission of Psychiatric Inpatients," 1992), and an analysis of "possible relations between GMF activity and electrodermal activity; rate of hemolysis of human red blood cells in vitro; psychokinetic influences of electrodermal activity; and attempted distant psychokinetic influence of rate of hemolysis, all of which showed direct correlations between higher and lower GMF activity, and higher and lower measurement values." (William G. Braud and Stephen P. Dennis, "Geophysical Variables and Behavior; LVIII. Autonomic Activity, Hemolysis, and Biological Psychokinesis: Possible Relationships with Geomagnetic Field Activity," 1989).

North Pole/South Pole

There is no doubt that the 2012 sunspot cycle peak will bring more opportunities to study the affects of GMF activity on humans, if we survive. And it is more than likely we will...perhaps just in time to be nailed by an even bigger catastrophe.

In a December 2005 *National Geographic* article titled "North Magnetic Pole is Shifting Rapidly Toward Russia," reporter Brian Vastag joked that Santa had better check his compass. The North Pole, it seems, is moving at a rapid rate of 40 kilometers a year, and is now heading toward Siberia.

The topic of magnetic pole shift has sent many 2012-awaiters into a tizzy, with worries of catastrophic disaster as the Earth flips end over end and the North Pole becomes the southernmost point on the map. But shift happens, and the current oscillation of the Earth's magnetic field may be more normal than we think.

The last pole flip occurred 780,000 years ago, and reversals may have occurred more than 400 times in the last 330 million years. Scientists look to magnetic clues "sealed in rocks around the world," according to Vastag. But Joe Stoner, a paleomagnetist at Oregon State University, says this is nothing dramatic. "It's probably just a normal wandering of the pole." Wandering poles? Flip-flopping fields? Sounds more like politics.

Stoner's team examined deep mud cores and clay from the bottom of frigid arctic lakes to determine that a recent drop in the strength of Earth's magnetic field is partially responsible for the north-south reversals and "jerks" in the magnetic fields, which occur often and not always during a complete reversal.

Dr. Peter Olson, a professor and geophysicist at Johns Hopkins University, is also heavily involved in pole shift research, which he believes is underway, and admits that the Earth's magnetic field is weakening. His research (available at *www.jhu/edu/~eps/faculty/olson/*) examines the links between theory, numerical models, and laboratory fluid dynamic models to interpret global geophysical data about the earth's deep interior, including the mantle and core, concentrating especially on how these interact to produce the GMF.

Scientists admit that a weakening magnetic field seems to be a precursor to a pole reversal. Geological records show these reversals have happened, but until fairly recently, it was believed to be random. In early 2006, a team of physicists from Italy's University of Calabria, led by Vincenzo Carbone, discovered that the sequence of polarity reversals follow a non-random distribution known as a Levy distribution, rather than a random Poisson distribution. Their research, reported on Physicsworld.com on March 21, 2006, suggests, "The result means that polarity reversals are not random events that are independent of each other.… Instead, there is some degree of memory in the magnetic dynamo processes giving rise to reversals."

The team also plans to research what physical mechanisms might be triggering pole reversals. But regardless of why they happen, how they happen, and what triggers them, a recent study by a team of scientists at the Utrecht University of the Netherlands, as reported in the October 12, 2006 journal *Nature*, posits that wobbling of the Earth's orbit might be behind a cycle of extinctions. By studying 22 million years of fossil data, the team of 22 scientists, led by Jan van Dam, found corresponding evidence between periods of extinction and changes in the Earth's orbit that act to cool the planet.

There appear to be two different cycles of turnover rates at play. A 2.5-million-year peak occurs each time the Earth's orbit is closest to being a perfect circle. The second cycle occurs every million years when the planet shifts its degree of tilt on its axis. Both cycles have the same end result of global cooling and expansion of ice sheets.

Van Dam believes the next 2.5-million-year cycle of turnover would peak in about 600,000 to 800,000 years, but does admit that global climate changes that have occurred throughout the past 3 million years add to the uncertainty of that prediction. In essence, though, global warming is on the fast track to occurring far sooner than any global cooling.

NASA's own Magnetic Field Satellite has proven that for the last 1,800 years or so, the Earth has been experiencing this decrease in the magnetic field, and that the field, according to satellite measurements, will hit "zero" in approximately 1,200 years (although some scientists suggest it will not hit actual zero, but perhaps about 20 percent of its normal field strength). Then, a reversal will take place, topping off a time of radical environmental and physical changes to both the planet and perhaps its people.

So, if NASA predicts the next reversal won't happen until well after 2012, what can we expect in the next five years? The effects of magnetic shift and reversal on humans are not entirely clear. We do know that, similar to many species of marine and animal life, our inner compass might be disrupted, and because our brains have magnetite, might we expect widespread confusion, mental illnesses, and gross incoordination? If the human neurological system is challenged, would we be able to continue living a normal existence?

Gamma Rays

Once the geomagnetic field has been compromised, we might be in for trouble, as high-energy particles from deadly gamma rays penetrate what little defense we naturally have, causing shutdowns of communications systems and electrical power grids, and also damaging humans at the cellular level with radiation, causing genetic mutations and who knows what else. Gamma-ray bursts are high-energy radiation beams that shoot from the north and south magnetic poles of a star undergoing a supernova explosion, in which the core of the massive star implodes into a black hole. Gamma-ray bursts (GRBs) are the most powerful explosions we know of in the universe. They occur rather randomly, and don't last long, which can be frustrating for scientists trying to study them by localizing the gamma rays and x-rays that follow the burst.

One of the closest GRBs recorded by scientists occurred on March 29, 2003, at 6:37 a.m. EST. Given the name GRB 030329, this burst and its afterglow were the brightest ever recorded, pouring out approximately 1,000 trillion, trillion times the gamma rays typically seen in a solar flare. The afterglow from this burst stayed strong even an hour later, but occurred almost 2 billion light years from Earth. Though it was too far to see with the naked eye, it was relatively close in astronomical terms, for a GRB, with a redshift measurement of 0.168—the second-closest redshift measurement recorded after a burst. Redshift refers to the measurement of light in distant parts of the universe. Light shifts to a lower energy level as the universe expands. Thus, the greater the redshift, the further away the burst is from Earth.

The chance of a gamma-ray burst hitting so close that it wipes out life on Earth is miniscule, at least in comparison to other more pressing disasters we face (many of which will be explored in the next few chapters). An article for Ohio State's *Research* titled "Deadly Astronomical Event Not Likely to Happen In Our Galaxy, Study Finds," examines the likeliness, or rather unlikeliness, of a potentially deadly GRB striking Earth, or even our own galaxy. The study, led by a group of astronomers at Ohio State, suggests that GRBs tend to occur in "small, misshapen galaxies that lack the heavy chemical elements. Even among metal-poor galaxies, the events are rare—astronomers only detect a GRB once every few years."

The Milky Way is a large spiral galaxy with plenty of heavy elements, but does that mean we are in danger?

The study looked at four nearby galaxies where GRBs have been recorded, and found that even in the one with the most metals, the one most similar to our own galaxy, the odds of a GRB happening would be approximately 0.15 percent.

As for damage to humans from GRBs, if the deadly gamma and x-rays constantly bombarded us from above, there would definitely be cause for concern. Gamma rays and x-rays cause chemical reactions in cells called "radiolysis," which breaks the atomic bonds within the molecular structure and destroys the chemical makeup. Gamma rays are the most intensely penetrating form of radiation, and even x-rays, which can be just as intense, but differ from gamma rays only in terms of origin (gamma rays are nuclear in origin, x-rays are generally of atomic origin), have enough energy to ionize matter. Ionizing radiation produces ion pairs that can destroy or alter molecular bonds. This creates free radicals, which continue to damage molecular structure.

What scientists are not so certain of is how much damage is being done by GRBs so far from Earth. Are we on a genetic "slow ride" to mutation from trickles of radiation from distant bursts?

Meanwhile, gamma-ray hunters use orbiting detectors, fast relays to observers worldwide via the Gamma-ray Burst Coordinates Network (GCN), and ground-based robotic telescopes, as well as the HETE (High-Energy Transient Explorer) satellite to keep a close watch on these mighty cosmic monsters. We might not be able to stop one in its tracks, but at least we will know when it's coming.

This same situation applies to what may be the most pressing threat from above, a threat often mentioned in discussions of 2012: asteroids.

Asteroids

Are you sitting down? According to the November 2007 issue of *Discover* magazine, in an article titled "What To Do Before the Asteroid Strikes," reporter Andrew Lawler reveals this tidbit of information:

"In 2004, as a massive tsunami rolled through the Indian Ocean killing hundreds of thousands of people, a dozen or so scientists quietly confronted an impending disaster potentially even more lethal."

The article continues, describing a 1,300-foot-wide chunk of rock and metal being closely watched by scientists, a chunk of rock hurtling toward "a possible collision with the most populated swath of Earth—Europe, India, and Southeast Asia." The scientists frantically crunched some numbers and put the odds of impact, in the year 2009, at 1 in 37 chance of that happening.

Yikes.

They gave the asteroid a name. Apophis—derived from the Egyptian god Apep, the "destroyer who dwells in eternal darkness."

Okay, you can stand up now, because by the end of that same day, the team turned up trajectory information putting the odds of a collision at nil. Still, they do admit Apophis will make a close fly-by, coming closer, in fact, than the global communications satellites do.

Maybe you want to sit down again. A 2-mile long monster rock named 2007PA8 has been discovered, too. This one, known as a "civilization ender," is large enough to send us right into the extinction zone. But the odds of it hitting us? Nil.

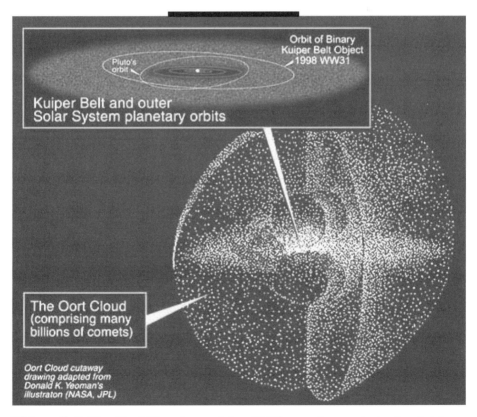

Figure 5.4: The Oort Cloud consists of billions of comets just outside Pluto's orbit. Image courtesy of NASA.

Figure 5.5: The Barringer Crater in Arizona is proof of past asteroid impacts and their amazing size and strength. Image courtesy of PDPhoto.org.

And therein lies the problem with these "doomsday rocks." There are millions of asteroids floating around in the solar system, many with the potential to wipe humanity off the slate for good. Even the smaller ones can cause another disaster similar to the impact at Tunguska, Siberia, that caused a smackdown of a huge swatch of forestland. The vast bulk of these nasty rocks, which range from pea size to the 560-mile-wide Ceres, make their home in the asteroid belt between Mars and Jupiter.

Many of these asteroids stay in their places, but often they veer off course, usually when closest to the planet Jupiter, and end up being pushed out of the procession into deep space. While some spin toward Pluto and beyond, others might find a new trajectory toward the sun, or begin a new orbit around another planet. Others swarm in the Oort Cloud outside our solar system.

But it's the near-Earth asteroids that cause the greatest concern. Many scientists believe that just such an asteroid impact caused the extinction of the mighty dinosaurs approximately 65 million years ago (although new research is leading more and more experts to believe that supervolcanoes right here on Earth may have been far more involved than previously thought!). Anyone who has ever visited the famous three-quarter-mile-wide Meteor Crater, also known as the Barringer Meteorite Crater, in Arizona, knows the power of an asteroid impact.

Asteroid detection has evolved considerably, and NASA can monitor changes in the orbit of asteroids in the nearby belt, and detect incoming threats from beyond the solar system. In addition, NASA is hard at work on ways to actually alter an asteroid's orbit or trajectory, and possibly prevent a direct hit. The B612 Foundation, a group of scientists at the Johnson Space Center in Houston, hope to have a plan to do just this by 2015. The European Space Agency is also putting their own concrete ideas into action as part of their Don Quixote, a conceptual spacecraft that might push an asteroid out of its intended path, while another spacecraft called Sancho monitors activity nearby.

Other ideas being tested involve vaporizing part of the asteroid, shooting projectiles into a comet, and even using the gravitational pull of a "space-tug" to gently change an asteroid's trajectory. Astronauts Edward T. Lu and Stanley G. Love are working on a unique plan using gravitational force to "tow" an asteroid off course, using an unmanned craft to fly close enough to the rock to form a gravitational bond. The force of the bond throughout two or three years, they suggest, would be enough to gently pull the asteroid out of its Earth-directed trajectory. The technology needed to pull this off is years away, but NASA has indeed begun developing the nuclear-electric motors that would be required to attempt such a feat.

This proactive approach may keep us from one day being vaporized, and going the way of the dinosaurs. Unlike gamma-ray bursts, which cannot at this time be prevented or deflected, at least we have a fighting chance when the big rocks com a-callin'.

But there may be a more pressing problem to deal with in the next few years that is right here on Earth, and this one cannot be deflected, altered, or stopped.

Supervolcano

The earth is never still, always restless…changing. Although most major seismic activity can result in regional, even national disasters, only one has the capacity to create a global disaster that would end a huge swath of human, animal, and plant life, and drastically alter life for those lucky, or unlucky enough to survive.

A supervolcano can radically and permanently alter life on Earth in a way that few other calamitous events could. Unlike "normal" volcanic activity, which can easily kill thousands and wreak environmental havoc with ashfall and cooling, a supervolcano does that to the utmost extreme, resulting in global cooling that can lead to mini ice ages. Volcanic winters and nuclear winters are the same thing, with one exception. We can prevent the nuclear version.

Supervolcanoes are identified as volcanoes that create massive eruptions of ejected material. Using a scale similar to the Richter Scale for earthquake activity, volcanism is measure by the Volcanic Explosivity Index (VEI), which measures:

∞ volume of ejected material.
∞ eruptive column height.
∞ subjective descriptions of the eruption (gentle, effusive, explosive, cataclysmic, and so on).
∞ plume head height.

The two most important measurements are the volume of ejected material and plume height. The VEI ranges from 1 to 8, with 8 being a supereruption or mega-eruption event. These eruptions eject at least 1,000 km^3 of pyroclastic material, which consists of rock, ash, and gases.

Supervolcanoes have been around since the dawn of time, helping to shape the planet, and even playing a role, as recent research shows, in the mass extinctions of species. But it's been 26,500 years since we've had a supereruption, when Lake Taupo in New Zealand's North Island ejected 1,170 km^3 of material.

The largest supervolcanic eruptions that we know of are, in order from biggest to smallest in terms of their volume of erupted material:

∞ **La Garita Caldera, Colorado**—The Fish Canyon Tuff is the biggest event we know of, putting out ~5,000 km³.

∞ **Lake Toba, Sumatra, Indonesia**—Erupted 74,000 years ago and ejected 2,800 km³. Also caused a population bottleneck that almost wiped humanity off the map, as documented in my book *Supervolcano: The Catastrophic Event That Changed the Course of Human History*, coauthored with geophysicist Dr. John Savino.

∞ **Yellowstone, Wyoming**—The Yellowstone Caldera erupted 2.2 million years ago, with 2,500 km³, and 640,000 years ago, with 1,000 km³.

∞ **Lake Taupo, New Zealand**—26,500 years ago, with 1,170 km³.

There have been many other massive eruptions that list below 7 on the VEI, with the 1815 Tambora eruption (160 km³) the largest in recorded history. But the geological record shows that the earth is constantly undergoing explosive volcanic activity, especially around the 25,000-mile-long Ring of Fire that arches over the land surrounding the Pacific Ocean, encompassing Japan, Indonesia, and northward, then across the Bering Strait and down the western coasts of Canada, the United States, and Central and South Americas.

The vast majority of all seismic activity occurs along the Ring. And in terms of which supervolcano might erupt next, we look to the sunny states of Wyoming and California.

When it comes to supervolcanoes, the Yellowstone caldera-forming eruptions are the most widely known, thanks in part to some greatly entertaining movies, TV, pseudo-documentaries, and a mythology built up around the gorgeous national park. A supereruption at Yellowstone is also the most widely associated with 2012 and predictions of seismic cataclysmic doom.

The Yellowstone eruptions have been said to include a third event, which occurred 1.3 million years ago, thus creating a recurrence interval that indicates the caldera is overdue to blow again sometime soon. As described in *Supervolcano: The Catastrophic Event That Changed the Course of Human History*, this recurrence interval to which most people refer is flawed.

"A recurrence interval of 600,000 to 700,000 years is often quoted for large caldera eruptions at Yellowstone, even though it is only based on two intervals, and, as a result, of highly questionable statistical significance. It should be noted that the 1.3-million-year event, while a very large eruption, was not a supervolcano, and casts additional doubt on the meaning of a recurrence interval at the Yellowstone hotspot."

Yet we still hear lay prognosticators talking about a pending supereruption, possibly coinciding with the year 2012 itself, as if the caldera was primed and geared for such an event. However, there are signs of restlessness and activity around Yellowstone, including 1,000 to 3,000 earthquakes each year, which is an indication of ongoing seismic motion. A greater indicator is deformation of the caldera, which has indeed been rising and falling for the past 15,000 years. Between 1997 and 2003 alone, the northern part of the caldera began to bulge, rising about 5 inches throughout a 25-mile-wide area. This was accompanied by a sudden rise in temperatures, new steam vents, and increased or new geyser activity around the area, including the erupting of the Steamboat Geyser in May 2000 after nine years of dormancy.

Earthquakes

Earthquakes and increased geothermal phenomena don't necessarily point to a pending supervolcanic eruption. Even with the added signs of "tree kill," in which swaths of trees die from large volumes of carbon dioxide seeping into soil due to magma movement and rising pressure, or "harmonic tremor," which is present when magma begins to really move beneath the caldera floor, it would still not indicate that a supervolcanic eruption was imminent.

If these signs of unrest are meant to scare, then perhaps our attention should be drawn further west and south, to the Long Valley caldera in central California. The Long Valley caldera is located near the Mammoth Lakes ski resort just south of Mono Lake near the Nevada state line. The Long Valley caldera is the result of a supereruption that occurred approximately 760,000 years ago, ejecting between 140 and 170 cubic miles of high-silica rhyolite, and approximately 50 times the amount of magma ejected during the 1991 Mount Pinatubo, Philippines, eruption. Long Valley was a massive, short-duration eruption (10 days), resulting in a 10×12-mile oval depression that is now the caldera we see today.

According to *Supervolcano*, another large-scale eruption at either Yellowstone or Long Valley could result in a drastic global climate cooling known as volcanic winter, as huge volumes of volcanic gases released into the atmosphere affect temperatures across the planet for several years.

Long Valley is showing all the signs of unrest, short of harmonic tremor. Similar to Yellowstone, it is being monitored 24 hours a day by the USGS. But unlike Yellowstone, Long Valley is potentially linked to another imminent natural disaster that could, as new research suggests, trigger a supervolcanic eruption.

On June 28, 1992, a magnitude 7.3 earthquake occurred 100 miles east of Los Angeles in the desert town of Landers. This quake actually triggered a swarm of small quakes beneath the Yellowstone caldera, and even temporarily altered the eruption rate of one of the park's most accurate geysers. At Long Valley, the Landers quake triggered the strongest "swarm" in the caldera during that entire year, with more than 250 small quakes in the six days following Landers alone.

On October 16, 1999, the Hector Mine quake, magnitude 7.1, hit the Mojave Desert area in Southern California. The distance between the Hector Mine quake and Yellowstone and Long Valley was comparable to the Landers event, yet this time, only Long Valley showed any deformation and quake swarms immediately following the quake.

San Andreas Fault

No Southern Californian is unaware of the San Andreas Fault. We who live here live with the daily threat of "The Big One," a massive quake that many earth scientists believe could happen any moment of any day…

This continental transform fault produces strike-slip quakes, that move the tectonic plates horizontally, so that a person standing on the western side of the fault would, during a quake, move left, and at the same time see a person on the eastern side move to the right. The San Andreas Fault has been the subject of countless "Irwin Allen–style" disaster movies, books, and TV shows, and all the hoopla may not be just Hollywood sensationalism. A June 2006 study by Yuri Fialko, an associate professor of geophysics at the Institute of Geophysics and Planetary Physics at Scripps Institute of Oceanography in La Jolla, California, found that the southernmost segment of the San Andreas Fault, from San Bernardino to the Mexican border, is primed for a massive earthquake. This particular section of the fault has not produced a quake above a magnitude 7 in more than 300 years.

It is long overdue. It is imminent. And it is only 280 miles from the Long Valley caldera (770 miles from Yellowstone). If smaller quakes measuring 7.1 and 7.3 on the Richter Scale could affect activity at Long Valley, one has to wonder what a seismic monster of an 8.5 or higher might do...and many scientists insist The Big One will be at least a magnitude 8, or possibly a series of larger quakes below an 8, but equally devastating.

Although no scientist could possibly come right out and say that a San Andreas quake could trigger a supervolcano at Long Valley, the evidence that points to the possibility of just such a scenario is growing. Still, there is no indication that this could or will happen tomorrow, or in 2012, or 10,000 years from now.

Unlike humans, the Earth doesn't always stick to a calendar.

6

The Now Explosion

By avarice and selfishness, and a groveling habit, from which none of us is free, of regarding the soil as property...the landscape is deformed.
—Henry David Thoreau, *Walden*

As I write this book, the world population clock on the United States Census Bureau's Website stands at approximately 6,700,000,000. By the time we reach 2050, if we do, that number will climb to a startling 9 billion. And if 2005 fertility rates remain at a constant state, that number could reach as high as 11 billion.

Population Situation

According to numerous sources, the global population has actually been slowing; even fertility seems to be on a downward trend. But the problem is not in the rates themselves, but in how fast those rates are being increased. Rapid population throughout specific periods of time is the problem. In the

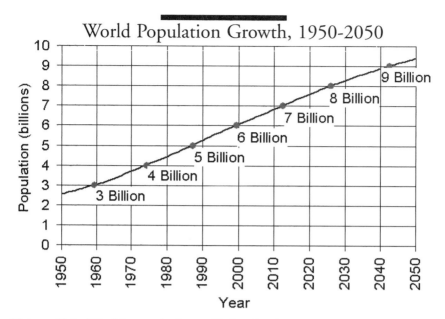

Figure 6.1: World population will rise by 3 billion by the year 2050. Graph courtesy of U.S. Census Bureau.

World Population Growth, 1750–2150

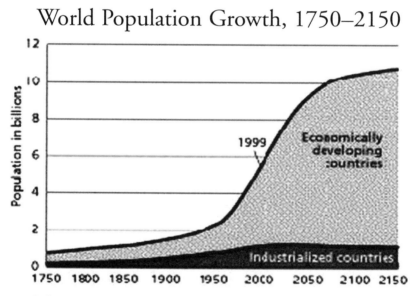

Figure 6.2: Note the rising population growth in economically developing nations. Courtesy of Population Connection in Washington, D.C.

September 2005 issue of *Scientific American*, Joel E. Cohen, professor of populations and head of the Laboratory of Populations at Rockefeller University and Columbia University, states that "Although the rate of population growth has fallen since the 1970s, the logic of compounding means that current levels of global population growth are still greater than any experienced prior to Word War II." Cohen describes how the first absolute increase in human population by 1 billion took from the beginning of time until the early 19th century. Today, we are seeing 1 billion people added to the human roster in just 13 to 14 years.

Human population growth is a major crisis, with between 74 million to 76 million people adding to the numbers annually. Death rates, along with infertility rates, may account for a drop of 1 to 2 billion people, but the growth rate far outweighs any of those numbers.

Cohen predicts that "virtually all population growth in the next 45 years is expected to occur in economically less developed regions." This means that, despite higher death rates, the populations of poor nations will outpace those of richer nations. More people, more poverty.

Between 2005 and 2050, Cohen sees tripled populations for nations such as Afghanistan, Chad, Congo, East Timore, Liberia, Mali, Niger, and Uganda, as well as some of the other poorest nations on Earth. "Half the global increase will be accounted for by just nine nations," Cohen writes. Those nine nations are: India, Pakistan, Nigeria, the Congo, Bangladesh, Uganda, the United States, Ethiopia, and China. The rise in U.S. population will be mainly due to immigration.

Poverty

Poverty is going to be one of the biggest, most challenging issues we as a species face. Many economically developed nations will actually decrease in population in the next several decades, leaving the poorer nations in a more demanding position for diminishing global resources such as fresh, drinkable water. And, as Cohen points out, most of that growth in the poorest nations will occur in urban areas, resulting in the equivalent of one new city, home to more than 1 million people, built each week for the *next 45 years.*

In truth, the number of people living in extreme poverty has actually shrunk since 1981, when there were approximately 1.5 billion people living in dire conditions. As the global economy increased throughout the next two decades, 2001 saw an estimated 1.1 billion poor. According to the Millennium Development Goals, part of the UN Millennium Project, projections show those numbers down to 0.7 billion by 2015. That is good news, but not good enough, because the number of people existing on less than $1 a day, with little access to fresh foods and water, is still staggering. And although the new global economy has supported the rapid economic advancement of nations such as China and India, other nations are largely forgotten; China exploded economically, but Africa suffered, and it is the area of the highest extreme poverty levels to this day. The future, for Africa and other poverty-stricken Asian and Latin American regions, does not look much better, unless real focus is placed on expanding development assistance.

Some of that assistance could come from the UN's ambitious project to give the poorest of people basic survival necessities: food, water, basic healthcare, and shelter, all of which can be covered by a combination of financing from domestic corporations and government institutions, with international institutions making up the gap. The UN Millennium Project estimates it would cost a total investment of $110 per person a year for tropical Africa alone, with a total of $160 billion a year needed to provide global poverty assistance. That is a lot of money indeed, but think about it in terms of the amount spent by the United States alone on the Iraq war, or the profits made collectively in one year by the leading oil companies.

With this kind of investment program, the UN Project estimates that global poverty could be drastically cut by 2015, possibly eliminated by 2025, placing more than a billion people above that mere subsistence level, even allowing them to look with hope toward a better economic future. Still, we must act quickly before population numbers rise too drastically to keep up with levels of available resources.

Shifting of the Ages

Before we get into a discussion of rising population versus diminishing resources, there is an even more startling population statistic. Even as we are actually seeing a slowing population growth rate (but again, the growth is happening so much faster, so that offsets the benefit), we are seeing a tremendous shift in demographics that could have major repercussions for the rest of the 21st century.

The 20th century is the last time in human history when we will see the population of younger people outpace that of older people.

By 2050, it is predicted that one in three people in more developed nations will be over the age of 60. This rate falls in less developed regions, where the ratio is one in five. With average life spans now at more than 65 years, and lower fertility levels in developed countries, this new demographic force will affect just about every aspect of human life, especially the labor force. In a February 2004 article in the *Monthly Labor Review*, reporter Mitra Toosi looked at projected trends in the labor force from 2004 to 2012. The results show that by 2012, the annual growth rate of the 55-years-and-older demographic will be approximately four times that of the overall labor force.

The rate of growth in the women's labor force is expected to stay the same, yet still increase at a faster rate than that of men, 1.3 percent to the men's 1.0 percent. Women's share of the labor force, however, is expected to jump to 47.5 percent by 2012, opposed to a decline in the men's labor force to 52.5 percent. And again, the aging Baby Boomers born between 1946 and 1964 will be the lion's share of the labor force growth, making up an eventual 66 percent of total labor for those between 25 and 54, and 19.1 percent for folks over 55.

This shift in demographics will of course determine the type of labor that will take precedence in the coming five years, with older workers, as well as increased presence of women, changing the way things are usually done "on the job." Even if the types of jobs that older workers and women hold end up shifting, these two demographic groups also face the challenges of medical care as the population of dependent elderly people skyrockets. Urbanization actually raises the "economic premium" for younger people, while diminishing it for less mobile older workers. This stronger population presence in cities also "weakens traditional kin networks that provide familial support to elderly people," Cohen writes. "An older, uneducated woman who could have familial support and productive work in agriculture if she lived in a rural area might have difficulty finding both a livelihood and social support in a city."

The looming elderly dependency crisis will depend largely on the health of the growing elderly population. Elderly people are seeing positive trends in health, as well as increased medical resources, with married elderly people having it much easier in terms of home care. Single, widowed, and divorced elderly will no doubt present a healthcare challenge to a planet already strapped with problems, as AIDS and other emerging diseases rise, the environment declines, and economic power shifts out of the West.

Can We Run Out of Water?

Human population trends seem most stark when it comes to the effect on the environment. Where ingenuity and creativity can often offset challenges to a changing workforce demographic, including the increase of telecommuting jobs and easier communication options, the environment poses problems to which no easy solutions come to mind.

The Washington, D.C.–based organization, Population Connection, has some shocking statistics:

- ∞ Every 20 minutes, we lose one or more entire species of plant or animal life.

- ∞ By 2025, almost 48 percent of the Earth's population will live in an area of water stress or scarcity, a problem that could not only affect humans, but also destroy delicately balanced ecosystems.

- ∞ Only 0.3 percent of the planet's water is available for human consumption. More than 40 percent of ground water in the United States alone is contaminated by industrial, agricultural, and household pollution, rendering it almost impossible or extremely costly to purify.

- ∞ The United States makes up only 5 percent of the world's population, yet consumes a stunning 25 percent of the world's resources, with countries such as China and India now looming as major "consumption" nations as well.

- ∞ In the United States alone, land that is currently used for urban sprawl is expanding by 305 percent, stressing the surrounding environment with higher carbon dioxide levels due to greater car dependency.

The issue of water alone threatens billions of people. Currently, more than 1.2 billion people do not have access to safe drinking water, and more than 3 million die each year because of unsafe water. More than half the world's major rivers are so polluted that they endanger human health; not to mention what that pollution does to surrounding ecosystems. In 2003, UN Secretary General Kofi Annan said, "Water is likely to become a growing source of tension and fierce competition between nations, if present trends continue, but it can also be a catalyst for cooperation." This is a widely held opinion. Brian Fagan, emeritus professor of anthropology at the University of California, Santa Barbara, said in the September/October issue of *Archeology Magazine* that "Many futurologists believe tomorrow's wars will revolve around water as much as they will territorial claims or weapons of mass destruction…. The short-term effects of a drought or hurricane may be catastrophic, but the subtler results such as major and minor social changes, shifting of capitals, or new agricultural methods, may surface years, or even generations later, as a society adjusts to changed circumstances…."

Obviously, more people means less clean, fresh water for consumption, and though there are things we can do to conserve water, such as implementing low-cost technologies like drip irrigation, curbing industrial air pollution, and instituting pricing policies that cut down over-consumption by rich nations (which will allow poorer nations to get the water they need for survival), those ideas have gained little ground. Greed and a lust for resources in rich nations seem unabated.

By 2025, projections show that two-thirds of the global population will suffer from water stress or serious water scarcity. Twenty-five years later, more than 4 billion people will be living on less than 50 liters of water per day. The danger of the planet's water resources being in the hands of rich nations, or, as is being discussed today, privatized to corporations, raises the specter of wars and geopolitical conflict. Where we now fight wars over oil, we may soon do so over water, and the spoils will no doubt go to the strongest nations.

In the January 2008 issue of *Discover Magazine*, Megan Mansall Williams reported on the waterless future facing Australia, a nation considered "the canary in the coal mine when it comes to the impact climate change on water resources," according to Ross Young, executive director of the Water Services Association of Australia. Williams also reported that water shortages will intensify in Australia, as well as China, Africa, Asia, parts of Europe, and the United States, affecting more than 3.2 billion people by the end of this century. "Environmental experts warn that Australia's plight should be making the whole world thirsty," as the country enters its seventh year of the worst drought in a millennium.

Population Connection quotes Joel E. Cohen as saying that "there is enough water on our planet for every living person, but it is often at the wrong place at the wrong time." In the United States, the effects of acute water shortage rear their ugly heads each time the southwest burns with massive wildfires, and in the southeast, where 40 to 50 percent of freshwater snail species are extinct or endangered, thanks to the redirecting of rivers coupled with increased pollution. The year 2007 saw droughts throughout the southeast—regions usually experiencing plenty of rainfall, and many states were forced to ration what little drinkable water there was.

The problem, of course, is worldwide. As China and India experience rapid human population and economic growth, they consume more and more of what little water there is, adding to political pressures already being experienced by competing nations eager to plant their flags on the existing supplies. Meanwhile, these nations increase their global carbon footprints. A perfect example of too much life living on too little resources is Bangladesh; more than 20 percent of freshwater wells are unfit for human consumption.

Lack of fresh water also leads to sanitation issues, with urbanization compounding the increase of infectious diseases. Water is so critical to agricultural development that many experts believe it is a crucial element in controlling poverty, and just may be the main cause of the poverty itself. Farmers suffer the most when water is scarce, and because half the world's poor are farmers who work their own plots of land, the connection between the two is palpable.

Agriculture

Water is not the only red-flag issue of the future. Food production may also struggle to keep up with consumption levels. As more and more people flock to urban areas, that arable land is removed from the agricultural production scenario, thus lessening the amount of available food in a specific region. Increased use of chemical fertilizing agents also threatens to destroy soil quality, thus affecting the ability of plantable ground to produce higher quantities of grains, vegetables, and fruits fit to be consumed.

In other words, the more we mess up the earth, the less she can hope to sustain us.

Earlier in the year 2007, the U.S. Department of Agriculture struggled to learn the reason behind a massive honeybee die-off that threatened the U.S. food supply. Because honeybees pollinate more than 90 percent of the flowering, edible crops, any decrease in their population raises a red flag. One-third of the human diet comes directly from insect-pollinated plants, of which, the USDA. says, honeybees are responsible for pollinating the vast majority. The die-off got so bad that Yahoo News quoted Kevin Hackett, the national program leader for the USDA's bee and pollination program, saying that the honeybee issue was "the biggest general threat to our food supply."

Not every scientist agreed that this particular bee die-off was so dire. Large-scale die-offs have happened in the past, including several in the 1960s and 1970s, but this particular Colony Collapse Disorder, which eventually spread through more than 26 states and into Brazil, Europe, and Canada, was considered highly unusual, because of the rate of collapse. There is also the concern that the top suspect is an unknown virus or parasite, possibly combined with excessive pesticide use, which has been instrumental in the declining rates of honeybees throughout the last several decades.

What this die-off suggests, whether the cause turns out to be perfectly natural or human-initiated, is that our food production system is just as sensitive as our water resource availability. If a little buzzing bee could disrupt the ability of a nation to produce fresh fruits and vegetables, it reminds us how delicate the entire balance of nature is. And by no means is the honeybee issue small—a Congressional study shows that honeybees add approximately $15 billion a year to the food supply! With added pesticide use, along with soil degradation, polluted water run-off, and a host of other negative factors, we can expect greater challenges to our food supply, including more "recalls" of products laced with toxins, especially those we import from other nations where testing standards are low or nonexistent.

Food Inflation

A coinciding problem is food inflation. Soaring food prices make it difficult for even middle class families to keep their refrigerators stocked with healthy, nutritional foods. According to a 2007 study by Advanced Economic Solutions, food-inflation is now at an all-time high, and will continue for the next five years, mainly due to growing world populations, expanding economies, an increased demand for supply, and the sharp increase of corn-based ethanol production. The study contends that during the next five years, food inflation may increase by an average of 7.5 percent, up from the average 2.3 percent during the last decade.

Ethanol production has taken a big bite out of corn crops, with 24 percent in 2007 utilized for ethanol, an increase from just 14 percent two years ago. But some economists argue that ethanol is not the main reason behind growing food inflation. Rising costs of global energy prices, labor, packaging, and other non-farm costs also contribute, and where previously the food industry itself—processors, store owners, restaurants, and so on—took the brunt of the higher commodity prices, those increases are now being passed directly on to the consumer.

Higher food, water, and energy costs obviously will translate into more poor, including the working poor, and increased poverty worldwide.

The Cost of Poverty

So how much money would be needed, say, to cut poverty levels in half? According to Paul Polak, founder and president of the International Development Enterprises (IDE), a nonprofit grassroots organization that helps bring small farmers out of poverty, it won't cost that much at all. In a *Scientific American* article titled "The Big Potential of Small Farms," Polak gives his educated guess that "on larger farms with good soils, where most of the gains in agricultural productivity have been made so far, I estimate that boosting harvests further will require a total investment of $20 billion over the next 10 years." Polak goes on to state that an additional $10 billion would be needed to support agricultural research at universities, national institutions, and other agencies focused on the issue, and perhaps another

$10 billion more to double the productivity of existing irrigation systems and build new dams. Perhaps add to that $1.5 trillion from wealthy countries to help developing nations through the next decade, providing them with food, education, energy, and road infrastructure. Again, one is encouraged to think about the amount of money we spend on war. Suddenly, the amount necessary to sustain life becomes miniscule...and doable.

The question remains, then, why don't we do it?

Oil Issues

By the year 2012, edible food and clean, fresh water will be the issues du jour, but so will our ability to be mobile in an increasingly bigger, more expansive world. Peak oil is a topic many 2012 theorists and experts believe presents an imminent challenge, one being felt right now at the gas pump and each time you open your utilities bill.

The term "peak oil" refers to a specific time frame during which the global production rate of petroleum reaches its peak, or maximum, and then enters a rate of irreversible decline. This tipping point, so to speak, was first theorized by American geologist M. King Hubbert. In 1969, Hubbert published his predictions that annual oil production would follow along a bell curve, and this curve was named "Hubbert's Peak." In his book *Beyond Oil: The View From Hubbert's Peak*, author Kenneth S. Deffeyes, professor emeritus at Princeton University, documents Hubbert's predictions and how they have played out in the last several decades.

Hubbert made two specific published predictions. In the first—his more optimistic, according to Deffeyes—Hubbert placed peak production at the end of the year 2000. His second prediction, formulated in the year 1956, stated that world production would peak as early as 1965–1970. Deffeyes, considered a petroleum industry expert, predicted the peak year as 2005. Yet some professional petroleum observers, according to Deffeyes, place the peak year much further down the road...at the year 2030. No matter which year, most experts agree that we are approaching the peak production stage of oil, if we haven't already entered it, and that the repercussions will be life-altering.

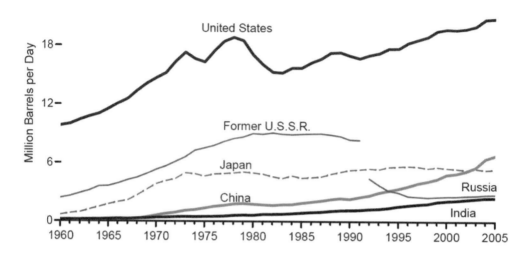

Top-Consuming Countries, 1980–2005

Figure 6.3: Crude Oil production skyrocketed between 2001 and 2007 alone, with little sign of abating, according to the U.S. Energy Information Agency.

It's not that we've run out of oil reserves. However, we have run out of most of the *easily accessible* oil reserves, leaving much harder reserves in terms of extraction. Oil reserves are classified by three P's: proven, probable, and possible. A proven reserve has at least a 90 percent certainty of containing a specific amount of extractable oil. A probable reserve has approximately 50 percent, and possible reserves have 5–10 percent. But current technology only allows us to extract less than 50 percent of these estimates, so it becomes critical to develop new methods to either extract harder-to-reach areas, or, find alternative sources of fuel.

There are even concerns raised about the projections of stated reserves, and many experts believe that these reserve levels are inflated, or point to resources that are simply not accessible with today's technology. No matter the argument, we will, and are, running out of easy, cheap oil to fill the growing needs of not only the United States and Europe, but also the rising powers of China and India. We have all heard about the issue of supply and demand, and how less supply creates higher prices as demand increases, but few people realize that this is not the only factor dictating oil availability and price. War, military conflict, and even political changes can create fluctuations in price, even in the supply offered to a public unrelentingly hungry for oil. Even hurricanes, such as Katrina, which crippled Gulf of Mexico oil rigs and production for months, can bring availability down, and prices up.

Solar Alternatives

The alternative would obviously be conservation, and the desire to find other forms of cheap, accessible energy. Oil is on the decline in terms of Energy Returned on Energy Invested. In other words, it is getting more and more expensive to extract less and less oil. And, with a human population showing little signs of abating, experts agree that worldwide demand for oil will significantly outpace availability as we approach 2030.

The U.S. Department of Energy published a report in 2005 titled "Peaking of World Oil Production: Impacts, Mitigation and Risk Management." Known as the Hirsch Report, this paper stated that the peaking of worldwide oil production would present the entire globe with "an unprecedented risk management problem. As peaking is approached, liquid fuel prices and price volatility will increase dramatically, and, without timely mitigation, the economic, social, and political costs will be unprecedented."

Oil and gas is essential to more than just transportation and home heating needs. Modern agricultural techniques require oil and gas, and if reserves decline, we could also see sticker shock at the grocery store, with famine spreading across the planet. Yet, we keep using fuel as though it is infinite in supply. Not to mention the fact that it takes oil to produce non-oil technologies, putting us in a catch-22 that renowned journalist Thom Hartmann describes in his seminal work, *The Last Hours of Ancient Sunlight*.

Take solar cells, a popular alternative energy source. Hartmann points out the following:

∞ Solar cells are made up of several rare-earth materials that require the mining of hundreds of tons of earth to extract only a few pounds. The mining is done by machines fueled with oil.

- ∞ The machines are also made of materials that are mined, smelted, and fabricated in oil-fired furnaces by oil-driven machinery.

- ∞ High-temperature oil-fired furnaces are required to smelt and purify the rare-earth minerals, and to make the glass that covers the solar cells.

- ∞ Last, but not least, the people who work at these factories drive cars fueled by oil and live in houses heated by oil.

This problem also applies to wind power, because the high-tech turbines built to capture wind energy are made from steel, and materials that can only be fabricated, Hartmann points out, with energy derived from fossil fuels. Hartmann also takes issue with green energy, stating that some so-called re-newable resource green energy is not at all what it seems, but is instead the product of methods fueled by, well, fossil fuel. Even the electricity we count on in our daily lives is the result of oil. Electricity production is responsible for 66 percent of all sulfur dioxide emissions, and 36 percent of all carbon dioxide emissions, thanks to the pollution created by burning oil to make electricity. Not quite the payoff many of us imagine when we flick on the lights.

But there are alternatives, such as "green electricity" or power generated by renewable sources that use sunlight: wood-fired boilers, hydroelectricity, solar power, and wind power. But there just may not be enough money, incentive, or time to turn these alternatives into realities. Mike Byron, au-thor of *Infinity's Rainbow: The Politics of Energy, Climate and Globalization,* and the follow-up *The Path Through Infinity's Rainbow: Crisis and Renewal in Interesting Times,* holds a PhD in political science at University of California, Irvine, and teaches all aspects of both political science and political economy. He is a leading authority on global political issues, and even ran for Congress in 2004.

Byron's extensive research examines the past, current, and future crises that face us, thanks mainly to global climate change, fossil fuel consumption, and geopolitical changes. When it comes to finding quick alternatives for fossil fuels, Byron points out, "There is no large-scale substitute for hydro-carbon energy…. Even if there were, there is now no time to convert the world's several billion vehicles to a new energy source. The growth in demand for oil is now nearly 3 percent compounded per year. Time is running out to deal with the economic ramifications of peak oil."

Byron points out how the peak oil discussion began more than 30 years ago during the Carter presidency, but the problem remained largely ignored. Carter recognized the huge sacrifice the public would have to make in order to deal with the problem. Carter was soon voted out of office. This may be in part, to the fact that the political system itself, as Byron suggests, was "captured by the very energy companies which profit most from maximizing the use of hydrocarbon energy and who have the least incentive to transition away from it."

Nuclear Energy

Nuclear energy is often touted as the "savior source" of fuel, yet nuclear power can only supply us with electricity in substantial quantities. Byron points out that nuke power is useless for transportation, and although it can provide the energy to manufacture the hydrogen that can be used as fuel, "building nuclear power plants is very energy intensive, as is the mining and refining of nuclear fuels. And of course these fuels exist in limited quantities themselves." Byron states that nuclear power options may only be limited to providing us with a very small amount of our power needs in the early 21st century, and for perhaps only a few decades.

Let us also not forget what nuclear power does to the environment. Yes, it is a greener method than fossil fuels, but, as Byron states, only as long as supplies of rich uranium last. After that, the less-rich sources would require a tremendous amount more energy to turn into the needed fossil fuels. "The mining and refining of nuclear fuel in conjunction with the vast amount of construction required to build the nuclear power plants would release enormous quantities of greenhouse gases—and other pollutants—into the atmosphere."

Other Alternatives

We face this same dilemma with coal. Kenneth Deffeyes, in *Beyond Oil*, calls coal the "best of fuels and the worst of fuels." Best, he states, because it is much less expensive per unit of energy, but worst because of the pollutants it creates, as well as mining hazards, of which we have all become familiar in the last few years. But because it is cheap and versatile, Deffeyes feels we have to make a choice between two necessary evils.

"Coal utilization is not a problem that we can ignore. Fantasizing about a fleet of nonpolluting fuel cell automobiles 20 years from now will not compensate for declining oil production in this decade. I hate to say it, but we will likely be forced to choose either increased pollution from coal or doing without a significant portion of our present-day energy supply."

What a choice. Worldwide coal reserves are, however, estimated to be big enough to get us through a few hundred years, at present production rates. But as Mike Byron reminds us in *The Path Through Infinity's Rainbow*, the rapid burning of coal "will have devastating effects on the rate of CO^2 increases in the atmosphere."

In any event, the year 2013 will see us waking up to less oil reserves, higher prices, and perhaps a much smaller pool of who can afford to actually purchase oil. Those with the resourcefulness and ingenuity to create new jobs based upon telecommuting, and new neighborhoods that are walker-friendly, may not feel the pinch as deeply as those totally enmeshed in a fossil-fuel lifestyle. In December 2007, at a two-week UN climate conference held on the resort island of Bali in Indonesia, an agreement was reached between some 190 nations to do more to fight global warming by 2009. Bitter divisions and criticisms were set aside to reach this important and urgent call to action, which would examine new ways to reduce pollutants, and empower poorer nations to better adapt to environmental challenges with technology and possible financial assistance.

But despite a hard push from the European Union to include specific emissions reductions for all industrial nations, none were adopted, making even this potential agreement weaker than what environmentalists had hoped for. Still, it is a start, and the coming years will tell if the urgent action spoken of by the leaders of the world will be taken.

Disease

Whether or not we continue to drive our cars and heat our homes to our hearts' content, as the year 2013 approaches, there may be an even greater threat, and one much smaller than any discussed in this or any other chapter. Because while hurricanes, global climate change, natural disasters, drought, and famine may threaten to diminish our numbers, the biggest challenge Gaia may throw our way could actually be the tiniest. Invisible to the naked eye, even.

Infectious diseases, including emerging diseases otherwise localized to specific global regions, threaten to derail the sturdy human from its steady track of evolution. Disease is directly related to issues of poverty, sustainability, overpopulation, and lack of food and water resources.

HIV/AIDS

HIV/AIDS alone is expected to kill more than 65 million people in the next 15 years, according to a 2002 study from the Joint United Nations Program on Hive/AIDS (UNAIDS). The study paints a stark portrait, stating that "the epidemic's global death toll could more than triple over the next two decades." This projection is a huge departure from earlier reports that say the epidemic might reach its peak in some of the hardest-hit countries.

Some of the report's findings include:

∞ New HIV infections are now spreading more quickly through central Asia and eastern Europe than any other part of the world.

∞ In eastern Europe, the epidemic is now entering the general population.

∞ Fifteen- to 24-year-olds account for half of all new HIV infections worldwide.

∞ Reported HIV infections in China shot up 67 percent in 2001 alone, and could soon be rivaling sub-Saharan Africa infection rates.

∞ Less than 2 percent of the 40-million-plus living with HIV/AIDS have access to antiviral medications.

Although most of the report's findings are chilling, Dr. Peter Piot, director of the UNAIDS program told amFAR.org in July of 2002 that some nations are succeeding in turning the epidemic around, including Zambia, which will soon join Uganda as the second African nation to reverse HIV rates. Other nations such as Brazil, Cambodia, and Poland have managed to slow the infection rate by using prevention efforts.

In 2006, UNAIDS joined with the World Health Organization (WHO) in claiming that AIDS has killed more than 25 million people since it was first recognized in June of 1981, a third of these deaths coming from sub-Saharan Africa. In 2005 alone, AIDS claimed more than 3 million lives; more than 570,000 of those were children.

There isn't time in this book to go into the details behind this terrifying epidemic. But suffice it to say that we can lower the number of deaths expected during the next decade drastically. The July 6, 2002 edition of *Lancet*, the British medical journal, stated that two-thirds of all HIV infections projected to occur in the next eight years (culminating now in 2010) could be prevented "if global AIDS prevention spending increases by $27 billion by 2010—or a cost of about $1,000 per infection avoided." This is an expensive program, but think of how expensive it will be if not implemented.

According to Dr. Helene Gayle of the Bill and Melinda Gates Foundation, global HIV prevention works. Gayle co-chaired the Global HIV Prevention Working Group, which put together a blueprint for just such a program—a blueprint that includes strengthening healthcare infrastructures, increasing access to AIDS treatment, and expanding existing proven programs.

Other UN population researchers project that by 2025, more than 100 million people in Africa alone could die from AIDS, along with 31 million in India (which just recently topped South Africa as the country with the most new infections, with 5.7 million to SA's 5.5 million), and 18 million in China. In a June 2006 AP story, Mark Stirling, director of East and Southern Africa for UNAIDS, said, "We will be grappling with AIDS for the next 10, 20, 30, 50 years. Especially since efforts to find a vaccine have led to virtually nothing, with over 30 vaccines currently being tested in small-scale trials as part of the International AIDS Vaccine Initiative."

Interestingly, many Americans think they will lead lives untouched by HIV/AIDS. Yet the 2006 report from UNAIDS and WHO shows that in 2005 alone, 1,200,000 adults and children became infected with HIV (not all will develop AIDS). This number is up by 100,000 from two years prior. In 2004, HIV/AIDS infected an estimated 4,883 young people between the ages of 13 and 24. Although HIV progresses to AIDS more slowly in young people, infection rates are up, especially in the African American community, where they accounted for 55 percent of the new infections among all persons in that age group. Overall, young people between 15 and 19 years of age are experiencing rising rates of HIV infection, with a 20 percent jump between 2001 and 2005.

Another shocking increase is occurring among women. The Centers for Disease Control's (CDC) own HIV/AIDS statistics for youth showed that between 2001 and 2004, 38 percent of diagnosed cases of HIV/AIDS were female. And young, ethnic women showed the greatest risk for heterosexual transmission, with African American women seven times more likely to get infected than white women, and Hispanic women eight times more likely.

The CDC does state that the annual number of new HIV infections has declined from a peak of more than 150,000 in the mid-1980s, and has stabilized since the late 1990s at approximately 40,000. But through time, unless increased prevention and treatment strategies are implemented, the numbers will continue to add up. In addition, there are fears that HIV will someday develop mutations that will render current AIDS drugs useless, and trigger a reemerging epidemic. And once again, according to amFAR, it will be up to the wealthiest nations to quickly pledge the tens of billions of dollars needed for AIDS prevention and treatment.

But HIV/AIDS is only one disease. Emerging infectious diseases, as well as reemerging ones, pose a multilayered threat that is costing lives, and billions of dollars, and shows little signs of abating.

List of NIAID Emerging and Reemerging Diseases

The National Institute of Allergy and Infectious Diseases (NIAID) is part of the National Institutes of Health.

Emerging infectious diseases:

∞ Anthrax.

∞ Antimicrobial resistance.

∞ Botulism.

∞ Campylobacteriosis.

∞ Dengue fever.

∞ E. coli.

∞ Flu (influenza).

∞ Group A streptococcal infections.

∞ Lyme disease.

∞ Plague.

∞ Prion diseases.

∞ SARS.

∞ Salmonellosis/salmonella.

∞ Shigellosis/shigella.

∞ Smallpox.

∞ Tularemia.

∞ West Nile virus.

Reemerging pathogens:

∞ Enterovirus 71.

∞ Clostridium difficile.

∞ Coccidioides immitis.

- ∞ Mumps virus.

- ∞ Prion diseases.

- ∞ Streptococcus, group A.

- ∞ Staphylococcus aureus.

- ∞ Coccidioides immitis.

Agents with bioterrorism potential:

- ∞ Bacillus anthracis (anthrax).

- ∞ Clostridium botulinum toxin (botulism).

- ∞ Yersinia pestis (plague).

- ∞ Variola major (smallpox) and other related pox viruses.

- ∞ Francisella tularensis (tularemia).

- ∞ Viral hemorrhagic fevers.

- ∞ Arenaviruses.

- ∞ LCM, Junin virus, Machupo virus, Guanarito virus.

- ∞ Lassa fever.

- ∞ Bunyaviruses.

- ∞ Hantaviruses.

- ∞ Rift Valley Fever.

- ∞ Flaviruses.

- ∞ Dengue.

- ∞ Filoviruses.

- ∞ Ebola.

- ∞ Marburg.

NIAID priority areas: Emerging infectious disease threats such as Nipah virus and additional hantaviruses.

∞ *Tick-borne hemorrhagic fever viruses.*

∞ *Crimean-Congo hemorrhagic fever virus.*

∞ *Tick-borne encephalitis viruses.*

∞ *Yellow fever.*

∞ *Multi-drug resistant TB.*

∞ *Influenza.*

∞ *Other rickettsias.*

∞ *Rabies.*

∞ *Prions.* *

∞ *Chikungunya virus.* *

∞ *Severe acute respiratory syndrome—associated coronavirus (SARS-CoV).*

∞ *Antimicrobial resistance, excluding research on sexually transmitted organisms.*

∞ *Antimicrobial research, as related to engineered threats.* *

∞ *Innate immunity, defined as the study of non-adaptive immune mechanisms that recognize, and respond to, microorganisms, microbial products, and antigens.* *

* Added January 2007

In 2007, the horrific disease Ebola made headlines all over again when a new strain was discovered in a western Uganda outbreak. More than 16 people, at the time this book was written, had died, and the WHO and CDC indicated that the virus belonged to a new subtype with new symptoms (vomiting) not normally associated with the dreaded hemorrhagic fever. Ebola currently kills most of those infected, causing victims to "crash and bleed out" from massive blood loss and damage to internal organs. The disease spreads through direct contact with blood and bodily secretions, and even via objects contaminated with infected blood and secretions. Currently, there is no cure or treatment.

SARS

While the three main subtypes of Ebola have killed more than 1,000 people in the Congo and Sudan regions since the disease was first identified in 1976, other infectious diseases such as SARS, avian flu, and West Nile virus pose graver threats globally. The Severe Acute Respiratory Syndrome (SARS) outbreak that made headlines in February 2002 started in Asia. During the next few months, SARS had spread into 24 countries across the globe, infecting a total of 8,093 that year alone, of which 774 died. Luckily, SARS did not spread widely through the United States, and was considered under control by the CDC, which quickly developed guidelines and recommendations for preventing a public health disaster.

However, a new SARS threat lurks on the horizon, at least in China. A December 10, 2007 article for Yahoo News titled "China Market May Be Breeding Ground for Deadly Viruses," examined the rising dangers of the exotic, and often illegal, wildlife trade at many busy Chinese markets. The 2002 SARS outbreak resulted in the black market status of the civet, a raccoon-like animal that was blamed for spreading SARS. Now, exotic wildlife is returning to the Quinping market among others, and infectious disease experts are concerned.

Most of China's wealthy shop at grocery stores, purchasing packaged and brand goods, but, as the article points out, right outside the "glitzy marquee cities of Shanghai, Beijing, and Guangzhou, traditional wet markets still account for the bulk of fresh food sales in China." These "wet markets" are often way below health inspection standards, with wet floors, and all kinds of exotic (usually illegal) beasts for sale. Though scientists say the odds of SARS spreading from another civet are rare, it is only a matter of time before a new disease may emerge from close contact with a sick wild animal.

Bird Flu

Globalization and global warming both contribute to the spread of new infectious diseases. SARS was spread to other nations mainly from person-to-person contact, most likely by those visiting the Asian countries where the viral respiratory illness lurked. Avian flu, or H5N1 Avian Influenza A virus, also created quite a scare, as this highly contagious bird flu entered the human population with mutated subtypes. Normally, avian flu is not a high risk for humans, but because Influenza A viruses are constantly changing, they can and do adapt through time and infect humans and other animals.

H5N1 did cause some human-to-human infection in Indonesia, where eight people of one family were infected. In 2007, China's Ministry of Health reported one new death from H5N1, adding to the 16 fatalities in that country alone.

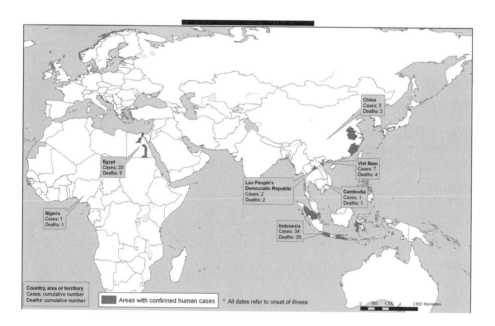

Figure 6.4: Areas with confirmed human cases of H5N1 Avian Influenza since January 1, 2007. Courtesy of the World Health Organization.

So far, the fatality numbers have been relatively low in the human population, but as global travel and commerce expands, especially in Asian countries where many of these viruses originate, we may one day see a pandemic (worldwide outbreak). So far, H5N1 is resistant to amantadine and rimantadine, the two viral medications that commonly treat influenza. That leaves two antiviral meds, oseltamavir and zanamavir, both of which are still being tested for effectiveness. And, should a pandemic occur, it will be a question of who gets the limited supplies of available vaccines first, if at all.

There is a vaccine that blocks bird flu. In early 2007, the FDA approved a two-shot vaccine made by Sanofi Pasteur that, in clinical trials, protected 45 percent of adults who received the highest dose against infection from H5N1. The goal now is to stockpile enough vaccine to protect at least 20 million people until an even more potent vaccine can be made available.

But even as vaccines for one bird flu strain are developed, there is always a new strain to contend with. In September 2007, Canada experienced an outbreak of another deadly avian flu, H7N3—a reminder of how quickly emerging diseases can appear, and mutate.

West Nile Virus

Perhaps the biggest threat facing the United States is the West Nile virus, thanks in part to global climate change. This potentially serious illness has become a seasonal epidemic that flares up in the summer months, and often continues into the fall. Mosquitoes carry WNV, and as global temperatures increase, and more regions experience rain that they might not normally get, the potential breeding grounds for mosquitoes increase, along with the risk they pose to humans. Standing water is the biggest problem, including backyard wading pools, puddles, and flowerpots. Birds, which are often infected by mosquitoes, can also carry WNV. In San Diego County, my hometown, dead bird warnings are a regular thing, with news alerts urging people not to pick up dead birds, or assist those that appear to be sick and dying.

According to the CDC Website on WNV, approximately 80 percent of people who get infected never show any symptoms, with the rest experiencing everything from flu-like symptoms to skin rashes and vomiting. There is no specific treatment for WNV, therefore, as climate changes bring more rainfall to specific regions, the necessity for keeping standing water to a minimum could be the only thing between an easy, breezy summer and a national epidemic.

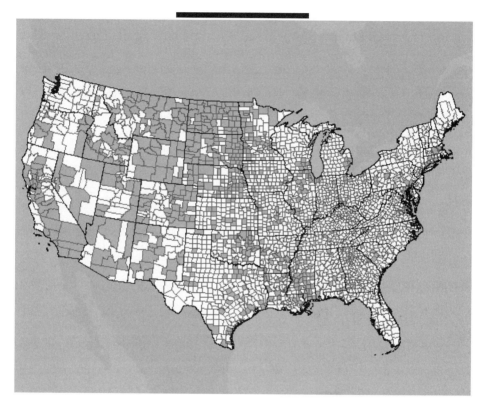

Figure 6.5: To date, there have been more than 3,300 cases of West Nile virus in humans. The darker squares indicate positive test result areas. Courtesy of the U.S. Dept. of Interior and USGS.

Malaria

Global climate change is also contributing to the rise of malaria in warmer highland areas of the western Pacific island of Papua New Guinea. AP Correspondent Charles J. Hanley reported on this new surge of an old disease in a December 8, 2007, in the Yahoo News article "Malaria Climbs Into Warmer Highlands." Hanley stated that the threat of collapsing ice sheets and super-hurricanes could be responsible for a warming Earth, and the introduction of disease-bearing mosquitoes into areas to which they have never had access before.

Naturally, the burden of handling these emerging and reemerging diseases will fall upon the poor nations hit hardest by overpopulation and climate change. Hanley commented, "Of the litany of ills linked to climate change, the slow spread of warm-weather diseases is more a quiet scourge, one whose ultimate cost remains incalculable." Per year, more than 1 million people die of malaria across the globe, mostly African children. But as the parasite responsible for the disease (which is transmitted by the bite of a female anopheles mosquito), finds more locations where the temperature for development is just right (64 degrees Fahrenheit or higher), those numbers will begin to rise. Interestingly, malaria may actually contract in range in places such as the Amazon, which are predicted to grow drier as global warming continues.

Similar highlands epidemics are also being reported in areas once considered malaria-free: east Africa, Madagascar, and West Papua. Dr. Vivo Mueller, lead scientist at the Papua New Guinea Institute of Medical Research, warns, "As the Earth warms...malaria epidemics in the highlands are now basically happening every year." Mueller also added that other factors add to increased malaria outbreaks, including deforestation, population movements, and failing health systems. These same factors will also contribute to rising numbers of West Nile virus and other pathogens.

Fighting Off Disease

In Mike Byron's *Infinity's Rainbow: The Politics of Energy, Climate and Globalization*, he cites an international study by Harvard University's Center for Health and the Global Environment, Swiss Re, and the UN Development Program. The study concurs:

∞ warming favors the spread of disease.

∞ extreme weather events create conditions conducive to disease outbreaks.

∞ coastal communities, coral reefs, and forests are especially vulnerable to warming and disease.

The mosquito is the common animal vector, or carrier, of many infectious diseases such as malaria, WNV, yellow fever, dengue fever, and St. Louis encephalitis. And because mosquitoes need wet places and warm weather to complete their life cycles, even small increments of global warming can cause both epidemics and pandemics. Byron's book also points out that ancient illnesses could also be unleashed once ice sheets drip away and bacteria and viruses defrost. Imagine polio reemerging once more, or new, deadly species of viruses currently unknown, lurking under the protective layers of ice.

As national borders blend and merge, the potential for regional diseases to spread into formerly uninfected areas grows as well. Pathogens can spread across the globe at breakneck speed, with little regard for borders and rules. Public health is a global issue, but in the United States alone, more than 45 million people don't even have health insurance, and millions more have the least coverage possible. Health disparities are massive, with poor nations bearing the brunt of fatalities, even for diseases that are quite easily preventable, such as malaria.

Globally, infectious disease is actually on the wane, according to the CDC, but public health disparity, as well as the potential use of pathogens for bioterrorism and environmental calamity, are among the threats that could cause a seriously deadly outbreak that could cripple many nations, unless we all pull together and combine money, resources, and research. Otherwise, we might be facing a serious dent in our population numbers, thanks to the tiniest of threats—ones with the potential to kill indiscriminately, kill quickly, and mutate each and every time we think we are one step ahead.

In 2008 antimicrobial resistance is the biggest public health concern we now face. Microbes are developing resistances to drugs far quicker than we humans can develop new drugs to resist the microbes. The National Institute of Allergy and Infectious Diseases (NIAID) reports that more than 70 percent of the bacteria that cause hospital-acquired infections are resistant to at least one of the most commonly prescribed antibiotics assumed to fight them.

In 2005, almost a dozen football players on the Bronte, Texas, high school team came down with signs of infection from staphylococcus aureus, or MRSA, a new and improved staph infection that had become more stubborn in the face of antibiotic treatments normally prescribed. Newly identified staphylococcus aureus strains are able to evade the immune system response in healthy people with no known risk factors for infection. These strains are resistant to many forms of antibiotics, and are often spread through cuts, wounds, and even sharing protective gear, towels, and soaps.

These staph infections are now a common occurrence at schools nationwide, as well as in hospitals. Known as "superbugs," these bacteria have been increasing steadily, according to researchers at Baylor College of Medicine and Texas Children's Hospital. Their combined study showed that MRSA, once mainly seen in hospital settings (an estimated 5 percent of hospital and nursing home patients are infected—30,000 at any given time), is now turning up all over the place, causing skin infections, severe bloodstream infections, and even death. MRSA attacks the skin and soft tissue, but might be surprisingly simple to fight. Remember Mom's advice? Use soap and water to wash the cut, don't share towels, and keep the cut dry and clean.

Still, as the staph infections spread, they also mutate, and continue to evade the various forms of antibiotic treatments available. It has been 60 years since Dr. Alexander Fleming discovered penicillin, and in the meantime, overuse of antibiotics has contributed immensely to superbugs and rising infection rates that can be so virulent, they turn deadly within days.

MRSA

MRSA can cause serious bone and skin infections, and even pneumonia, in ordinarily perfectly healthy children and adults. The penicillin group of antibiotics is no longer effective against these new superbugs, and as the threat of an epidemic looms, with more than 10,000 cases reported so far (not including all the cases of undiagnosed MRSA), even multiple antibiotic treatments no longer work. Sadly, many Big Pharma companies are rejecting further antibiotic research altogether, simply because it is not as profitable as investing time and research into the next "chronic illness drug," such as Lipitor. In a May 2, 2004 CBS News.com article titled "Super-Resistant Superbugs," Dr. William Shaffner, head of preventative medicine at Vanderbilt Medical Center, said, "For example, in the year 2002, something like 400 new pharmaceutical agents were licensed by the FDA. In that year, there were no genuinely new antibiotics among them." The reason, he says, is simple. "If I were the CEO of a pharmaceutical firm, I would point out that our research is benefiting the health of the public. A lipid-lowering drug reduces heart attacks. But how can I responsibly invest my shareholders' money—$900 million—to create a new antibiotic? Those are the estimates. That's not fair to the shareholders."

Because antibiotics are usually taken for one or two weeks, and chronic disease drugs are taken for a lifetime, do the profit-bearing math. It is estimated that $2.1 billion alone would be needed just to fight drug-proof strains of TB, and because superbugs seem to be spreading to the poor, again the motivation and monetary resources must come first from the wealthiest nations.

On the good news front, a group of University of Pennsylvania scientists are working on a potential "miracle drug" inspired by frog skin that they claim could put an end to drug-resistant bacteria. This drug consists of a compound that mimics the molecules in frog skin that stab bacteria to death. Nick Landekic, CEO of PolyMedix, the company working on the drug based upon the U Penn research, is quoted in the January 2008 *Popular Science* as saying, "The possibility of bacteria developing resistance to this class of drugs would be like people developing bulletproof skin." So, perhaps superbugs are not as invincible as we think.

Rotavirus

There is also hope of a vaccine effective against one of the biggest viral killers of children: rotavirus. This virus is said to infect nearly all children in the first few years of their lives, causing vomiting and then diarrhea. But if left untreated, the diarrhea can become so severe that it can cause shock, dehydration, and death. More than 610,000 children die from rotavirus every year, but the World Health Organization and the Global Alliance for Vaccines have committed to finding a rotavirus vaccine, making it a top global priority. There are at least two rotavirus vaccines now proving successful in clinical trials. Perhaps, by 2013, a child dying of rotavirus will be a thing of the past. It would be nice to see the extinction of such a deadly virus.

Speaking of extinction...

Is Extinction Possible?

The chances of the human species becoming extinct by 2013 are close to nil. With a population set to top between 9 and 11 billion, it would take several acts of God so utterly catastrophic, one on top of the other, to totally decimate humanity into nothingness.

We would need a supervolcano or two, followed by a massive asteroid impact, gamma-ray burst, and perhaps 12 or more plagues unleashed across the globe…and still, there would be pockets of survivors to carry on. Complete extinction seems almost impossible, unless some genetic switch were to be suddenly activated in each and every human, causing us to drop dead on the spot (now there's a great movie idea). Still, with wars and violence and terrorism and famine and poverty, we do a pretty good job of trying to cull our numbers without nature's, or God's, help.

But extinction is a problem we need to take seriously, because according to the Washington, D.C.–based Population Connection Website, we lose one or more entire species of animal or plant life every 20 minutes. That adds up to 27,000 species each year, a rate and scale of extinction that has not occurred in 65 million years, since the mighty dinosaurs made their exit due to what scientists now believe may have been the result of a combined asteroid impact and supervolcanic activity.

Throughout the last 500 million years, the Earth has periodically cleansed itself of more than half of all life. This repeated extinction pattern was often ascribed to natural disasters of cosmic proportions, but sometimes, the plunge toward zero could not quite be adequately explained.

According to new fossil and geochemical evidence, there may be an environmental mechanism behind some of these massive extinctions—one directly related to global warming.

In the October 2006 issue of *Scientific American*, Peter D. Ward writes, in "Impact From the Deep," that an oxygen-depleted ocean that spews poisonous gas resulting from global warming could be the cause. This new model of extinction, called the "killer greenhouse effect," could explain the great Permian mass extinction 251 million years ago, as well as the more recent Triassic extinction, 50 million years ago. The trouble, Ward states, begins with "widespread volcanic activity that releases enormous amounts of carbon dioxide and methane. The gases cause rapid global warming. A warmer ocean absorbs less oxygen from the atmosphere…" and the process continues until the ocean waters are exposed to more radiation from UV rays, due to the release of excess gases into the troposphere.

These complex processes often depend on the intricate balance of nature, and even the slightest disruption of that balance can create environmental havoc. This new evidence of the slow poisoning of the world's oceans, "reveals that the earth itself can, and probably did, exterminate its own inhabitants." And if it happened before, it can happen again.

Ward ends his report with this warning:

The so-called thermal extinction at the end of the Paleocene began when atmospheric CO_2 was just under 1,000 parts per million (ppm). At the end of the Triassic, CO_2 was just above 1,000 ppm. Today with CO_2 around 385 ppm, it seems we are still safe. But with atmospheric carbon climbing at an annual rate of 2 ppm and expected to accelerate to 3 ppm, levels could approach 900 ppm by the end of the next century, and conditions that bring about the beginnings of ocean anoxia may be in place. How soon after that could there be a new greenhouse extinction? That is something our society should never find out.

Animal Extinction

Although widespread extinction seems more of a distant possibility than an immediate threat, some species are on a rapid decline. Many of the most common, beloved bird species are experiencing stunning drops in numbers, rendering the forests in many locales free of birdsong. Some species, such as meadowlarks and farmland birds, are losing populations due to suburban and industrial sprawl, and, according to the Audubon Society's "State of the Birds" report, intensive farming during the past 50 years. Others, such as the Greater Scaup and tundra-breeding birds, are dying off due to dramatic changes to their breeding habitats, as global warming melts permafrost. Boreal forest birds, such as the chickadee, are threatened by deforestation wiping out their habitats, as well as from increased insect outbreaks, mining, logging, and fires.

The Audubon Society states: "Since 1967 the average population of the common birds in steepest decline has fallen by 68 percent; some individual species nose-dived as much as 80 percent." All 20 birds currently on their Common Birds in Decline list lost more than half their population in just four decades. "The dramatic declines are attributed to loss of grasslands, healthy forests and wetlands, and other critical habitats from multiple environmental threats such as sprawl, energy development, and the spread of industrialized agriculture." Add to that the growing influence of global warming, and we can pretty much surmise that although humans may not become extinct any time soon, we sure are doing an awful lot to guarantee that other species meet such a fate.

In the May/June 2007 issue of *Mother Jones*, reporter Julia Whitty wrote in her shocking story, "Gone," that by the end of this century, half of all species on earth will no longer be around. She points to the research of Harvard biologist Edward O. Wilson, who estimates that "the current rate of extinction is 1,000 to 10,000 times greater than the normal background rate, and predicts that half of all plants and animals will be extinct by 2100." Currently, one in four mammals, one in eight birds, and one in three amphibians are on the brink of disappearing forever. At this rate, we are seeing between 2.7 and 270 species erased from existence every day!

Whitty offers a poignant description of the death of a species: "Beyond a critical point, the collective body of a unique kind of mammal or bird or amphibian or tree cannot be salvaged, no matter the first aid rendered…eventually an entire genetic legacy, born in the beginnings of life on Earth, is smote from the future."

Today, we are living in what is called the Sixth Great Extinction, also known as the Holocene extinction event. And now, we humans have more power than ever before to decimate a species in entirely new, and unalterable ways. Witty points out, "The World Conservation Union's Red List—database measuring the global status of Earth's 1.5 million scientifically named species—tells a haunting tale of unchecked, unaddressed, and accelerating biocide."

That Red List, which is updated every two years, "continues to show metastatic growth." We are the cancer.

The disappearing species are all part of a delicate grid of life, a complex web of coexistence that holds the key to our own mortality. Yet, we take no heed as we rape, pillage, use, and abuse it. Here are a few examples:

∞ Polar bears, a true sentinel species at the top of the Arctic food chain, are now estimated to carry some of the highest toxic compounds of all living animals.

∞ The northern white rhino has been on Earth for more than 8 million years, yet today only five to 10 remain.

∞ Honeybees are dying off.

∞ There are only 150 Chinese alligators left.

∞ One in five bird species faces extinction, for a total of about 2,000 of the 9,775 named species.

∞ A quarter of all land mammals are in danger of extinction.

∞ The African lion population has fallen almost 90 percent in the last 20 years and is close to extinction.

∞ African predator populations are plummeting, thanks to overhunting, land degredation, and habitat loss.

∞ Only 10 percent of the ocean's large fish species remain.

∞ Synthetic estrogens from birth control pills in waste water are decimating the fathead minnow, and could one day wipe out the entire fish population.

∞ Acid rain is posing a greater and greater threat to coral reefs and the third of the world's fish species that depend upon them.

∞ Loss of biodiversity due to human influence is the number-one cause of extinction rates.

∞ Frog extinction patterns show a direct relationship with lethal fungus outbreaks, implicating global warming, which stimulates fungal growth in warmer climes.

These examples are but a drop in the bucket, as many species face a grim future. If they face a future at all. Witty states that seven in 10 biologists believe that mass extinction poses an even greater problem to humanity than global warming. With some attention and focus being placed upon this crisis at annual Earth Summits and Conventions on Biological Diversity, as well as studies and actions on behalf of the UN, one has to wonder if it is all too little, too late. Both catastrophes of global warming *and* extinction could be prevented, or could have been, for perhaps the tipping point was reached long ago.

7

Power Plays

Who controls the past controls the future: who controls the present controls the past.
—George Orwell, *1984*

By 2013, the shift of power from West to East may be complete. Though the United States and Europe will always have a huge role in global affairs, the unprecedented rise of China and India has led to many geopolitical predictions of things to come.

Forbes Senior Editor Robyn Meredith says in her book *The Elephant and the Dragon: The Rise of India and China and What It Means To All of Us*, "Before our eyes, two giant nations—India and China—are simultaneously embracing both capitalism and globalization. The world economy is being transformed as a result."

Meredith points out that up until the year 1600, both nations accounted for more than half the globe's economic output, exporting tons of goods over land and sea. Protectionism closed off the two nations from the rest of the world, and by 2003, India and China combined accounted for only 20 percent of the global economy.

But industrial revolutions have skyrocketed the economic output of both countries, and now these two nations are richer, more powerful, and more modernized than ever before. Even their militaries have become fine-tuned. Along with progress comes a price, for both nations are experiencing rising energy demands and increased pollution. The combined populations of India and China hit the 2 billion mark, and both nations have doubled their oil consumption since the early 1990s.

As the United States goes to war in Iraq for oil, and poises itself for new invasions into other oil-rich nations such as Iran, both India and China are protecting their rising resource needs by making deals with less-than-savory nations, even going as far as securing relationships with former enemies. The rush to grab up what resources remain on Earth is creating some awfully strange bedfellows.

China

China in particular presents a major challenge to the United States and the world. The news in past years has been filled with stories about lost manufacturing and blue-collar jobs to Chinese competition, and the closing of factories in the industrial heartlands of the American Midwest. But not many people understand that this Chinese economic challenge is also targeted toward the more high-tech and white-collar jobs, as more competition from the mighty nation threatens to push even more companies to seek cheaper ways and means overseas. One of the reasons for this, according to author James Kynge in his book *China Shakes the World: A Titan's Rise and Troubled Future—and the Challenge for America*, is that the Chinese are more open to the idea of foreign companies setting up shop on their soil.

Many people argue that the importation of cheap Chinese products offsets the loss of jobs to outsourcing. Wal-Marts and other superstores across the nation carry Chinese-made products, and though consumers enjoy the cost, they rarely think about what their thirst for cheaper things is doing to our economy, not to mention how many of those cheap products come from underpaid Chinese migrant workers. Add to that the increasing environmental degradation from China's burgeoning economy, and paying two dollars less for a pair of jeans suddenly doesn't seem to make so much sense.

It isn't only exporting cheap products that make China such a potential world power. Between 1999 and 2004, trade among Asian nations jumped more than 80 percent according to the World Trade Organization. In a November 2006 *New York Times* article, reporter Stephen Kotkin writes that trade between Asia and the United States has been surpassed, with China as the largest trade partner of the Asian nations.

Kynge describes the growing conflict between America and China as "two powerful economies powered by incompatible political systems," and cites the clash between the goals of Washington and the actions of the Chinese leadership. Adding fuel to that fire are the many "oil-inspired alliances" between China and Iran, and Sudan and Venezuela, among other nations often at odds with the West. China is now only second to the United States in oil consumption, with Chinese consumers going through approximately 7.6 million barrels a day.

China, though, is not immune to collapse, and Kynge suspects that could come either internally—from conflicts between the central government in Beijing and the many local governments that act more like fiefdoms of old, "a law unto themselves, virtually devoid of checks and balances"—or externally, from the rising reliance of China on foreign investment and trade, which, if the world's nations were to begin closing themselves off to China, could cause its complete economic shutdown. Strains with Taiwan pose a future problem, as does growing nationalism, but it is possible that Chinese leaders can curb political strife and keep foreign relations at a peaceful level, even as they continue their quest for global economic domination.

One interesting export trend has seen Chinese students moving out of the nation to study abroad at universities in Europe and the United States. But because the cost of building a university in China is a fraction of what it would be elsewhere, more and more nations are considering placing campuses on Chinese soil, creating what Kynge calls a "mini gold rush," as Western universities either build entire campuses outright, or at the very least, offer courses at existing Chinese universities. The lower cost of a complete education in China may also see a rise of foreign students studying at cheaper campuses, with cheaper textbooks, and of course, the increase of Internet classes, changing the face of education itself in another shift from West to East.

One major issue that will continue to plague China is its reliance on coal as a primary source of energy. Large coal deposits, thousands of factories that burn coal, and its many coal-producing plants all add to a soaring pollution crisis, posing both an immediate danger to the nation's citizens, and a coming danger to the entire world. In a June 2006 *New York Times* article titled "World Business: Pollution From Chinese Coal Casts a Global Shadow," it is projected that in the next 25 years, China's coal use will produce enough global warming gasses to exceed those of all industrialized nations combined. Making matters worse, "India is right behind China in stepping up its construction of coal-fired power plants—and has a population expected to outstrip China's by 2030."

If current trends persist, some experts believe that in 30 years, China will be the leading global economic power, as well as Asia's most powerful military force. Though America is estimated to take in about $70 billion a year in trade with China, it will be the jockeying for rail position that will make the next five years an intriguing power play between East and West.

India

India's influence on the United States can no longer be denied either. There are more than 2 million Indians who call themselves American citizens, and that population is predicted to rise in the next five years. Indian clothing, food, music, handicrafts, and entertainment hold great appeal to the American public.

But the nation itself, home to one in six members of the human race, is undergoing a massive transformation, finding new allies in both the East and West, and rising numbers of outsourced U.S. jobs hitting its shores. In an exclusive interview with rediff.com, Indian Ambassador David C. Mulford told readers that India was just as attractive an investment destination as China because "it has a strong economy, a large, articulate and well-educated population, it is a democracy, it believes in rule of law and it has a sophisticated and well-supervised financial system. It also has a large market with a relatively youthful population." Mulford believes these reasons give India the advantage over China, and he predicts India will soon be "a major world power." This despite epidemic problems of poverty and associated disease that continue to plague the nation. Three hundred million Indians are estimated to be living on less than one U.S. dollar a day, compared with 85 million in China (which is the more populous nation). Malnutrition plagues almost half of all Indian children under the age of five, and only half of all Indian villages even have electricity.

In its quest to plunge forward as a major consumer and capitalist machine, India may be forgetting its own, for more than half of its population live in poor, rural areas untouched by the benefits of globalization and the free market. Where once state-directed socialism took care of the basic needs of the poor, the new democracy and capitalist attitudes leave the poor to fend for themselves, adding to an already crippling poverty rate that could derail the prosperity of a rising global economy.

The Fight for the Title of "Superpower"

In the August 22, 2006 *Business Week* article titled "A New World Economy," the balance of power from West to East is seen as both a plus and minus, depending on your country of origin. The article states that both China and India are poised to make huge inroads in almost every dimension, including consumer markets, investors, producers, and users of energy and commodities. The two nations are referred to as "21st-century heavyweights," predicted to also advance at incredible rates in the fields of software technology, multimedia production, and even the medical and pharmaceutical industries. One of the reasons for these surges of growth? Increased brainpower at a fraction of the cost.

"An obvious reason is that China and India graduate a combined half a million engineers and scientists a year, versus 60,000 in the United States. In Life Sciences...the total number of young researchers in both nations will rise by 35 percent to 1.6 million in 2008. The U.S. supply will drop by 11 percent to 760,000.... Because these nations can throw more brains at technical problems at a fraction of the cost, their contributions to innovation will grow."

India is even predicted to one day surpass China in long-term market potential. According to Chief Economist William T. Wilson of Keystone Business Intelligence India, "The pace of institutional changes and industries being liberalized is phenomenal...I believe India has a better model than China, and over time will surpass its growth." By the year 2015, China's work-age population is expected to peak, and then begin to decline. India, on the other hand, will have a population close to 1.6 billion by 2050; it has higher fertility rates than China, and more people under the age of 19, which will make it a major economic force with a rising middle class ready to spend, if, and only if, its governing bodies can contain three things: (1) potential instability of a rising population, (2) increasing poverty and disease, and (3) pressures from nations with whom it depends for resources it alone cannot provide.

India is aligning itself with the United States in terms of defense, aeronautics, and space development, showing increased cooperation in working out beneficial deals for expansion. The nation, recognizing its own growing need for oil and natural resources, is also aligning itself with nations in the Middle East and Africa which may irk the United States and cause future conflicts. Similar to China, India is on the verge of becoming a major player in both consumerism and politics. If the "slumbering elephant" awakens, it could change the way we do business and live our lives, even on Western shores, in the next five years.

Obviously, the Middle East will continue to play a major role in global politics throughout the next five years, with Iran rising as a key player. In early 2007, a British Ministry of Defense (MoD) team at the Development, Concepts and Doctrine Centre, got together to envision the world in the next 30 years. Their 90-page report is an assessment of "probability-based, rather than predictive" events we might expect to see during the next three decades.

Some of the report's findings include:

∞ the rise of China and India as global superpowers.

∞ massive population growth in the Middle East, and to a lesser extent, North Africa.

∞ increased instability in Saudi Arabia due to a rising youth population and unemployment levels.

∞ rising Islamic militancy, especially due to increased youth population resenting the globalization of the Islamic community.

∞ tension between the Islamic world and the West, but also against China, whose "new-found materialism, economic vibrancy, and institutionalized atheism, will be an anathema to orthodox Islam."

∞ Iran's rising population and steady economic growth, which places it in a key leveraging position with the West and other nations, increasing access to globalization and diversity, and possibly transforming it into "a vibrant democracy."

The Middle East

As Iran sits on the verge of acquiring a seat at the nuclear power table, despite growing pressure from the United States and its allies, words of a possible military strike are everywhere. But Iran's deal with Russia, resulting in its first shipment of nuclear fuel in December 2007, could temper flaring conflicts with the West. The fuel is for the Bushehr power plant, which is near completion and could begin operating as early as 2008. Nuclear capability will give Iran world power status, with the ability to hold a strong influence over the international political landscape. Though the current Iranian president, Mahmoud Ahmadinejad, insists his nation's enrichment program is for peaceful purposes, the potential for political and terrorist purposes sends chills down its enemies' backs, especially the nation of Israel.

Rival Middle Eastern nations are also beginning to clamor for nuclear power. An April 15, 2007 *New York Times* article commented on the recent interest of Saudi Arabia's leaders in entering the nuclear power game, this after years of insisting to international atomic regulators that they had no interest in doing so. "The rules have changed," Jordan's King Abdullah II told Israeli newspaper *Haaretz*. "Everybody is going for nuclear programs."

This new nuclear arms race among Middle East states presents a challenge for the West. Although the nations' leaders say they only want atomic power, anti-U.S. sentiment and growing terrorism potential serve as a reason for distrust. Yet, ironically, it won't just be the United States doing the distrusting. The *New York Times* article quotes Geoffrey Kemp, a Middle East expert at the Nixon Center in Washington, D.C., as saying, "The Iranians have to worry, too. The idea that they'll emerge as the regional hegemon is silly. There will be a very serious counter reaction, certainly in conventional military buildups but also in examining the nuclear option."

This isn't the first time the Middle East has engaged in a race for nukes. Israel got their first nukes more than 40 years ago, which triggered surrounding countries to begin their own walk down the nuclear path. But "it is Iran's atomic intransigence that has now prodded the Sunni powers into getting serious about hedging their bets and, like Iran, financing them with $65-a-barrel oil."

So far, analysts state that the nuclear push is being led by the Saudis, within their Gulf Cooperation Council in Riyadh. Other nations that serve on the council include Bahrain, Kuwait, Omar, Qatar, and the United Arab Emirates, all United States allies, and the controllers of about 45 percent of the world's oil reserves. So far, 85 percent of the Gulf States, excluding Iraq, have stated their interest in pursuing nuclear power, including Egypt, which in 2006 announced plans for a nuclear reactor at El-Dabaa near Alexandria.

Few other nations appear to be on the brink of achieving superpower status, but the European Union is certainly the main contender, showing increasing effectiveness and influence in global affairs. Some academics and analysts see the EU achieving such status in the 21st century, due in large part to the region's large population, large economy, low inflation rates, high quality of life, and a sense of anti-U.S. foreign policy sentiment. Two EU states have nuclear weapons—Britain and France—and the military spending of the combined member states is second only to the United States. Though the EU is far behind the United States in research and development investment and advanced technology, it is in the same position to work with other nations such as China and India to import cheap physical and "brain" labor, just as the United States is doing to advance its global position.

The International Monetary Fund (IMF) released its 2006 list of the top 17 world economies. Already, almost two years later, India and China are rising higher on the chart.
Statistics courtesy of Worldwatch Institute State of the World 2006.

The world's 17 largest economies are:

1. *United States.*
2. *Japan.*
3. *Germany.*
4. *China.*
5. *Britain.*
6. *France.*
7. *Italy.*
8. *Canada.*
9. *Spain.*
10. *Brazil.*
11. *Russia.*
12. *South Korea.*
13. *India.*
14. *Mexico.*
15. *Australia.*
16. *The Netherlands.*
17. *Turkey.*

Gross Domestic Production per person in 2006:

∞ *China: $4,600*
∞ *India: $2,500*
∞ *Europe: $26,900*
∞ *Japan: $29,400*
∞ *U.S.: $40,100*

Barrels of oil used per person every year:

∞ *China: 1.9*
∞ *India: 0.9*
∞ *United States: 25.3*

Japan

Obviously, in sheer economic power, no less military might, Japan continues to hold a top spot as a world mover and shaker, and even Russia continues to be considered a potential for the 21st-century superpower list, although not in the very near future. Russia continues to prove itself as a power player in the energy industry, striking deals with nations that the United States often won't contend with. Along with its nuclear weapons capability and military strength, the nation continues to exert its influence on the rest of the world.

Brazil

One interesting key player from whom we may hear more in the next five years is one of only two Latin American nations to make the top economic lists. According to the Global Trade Negotiations Brazil summary, the nation of Brazil has emerged "as a major voice in trade negotiations, especially within the context of the Doha Development Round. Along with India, Brazil has been a principal agent in the mobilization of the G20, a block of developing nations joined to protect their common interests against developed nations in multilateral negotiating forums." Brazil has taken on the position of a powerful leader in the regional and global trade negotiations, as well as a bio-energy superpower that exports billions of dollars worth of fuel alcohol from sugarcane. As higher oil prices and increased attention to global warming challenge the fossil fuel industry, Brazil is in a key position to promote itself as the world leader in bio-energy.

Brazil's new biodiesel program is intended to promote research and development that will reduce the nation's need to import fuel and add more harmful emissions to the environment. But a secondary benefit is the creation of hundreds of thousands of jobs and increased family farming in rural, poorer areas, contributing to the rising influence of this popular tourist destination. Brazil is also a major producer of biomass, the agricultural and forestry waste that is now being used to make biomass energy for the South American nation, with the hopes of one day taking the production to a global, rather than local, level. That move alone could propel Brazil into a top spot as a future superpower.

Gender Imbalance

As a result of booming populations and increased economies, many of the new superpowers struggle with another issue that will no doubt rise to a critical mass by the year 2013. Gender imbalance plagues both China and India in terms of sheer demographics. Mainland China is now experiencing a mass shortage of marriageable women, due to years of selective abortion and infanticide against female babies. The *China Daily* newspaper states in a January 12, 2007 story that within 15 years, China would see 30 million more men than women because of the nation's tough one-child policy. Sex-selective abortion is prohibited in China, but the practice is widespread, mainly in the poor rural areas, where ratios of male-born to female-born are jumping drastically.

One of the suggested solutions for gender preference, according to the *China Daily* article, would be to initiate a stronger social security system, so that poor, rural couples don't feel pressure to have a son on which they depend in their later years.

India, meanwhile, struggles with a gender imbalance of its own. Again, booming population growth and a preference for male children have created unbalanced ratios of male to female born. But in India, a couple will continue to have more children until they finally obtain a male, leading to additional population issues. In 2005, the Indian government initiated a program that offers free and reduced-cost education for girls in an attempt to not only encourage couples to stop infanticide, but to promote education overall.

Because gender imbalance can cause social unrest, especially with high numbers of marriageable males who are unable to find spouses in traditional regions where family is of utmost importance, it is imperative for these nations, and others like them, to find solutions to the stigma against female babies and women in general. This stigma is often rooted within the class system and religious beliefs that label women as second-class, with little economic and political power, if any at all.

The Future of Terrorism

Religious beliefs that give rise to infanticide and gender preference also promise to be a challenge as the East and the West continue to clash during the next five years. Islam is the fastest-growing religion in the world, giving rise to concerns of more terrorism as militant fundamentalism spreads into other parts of the globe. The terrorism of the future may be more about small attacks from localized "cell" groups and less about the big, explosive events such as September 11. Other trends in terrorism, according to the 2006 Congressional Research Service report for Congress, include:

∞ the emergence of "micro actors." These are small, savvy, decentralized cells of terrorists acting autonomously, with the major al Qaeda leadership resulting in a more subdued operational and idealistic role.

∞ the trend toward sophistication, with terrorists using and exploiting the global flow of information, finance, and ideas via the Internet.

∞ an increasing overlap of terrorist activity with international crime, with terrorists using the same money-transfer, supply, and transport networks as criminal groups.

∞ an overall increase in suicide bombings, especially in Iraq, although state-sponsored terrorism is on the decline in most Islamic nations, with the exceptions of Iran and Syria.

∞ an increase in attacks, such as attacks on infrastructure, tourism, and oil installations, which are aimed at causing economic damage.

∞ a rise in unattributed terrorist attacks.

∞ the growing power of radical Islamist political parties in foreign nations.

The Future of Terrorism

The Congressional Research Service Report also states that the immediate future will see much more "smaller attacks, less meticulously planned, and local rather than transnational in scope." This shift will require changes in the United States's anti-terror strategy and tactics to reflect a more international law enforcement–focused approach. One statistic offers hope: The high levels of terrorism and violence cited in the report come from Iraqi casualties from sectarian violence, insurgency, and rampant criminal activity associated with the Iraq War. In 2005, the total number of terrorism incidents outside of Iraq that killed more than 10 people remained at the 2003–2004 levels of 70 per year. Iraq alone accounted for almost 30 percent of worldwide terrorist attacks and 55 percent of all fatalities.

Other 2005/2006 reports by the Netherlands Central Intelligence and Security Services, along with the RAND Corporation, added the following trends:

∞   Increasing homegrown terrorism.

∞   Decentralization and implantation of international jihad.

∞   Radicalization and emergence of local networks, and greater incitement of jihad via the Internet.

∞   Increased focus on soft-civilian-focused targets.

∞   Continued reliance on suicide attacks.

∞   Desire to use weapons of mass destruction, but little ability to execute attacks.

∞   Decrease in average age of terrorist recruits.

∞   Greater roles of women and non-Muslims in organizational/operational areas.

∞   Rising terrorism encompassing a greater variety of causes committed by a growing diversity of groups and individuals.

As growing and developing nations struggle with issues of poverty, limited resources, and gender imbalances, increased terrorism may arise out of a means of survival and the growing worldwide gap between the haves and have-nots. Coupled with deeply entrenched religious beliefs, there does not seem to be an end in sight to the threat of an attack, whether small in scale or massive and catastrophic, and no nation seems to be immune. It will be up to the leader nations of the world to work together to find the ways and means of staying one step ahead of the terrorists.

Religion

The links between terrorism and fundamentalism suggest that religious beliefs will continue to play a large role in politics and global affairs for the next five years. Recent trends in religion point to the rise of the Eastern traditions of Islam, Buddhism, and Hinduism, which of course parallel population growth in these regions. Buddhism alone has reached one hundred million followers, mainly in Asian countries, but there is marked increase of Eastern traditions on American soil.

Obviously, the rise in fundamentalist Islam is to continue, as well as a shift to non-white Christianity in nations outside of the United States. Other global trends see an increase of women in pastoral roles. Charismatic Pentecostalism is on the rise in Africa, and more and more Australian teens are experimenting with Wicca. But here in America, some obvious trends are emerging that will no doubt shape the next five years. Recent Gallup polls show the following:

- ∞ Religion is more important to blacks, women, and older Americans.
- ∞ Fifteen percent of Americans say they have switched religions, and 10 percent say they have dropped religion altogether.
- ∞ Thirty-two percent of Americans are dissatisfied with the role of organized religion and its influence on the nation.
- ∞ Just under a third of all Americans have an unfavorable view of Catholicism.
- ∞ Americans are slightly more likely to view the Mormon religion in a negative light.
- ∞ The most recent Gallup poll says 55 percent of Americans claim religion is important to them.

Other noticeable trends include a rise in the Pentecostal movement, with increasing numbers of megachurches sprouting up all over the country, many with thriving memberships in the tens of thousands. The megachurch trend is making inroads into urban black communities, many of which are using these massive facilities not just as places of worship, but also as a link to charitable service and a newfound respect of their African homeland, which is also experiencing its own charismatic wave. Even in suburban white communities, megachurches provide an opportunity for some old-time religion while building friendships and communities; something smaller churches do in rural areas.

According to a September 2001 issue of *Religious and Ethics Newsweekly*, 10 important movements that continue to influence religion, and are predicted to do so for the next five years, are:

1. **Spiritual seeking**—a renewed interest in spirituality, both traditional and non-traditional outlets, as more and more people seek to connect with their inner spirit. This includes an increasing interest in retreats, meditation, prayer, and even New Age practices.

2. **Church-State controversies**—as religion continues to be a main talking point for politicians eager to prove their value-based platforms, the debate to keep church and state separate shows little sign of abating. Republicans are more often associated with combining religion with politics, although many Democrats now say faith is a distinct part of their beliefs and ideals.

3. **Ethical dilemmas**—the continued debate over stem cell research will raise even more moral questions as biotechnology advances rapidly. Science, it seems, will continue to be at odds with religion.

4. **Religious diversity**—a definite increase in the styles and types of religious beliefs to which people ascribe, with more and more people being drawn to religious traditions outside of their "childhood faith." Also, an increase in "homemade" spirituality.

5. **Cyber power**—the rise of the Internet allows religious people to develop online communities and attract new converts.

6. **Sexuality debates**—gay marriage will continue to challenge old-school religions as more and more gays and lesbians step up the pressure on legislatures. Southern Baptists will continue to argue over the role of women, while mainline Protestants will debate about allowing gays to be ordained.

7. **Evangelical vigor**—as stated earlier, evangelicals, charismatic Pentecostals, and even nondenominational evangelical-oriented megachurches are on the rise. Parachurch movements, Women of Faith, Promise Keepers, and so on, are powerful groups that attract members in the tens, sometimes hundreds, of thousands.

8. **Hispanic influence**—the rising Hispanic population is seeing a definite influence on both Catholicism and Pentecostalism. Latino churches are booming as changing demographics challenge traditional white and black churches with new leadership styles.

9. **Varied papal influence**—the Catholic Church has lost credibility and members due to the recent sex scandals, and some question the Pope's continued influence over national affairs, especially the debates about abortion, birth control, and the death penalty.

10. **Increased God talk**—more and more public figures are openly talking about their religious beliefs, and religious-themed books and movies are seeing record audiences.

One sad note is the apparent decrease in tribal religions, as many indigenous populations are brought into the more traditional religions via missionaries and evangelical movements. However, native traditions are being adopted by more people who are dissatisfied with what the big three of Christianity, Judaism, and Islam have offered in terms of violence, conflict, and war.

Although religion continues to be a vibrant part of American life, I could not conclude this chapter without pointing to the September 2, 2007 issue of *Times U.K.* Reporter Richard Brooks presented the results of a British YouGov poll commissioned by broadcaster and writer John Humphreys, that found that nearly 42 percent of 2,200 Brits polled think religion is harmful. Yet more than half believe in God, or "something." Although the dominant faith is Christianity, only 17 percent thought the influence of religion was beneficial. A far cry from the more than half of all Americans who don't mind mixing church with state.

III

Ascendance: The Coming Evolution Revolution

8

Medical Miracles

The reasonable man adapts himself to the world: the unreasonable one persists in trying to adapt the world to himself. Therefore all progress depends on the unreasonable man.
—George Bernard Shaw, *Man and Superman: The Revolutionist's Handbook*

"Human Evolution Is Speeding Up." So states a December 11, 2007 article for BBC News by science and nature reporter Anna-Marie Lever. In the past 5,000 years, it appears genetic change in humans has occurred at a rate roughly 100 times higher than any other period. This contrasts a popular belief that human evolution has halted as of late.

Professor Henry Harpending, author of a study that appeared in the proceedings of the National Academy of Sciences, stated: "Genes are evolving fast in Europe, Asia, and Africa, but almost all of these are unique to their continent of origin...we are getting less alike, not merging into a single, mixed humanity." Harpending also stated that there is no sign of human evolution slowing down. He and his team point to two main factors behind the speeding-up process:

1. Because there are a lot more people, there are more opportunities for an advantageous mutation to show up. A large population has more genetic variation, and allows for more positive selection.

2. Environmental changes, including new diets, and lots of new diseases associated with larger populations.

Evolutionary changes in the human genetic makeup aside, we are on the verge of an evolution revolution in the way we view our bodies, our health, and our ability to merge science with biology. Major advances in medicine, bioengineering, and genetics loom on the horizon, promising hope and longer life spans for millions.

Medicine

Nearly 50 percent of all Americans will have Alzheimer's by the age of 85, according to the Alzheimer Association's Website, *www.alz.org*. There are currently four drugs on the market that can slow the progress of this horrible disease, but they only work in half the patients to whom they are prescribed. Thirty-five new drugs are currently undergoing testing, and Maria C. Carrillo, director of medical and scientific relations at the Alzheimer's Association in Chicago, says, "We're on the cusp of major breakthroughs. In three to four years, we may have a treatment for Alzheimer's that slows down the progression of the disease dramatically." She did not comment on when we might find a cure.

For those suffering from another major killer, breast cancer, the future looks even more promising. Some research has found a virus present in a large percentage of breast cancers, prompting the examination of a potential vaccine, much like the HPV vaccine for cervical cancer. Researchers have also identified key cancer gene mutations that increase the risk of developing the disease tenfold, and several new genes that can increase the risk by up to 60 percent. When there are tests for these genes, doctors will be able to catch the disease in much earlier, and more treatable, stages. We are also about one year away from seeing a new ultrasound technique that would let radiologists use elasticity imaging to distinguish between malignant and benign lesions, which would reduce the number of biopsies. Finally, nanotechnology may be behind the quest to build a machine that could screen blood, and detect the presence of molecules associated with breast cancer years before a mammogram could.

A number of new stroke technologies are also in development to more effectively remove blood clots that cause strokes. New drugs to dissolve blood clots hope to improve performance by delivering them to the blood clot through small tubes threaded directly into arteries or the brain itself. Researchers are also trying to develop very small mechanical devices that can be delivered through these small tubes to break up or remove blood clots.

The March 2007 issue of *Reader's Digest* reported on the top medical breakthroughs and innovations we can expect to see in the next five years:

∞ The Hemopurifier is a blood-filtering device designed by a biotech company in California that could, within one to two years, stop a pandemic in its tracks.

∞ Tufts University researchers are looking at spider silk as a potential source of material that could, within five years, be used in growing and repairing human bones.

∞ In four to five years, there may be a less-invasive technique than open-heart surgery for replacing heart valves, involving entering the body via the groin vessel, and using thread tools and devices to perform intricate procedures while watching live images from an x-ray machine and echocardiogram.

∞ A cure for smallpox is perhaps one to three years away, with the discovery of a new drug, SIGA-246, in the final stages of development.

∞ In three to five years, the 20 million Americans who suffer from asthma may find relief in a new outpatient procedure called Bronchial Thermoplasty, which reduces the amount of muscle in the airway passage without causing damage or scarring.

∞ Blood shortages plague many communities, especially following natural disasters, but in one to three years, scientists may be able to deliver a substitute called PolyHeme.

∞ In five years, we may never have to worry about taking pills again, as MicroCHIPS, Inc. has created a device that can be preloaded with up to 100 doses of meds, and administered into the body via wireless signals.

The Cost of Advancement

All of these amazing breakthroughs require three things: money, brain power, and additional research, but with advances in technology, especially the focus on stem cell research, it may only be a matter of time before we can, and do, cure just about everything. A startling new breakthrough in 2007 has put stem cell research back into the forefront of medicine...and politics. Scientists and laboratory teams on two continents succeeded in making ordinary human skin cells take on the powers of embryonic stem cells, all without using embryos themselves. Called "direct reprogramming," this stunning new development avoids the ethical complaints of religious groups, while potentially providing all the benefits of embryonic stem cells, prompting even President George W. Bush, who twice vetoed stem cell legislation, to laud the discovery.

But there is a drawback. More research is needed in order prevent the disrupting of skin cell DNA that occurs during the technique, which means this would be of no help to treat major diseases such as diabetes and spinal cord injuries. However, this new technique qualifies for federally funded research, unlike projects involving human embryonic cells, so researchers can fine-tune the process and make it applicable for a host of diseases, including Parkinson's, Leukemia, Cerebral Palsy, Multiple Sclerosis, and a variety of cancers. Researchers from the UCLA AIDS Institute and the Institute for Stem Cell Biology and Medicine state that AIDS can also benefit from stem cell research. In 2007, they demonstrated for the first time that human embryonic stem cells can be genetically manipulated and coaxed to develop into mature T-cells, raising hopes for a gene therapy to combat AIDS.

Meanwhile, advances in genetics and molecular medicine, due mainly to the completion of the Human Genome Project, in which scientists mapped the entire human DNA sequence, promise incredible breakthroughs by the year 2020 or before. These include: more effective new drugs manufactured by recombinant DNA technology; medical records that include each individual's complete genome and a catalog of single base-pair variations to better determine responses to drugs and treatment; more gene therapy for single-gene diseases, with neonatal testing to detect diseases far in advance; and an advanced understanding of human embryonic development. Some researchers predict that by 2020, there will be 1,000 complete genomes, giving us greater insight into evolution and biological complexity. Already, scientists at biotech firms such as the J. Craig Venter Institute and Synthetic Genomics are trying to make a genome from scratch in a complicated procedure that involves identifying the fewest number of genes a microbe needs to survive in a lab setting, then synthesizing that minimal genome from raw ingredients, inserting it into a host cell, and allowing it to make its own proteins to gradually transform the host cell into a new microbe. The project, headed by Craig Venter, one of the scientists who mapped the human genome, could be the beginning of an opportunity to literally build life from the ground up.

Bionics

Because all diseases have a genetic component, either from heredity or resulting from a physical response to an environmental stressor, the Human Genome Project is enabling researchers to find the smallest errors in genes that cause or contribute to disease. As increasing numbers of genetic tests become available, and biotech companies race to design and produce new diagnostic tests, the ultimate goal is to find new and effective ways to treat, cure, or prevent thousands of diseases. We are far from achieving this goal, but the HGP has spurred the rapid advancement of genetics that will be felt with each passing year.

From creating new cells from existing cells, and identifying and manipulating specific genes, we move to creating actual body parts. Most Baby Boomers remember Lindsey Wagner as *The Bionic Woman*, and Lee Majors as the Six Million Dollar Man, but few could have ever imagined that bionics would become a reality. Some sources point the origin of the word *bionic* to Jack E. Steele of the Aeronautics Division House at Wright-Patterson Air

Force Base in 1958, with its roots in the Greek *bion* for "unit of life" and the suffix *-ic* meaning "like"—or "lifelike." Others think the term is from the combination of *biology* and *electronics*.

Either way, bionics, also referred to as biomimetics, is a booming field of research and development. According to Wikipedia, a simple explanation for bionics is "the application of biological methods and systems found in nature to the study and design of engineering systems and modern technology." In the field of medicine, bionics refers to the replacement or enhancement of organs or body parts by mechanical versions. Unlike prostheses, bionic parts actually mimic the original bodily function, and can even surpass it.

In July 2007, biomechatronicist Hugh Herr and his team at the MIT media lab succeeded in creating a robotic ankle that adjusts to the user and the terrain. Developed throughout a three-year period, this robotic ankle uses sensors and microprocessors to determine just the right amount of power needed for the prosthetic joint to provide the forward boost. Now a company called iWalk is taking that one step further to develop a robotic system for commercialization that is smaller, quieter, and lighter in weight.

In Germany, a biped robot has been developed that will one day help researchers create circuitry for artificial legs that will give amputees a more natural gait. Known as RunBot, this amazing walking robot, developed in the lab of computational neuroscientist Florentin Worgotter of the University of Gottingen, can also adjust its stride to new terrain and use data fed into sensors in the legs to make minor adjustments as it moves.

Although bionic technologies for medical purposes are still in the infancy stage, there has been some success, mainly with cochlear implants that help the deaf hear, artificial hearts, mechanical heart-assist pumps that keep people alive while awaiting a transplant, and a newly developed silicon retina that can process images in the same manner as a living retina. Bioengineering has made major advances in providing implants for hips, knees, and damaged joints, helping people with injuries and diseases such as arthritis maintain active lifestyles.

Scientists at the University of Michigan's Medical School of Medicine are now testing the world's first bionic lung in animals. At the same location, bionic kidney and an artificial liver support system are undergoing clinical human trials. And scientists at the University's Kresge Hearing Research Institute are looking at how the brain perceives sound and the effects of drugs on the inner ear, with the goal of developing new bionic devices for hearing loss. Michigan University is also at the forefront of what is called extracorporeal life-support technology (ECLS), which is showing impressive success rates in saving newborn infants with neonatal respiratory failure, as well as adults with acute respiratory failure. Robert H. Bartlett, professor of surgery at the U of M, along with colleague Ronald Hirschl, have developed an artificial lung now being tested in sheep. Known as MC3 Biolung, the device attaches to the pulmonary artery and replaces 100 percent of the normal lung functions. The Biolung can be used inside or outside of the body. Bartlett and Hirschl will undergo complete animal studies, then clinical human trials, in the next five years, thanks to a $4.8 million grant from the NIH.

Bartlett and his research team are now working on an artificial liver life-support system that could help prolong the lives of the approximately 18,000 Americans with end-stage liver disease who are waiting for a transplant. Meanwhile, colleague David Humes, MD, a professor of internal medicine, is busy developing a bioartificial kidney using living cells—one that will help people with kidney disease not have to rely on renal dialysis machines, which are known to have long-term negative affects such as potential increases in heart attacks, strokes, infections, and blood clots. Before too long, with this kind of ingenuity (and all at just ONE university!), there will be a replacement part for every part of the human body.

Computer Technology

Computer technology is also allowing researchers to make great strides in medical advancement, some of which we will no doubt benefit from in the next five years. Neuroscientist Henry Markram of the Brain Mind Institute in Lausanne, Switzerland, is one of the researchers at the forefront of this brave new world. Markram is designing a computer model of the brain based on more than 15 years of mapping the living brains of rats to create a neuron-by-neuron simulation. Now, with the help of IBM, the Blue Brain Project, named in part after IBM's nickname of Big Blue, hopes to create a model of the human brain that can mirror the real brain's behavior and mathematically imitate the interactions between neurons and the effects of neurotransmitters. Using a supercomputer courtesy of IBM, Markram has succeeded in creating a preliminary model of the neocortical column, and hopes to have a complete model active soon. Markram has expressed interest in seeing if this Blue Brain can then take on the ability to make decisions and assume consciousness. As he is quoted in the December 2007 issue of *Discover Magazine*, "Once we build the whole brain, if consciousness emerges, we will be able to study it systematically and understand exactly how it emerges."

In the next chapter, we will look at how computers and bionics are changing the face of non-medical technology, but first, we turn to the one field of medical study that could change our lives, maybe even make them longer than we ever thought possible.

The Fountain of Youth

Would you, if you could, live to be 150 years old? Would you desire immortality? To never die? To live forever?

These questions bring up all kinds of reactions, but one thing is certain: As we move closer to the year 2012, scientists the world over are looking for ways to keep human beings alive longer, and preferably healthy enough to enjoy the extra years. Longevity research is at the forefront of medicine, reflecting an age-old (pardon the pun) quest to find the Fountain of Youth.

In the year 1900, life expectancy for the average human was 49. Today, it is approximately 76–80 years of age, mainly in wealthy countries. Centenarians, people living to age 100 or older, are the fastest-growing segment of our population. Because of advances in public health, nutrition, and healthcare, the overall standard of living has improved for most Americans, who seem to be living longer, and healthier than ever before. According to Richard J. Hodes, MD, the director of the National Institute on Aging, a recent meta-analysis of demographic studies also confirmed that disability among American seniors has been declining steadily throughout the past 10 years.

In his statement before the Unites States Senate in 2003, Hodes reported that more older Americans are able to participate in daily life activities, while fewer are experiencing limitations in basic physical tasks such as walking or climbing stairs. Though he tempered his good news with some bad—diseases continue to diminish the quality of life for many older Americans—he speculated that advances in the coming years will come from a number of emerging fields, including medical imaging, computational biology, proteomics, regenerative medicine, and nanotechnology. Fortunately, the National Institutes of Health (NIH) is supporting research into all these areas.

One of the most important study areas is the analysis of genetic contributions to longevity. In 1993, the Longevity Associated Gene Initiative was launched to identify genes and processes that regulated longevity across species. The ultimate goal of LAG is to hopefully translate this information to human biology and identify age-related changes in human physiological systems. The NIA is also supporting research into diseases and conditions that shorten human life spans, focusing on two major life-debilitating illnesses: Alzheimer's disease (AD) and obesity.

As America's aging population increases, the incidences of AD will rise dramatically, Hodes reports, with the sharpest increase around the year 2011 when Baby Boomers reach 65. Hodes believes considerable progress is being made in terms of new ways to treat and even prevent AD, utilizing advances in imaging technology that target anatomical, molecular, and functional process in the brain. PET (positron emission tomography) and MRI (magnetic resonance imaging) scanning are being lauded as useful tools to predict decline associated with AD and degenerative disease. Other emerging technologies are offering exciting advances in therapeutic approaches, such as blocking plaque and tangle formation, stimulating repair of brain tissue, and even improving the delivery of time-released medications.

Obesity

RNA interference (RNAi) is making genetic advancements into identifying obesity-related genes involved in the regulation of fat metabolism. Similar to AD, obesity is a chronic illness that threatens to derail healthier advances, especially in developed, wealthy nations such as the United States.

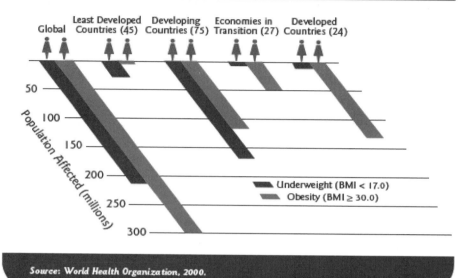

Figure 8.1: Global obesity rates are on the upswing, according to this chart courtesy of the World Health Organization.

According to ObesityInAmerica.org, individuals described as obese are on the upswing, and the increase is dramatic nationwide. Most notable increases in obese adults are occurring in the South, with states such as Alabama, Kentucky, Mississippi, Tennessee, Arkansas, Louisiana, Oklahoma, and Texas reporting record numbers each year.

Even in the "health-oriented" West and mountain regions, rates are up, with 35 of the 50 states having obesity rates as high as 20 percent or greater in the year 2000. Almost 10 years later, we can be sure those rates have skyrocketed. Because obesity is such a large contributing factor to other chronic diseases, such as cancer and heart disease, the focus of public health in recent years, and the biggest obstacle to longevity, has moved from infectious diseases to chronic diseases.

Sadly, one of the largest demographics affected by obesity is children. In 2007, pair of studies conducted in the United States and Denmark both confirm that obesity rates in children will see sharp increases in the future, leading to more prevalent heart conditions, particularly among boys. The studies appeared in the *New England Journal of Medicine*, and both teams of researchers found that more children than ever are facing problems caused by coronary heart disease due to obesity, and that these statistics show no signs of slowing down. It is estimated that by 2035, the prevalence of heart disease in youngsters will increase from 5 percent to 16 percent. The research studies both concluded: "Current adolescent overweight will have a substantial effect on public health far into the future."

Scary Statistics

The World Health Organization (WHO) released some projections of leading causes of DALYs, or "disability adjusted life years"—healthy years lost to disease, injury, or otherwise—and the changes in rank between 1990 and projections for 2020 are telling. In 1990, pneumonia and other respiratory infections topped the list, with heart disease and stroke at fifth and sixth places respectively. By 2020, heart disease will top the list, with depression in second place, and stroke in fourth (behind vehicular accidents). Emphysema and bronchitis will be fifth.

Currently, 80 percent of all seniors suffer from at least one chronic condition, with 50 percent having two or more with which to contend. Heart disease is now a killer of more than 33 percent of seniors, with cancer taking 22 percent and stroke 8 percent.

All of these are chronic diseases, and the sad thing is, most chronic disease is preventable with changes in nutrition, physical movement, basic treatment, and plain common sense.

A statement released in November 2007 by Linda Milan, director of the WHO's Building Healthy Communities and Populations, had some shocking statistics. Milan stated that chronic disease death rates are predicted to rise 17 percent in the next 10 years, and that chronic noncommunicable diseases (NCDs) were "a global problem that required comprehensive and urgent responses." The leading NCDs are identified as: cardiovascular disease, diabetes, cancer, obesity, and chronic respiratory disease—and all, Milan pointed out, can be drastically prevented by doing simple things such as eliminating smoking, getting more exercise, eating better, and using safe sex practices.

Milan reported that, just by addressing the underlying behavioral risk factors, 80 percent of premature heart disease could be prevented, along with 80 percent of premature stroke, 80 percent of type 2 diabetes (an epidemic today), and 40 percent of all cancers. These are stunning statistics, especially in light of the growing obesity rates, which appear to indicate that while Americans don't want to die of chronic diseases, they are not doing much about preventing it.

Depression

Most surprising is the expected rise of mental illnesses, such as depression and anxiety, which the WHO suggest may become the second leading cause of disability-related lost years. These mental illnesses may not cause a great numbers of deaths, but they do contribute to the world's burden of disease and lost productivity. In the vast majority of cases, mental illness is easily treated with medications, behavioral therapies, or some combination of both, as well as increased exercise and better nutrition.

Increasing longevity will be impossible for a vast number of Americans, and indeed, people worldwide, unless chronic disease rates are brought under control. The idea is to have a longer, healthier life, not just a life that takes longer to end. As genetics and molecular biology make advancements concerning aging causes and prevention, one major key to understand how and why we age, and how to stop it, is inflammation. And the study of how inflammation affects the body is where many researchers think the Fountain of Youth may finally be found.

Inflammation

In the December 2007 issue of *Discover* magazine, Kathleen McGowan asked the question, "Can We Cure Aging?" Interviewing a number of scientists and medical experts, McGowan presented a strong case for inflammation as a main cause of aging and chronic diseases. It appears that many prominent gerontologists look to aging as an actual consequence of inflammation, and their hopes are high for an anti-inflammatory drug that might ultimately treat diabetes, dementia, heart disease, and cancer, allowing us to live longer and better. The best thing is, these gerontologists think we might have that drug within our lifetime.

But first they need to fully understand inflammation's grip on the demise of human health. It seems our biological history may be to blame. Because infectious diseases have long been the top killers of humans, our immune systems have been primed and geared to act on this threat to keep us alive. Inflammation is how we did that. "It serves as an all-purpose protection against invaders and traumatic dangers," McGowan writes. To put it simply, the problem is that inflammation responses can kick in even when no apparent threat is visible, thus causing all kinds of problems that normally would have protected us, but now can kill us. "Over a lifetime, this essential set of defensive mechanisms runs out of bounds and gradually damages organs throughout the body," the author continues.

Biologists have been aware for a long time that inflammation increases with age, but only when it was found to be a factor in predicting heart disease in the 1990s did it take center stage. According to Russell Tracy, the University of Vermont's professor of pathology and biochemistry, who identified that C-reactive protein (CRP) is an accurate predictor of a heart attack, inflammation is now considered a "critical factor" in predicting heart attacks, heart failure, diabetes, cancer, and even fragility in old age.

Hormones

Other researchers are focusing on the hormonal system as the key to longevity and enduring health. Endocrinologists know that muscles atrophy along with a decline in human growth hormone, and that sex drives dwindle as testosterone decreases. Bones become more fragile as the body produces less estrogen. By finding new ways to utilize hormones and hormone therapies to reverse these shortages, researchers hope to soon be able to turn back the aging clock, or at least give it a good rewind.

Hormones may not play as big a role in aging as inflammation, but we do know that estrogen prevents osteoporosis, one of the most debilitating and widespread conditions the growing elderly population faces, especially women. Endocrinologists are pursuing anti-aging therapies involving the hormonal system that promise to be safer and more effective than the over-the-counter therapies offered by the pharmaceutical giants, including poorly regulated compounding pharmacies that whip up "bioidentical" hormones that are rarely tested.

Caloric Restriction

Interestingly, one of the most famous and seemingly effective ways to extend life span is caloric restriction. The idea is that restricted caloric intake, usually a reduction of between 30 and 40 percent of normal consumption, could result in mice and dogs living longer and healthier. Not only that, but these test animals also experienced less cancer and neurodegenerative diseases. The only downside? A decrease in fertility.

The phenomenon of caloric restriction was thought to be related to a slowing of the metabolic rate in response to less food intake, but now researchers find that metabolism does not slow down at all in mammals, and in things such as yeast and worms, it actually speeds up. Researchers David A. Sinclair and Lenny Guarente, writing in the March 2006 *Scientific American*, believe that "calorie restriction is a biological stressor like natural food scarcity that induces a defensive response to boost the organism's chances of survival." Sinclair is director of the Paul F. Glenn Laboratories for the Biological Mechanisms of Aging at Harvard Medical School. Guarente is a Novartis professor of biology and MIT faculty member. Both are immersed in looking at the presence of a longevity gene they call SIR2 and its relationship with caloric restriction and the aging process. Their research, reported in the article "Can DNA Stop Time? Unlocking the Secrets of Longevity Genes," has found that SIR2, and its gene relatives called Sirtuins, have some amazing affects that enhance longevity. One such example involves worms and the gene that encodes cellular receptors for insulin and the insulin-like growth factor (IGF-1). This gene is called daf-2. Suppressing daf-2's activity in adult worms interferes with signaling via insulin and IGF-1, resulting in an extension of the worm's life *by as much as 100 percent*. Sinclair and Guarente are continuing to examine the role of Sirtuins and aging, with hopes that they will soon know exactly how these genes orchestrate a "master regulatory network for aging."

Telomeres

As we attempt to understand, and one day overcome, the challenges of aging, the biggest answers seem likely to come from the smallest of places. Take the recent discovery of telomeres, which are tiny strips of DNA that cap the ends of chromosomes. Research into the role telomeres play in diseases associated with aging, such as cancer, is helping us to understand why some cells turn malignant. When a cell divides, the telomeres fray and shorten, which may explain why cells age and die, according to the research of Elizabeth Blackburn, a Cambridge-educated biochemist with a long list of awards to her name. Blackburn, named as one of *Time* magazine's 100 most influential people in 2007, has found that telomerase also influences aging and disease. "The enzyme telomerase seems to accelerate certain diseases of aging, which include the biggies—cancer, heart disease and diabetes," Blackburn stated in the December 2007 issue of *Discover* magazine. "If you say that a part and parcel of aging is susceptibility to these common age-related diseases, then the telomerase-telomere length maintenance and telomere protection is tying in more and more intimately with that aspect of aging."

Blackburn is currently involved in animal and human tests with telomerase that may one day lead to a major breakthrough in the treatment of cancers. So far, tests have shown some progress in affecting telomerase and making attacked cancer cells less metastatic and less malignant, but more money and research is required to turn lab tests into a tangible form of treatment.

Artificial Life

Perhaps the most shocking medical advancement on the near horizon involves the stuff of horror or science fiction novels. A September 2007 CNN.com story titled "Artificial Life Likely in 3 to 10 Years" reports on the progress of a handful of scientists across the globe striving to create "life from scratch." According to the article, they are getting so close that a predicted announcement of success will occur sometime in the next three to 10 years. The researchers are using the basic chemicals in DNA to create synthetic life, and right now, the results are, shall we say, microscopic. But within six months, the researchers involved in the field of "wet artificial life" will have created a synthetic cell membrane, and the next step will be getting nucleotides to form a working genetic system. Beyond that, one can only imagine, but the team promises to continue until they can keep this "new life" alive for more than just an hour or so in a lab.

Whether we live to be 100 or 200 years old, and whether our bodies are natural or partially synthetic, the quality of life is what will matter most. We can look to technology for progress at the speed of light that will change the way we operate in the world, and the way we access information, keep in touch, learn, communicate, drive, work, and, well, even think.

Welcome to the brave new world. Come inside and take a peek, if you dare.

9

Quantum Leaps

Is it progress if a cannibal uses knife and fork?
—Stanislaw Lec, *Unkempt Thoughts*

By leaps and bounds, technology moves forward into the future, dragging us along with it, breathless and awestruck. Some of us hold on for dear life as the amount of information to which we are exposed doubles, triples, and quadruples, snowballing until it reaches a point of "technological Singularity," leaving us stunned and blindsided, with a distinct sense of unease and the constant complaint of a lack of time. At least, that is, lack of time to stop and get our bearings. We are swept up in the wave toward progress.

Fear not, though, for what we lack the time to do, there is no doubt a computer or machine at the ready to do it for us. Even think.

Artificial Intelligence

Artificial intelligence, or AI, may be on the brink of taking technological progress to a whole new level, one that might make the machine smarter than the man making the machine. Many futurists predict we are about to reach a point of technological Singularity, a concept that suggests an explosion of intelligence that allows machines to potentially outpace human intellect. In other words, we are talking about brain-computer interfaces that, according to the description in Wikipedia, "rapidly accelerate technological progress beyond the capability of human beings to participate meaningfully in said progress."

Okay, if that is still too confusing, let me put it this way. Machines are going to think for us, and be better at it, too.

This idea was first explored by statistician I.J. Good, who argued that as machines surpassed humans in intelligence, they would also be able to recursively augment their mental abilities, and, in a snowball effect, exceed the abilities of their human creators. The concept was further strengthened and expanded by science fiction writer Vernor Vinge, who wrote about "online reality" as early as 1981 in his novella *True Names*. Vinge also explored artificial intelligence in future novels, and his work even influenced William Gibson, who is usually credited for defining "cyberspace" in his writings.

Vinge became known for his opinions on technological Singularity, suggesting that self-programming computers will "have a learning curve that points straight up," and that in a short time would become so intelligent and powerful, they could change the face of civilization...if left unchecked. In an interview with Salon.com, Vinge, a math professor at San Diego State University, discussed how the problem of computer software complexity is all that stands between programmers and their desire to create intelligent computers. But at the current rate of progress, research is exploding.

Vinge points to open source software's rising popularity as a potential for increasing the collective intelligence, and is happy to see the collaborative effects the Internet provides. But that is only as long as we humans stay on top and not allow "trans-human intelligence" to overtake us and make us obsolete. Because, as superhuman intelligences enhance their own minds at a rate far quicker than that of their creators, the progress becomes more rapid in return.

The technological Singularity we may all be tumbling toward will consist of two different types of AI:

1. Intelligence amplification of the human brain.
2. Artificial intelligence.

The former would include things such as bioengineering, genetic engineering, the use of nootropic drugs, brain-computer interfacing, and even mind transfer. Most organizations involved in trying to bring about this Singularity insist that the latter, AI, is the much more productive choice. Non-human artificial intelligence is often referred to as "seed AI," and is considered much easier to accomplish than trying to enhance human intelligence to higher levels necessary for such explosive progress.

The exploration of AI, though, leads to all kinds of concerns over potential dangers, many of which are being argued by AI researchers at The Singularity Institute for Artificial Intelligence, which uses the Three Laws of Robotics created by Isaac Asimov as a foundation for safety issues that come with AI. While many researchers like to try to diminish the dangers of over-thinking machines, others warn that by creating superhuman intelligence, we run the risk of making mistakes that would one day lead to our own annihilation at the hands of what we have created.

In 1958, Stanislaw Ulam reported in the Bulletin of American Mathematical Society's Tribute to John von Neumann, that he and von Neumann had discussed the concept of Singularity. This is one of the first times, if not *the* first, that the word was used, and Ulam wrote: "One conversation centered on the ever accelerating progress of technology and changes in the mode of human life, which gives the appearance of approaching some essential Singularity in the history of the race beyond which human affairs, as we know them, could not continue."

This idea of accelerating change is behind the work of the Acceleration Studies Foundation, founded by John Smart. The ASF engages in education and research into concerns about accelerating change on humanity (*www.accelerationwatch.com*), and even hosts an annual conference at Stanford University.

Not every futurist predicts that this point of Singularity will be reached in a speedy burst of progress. Ray Kurzweil is the author of two important books about the potential for humans to transcend biology. In *The Age of Spiritual Machines* and his more recent *The Singularity Is Near*, Kurzweil proposes that technology follows a pattern of exponential growth that follows what he refers to as the "Law of Accelerating Returns." Again, this law proposes that technology reaches barriers that, when crossed, lead to huge leaps forward as new technologies are created in its wake. Kurzweil also believes leaps in technology also create major paradigm shifts that change civilization. The Internet could be described as just such a leap, followed by a huge paradigm change that now is a part of our daily lives—one we could not have imagined 25 or 30 years ago.

Kurzweil takes on a more conservative approach, putting the date more into the future, say around 2045, but definitely before the end of the 21st century. Thus, a more long-term pattern of accelerated change may be unfolding.

On his Website, Kurweil states "An analysis of the history of technology shows that technological change is exponential, contrary to the common-sense intuitive-linear view. So we won't experience 100 years of progress in the 21st century—it will be more like 20,000 years of progress (at today's rate)."

Kurzweil goes on to state that this rate of progress will lead to "the Singularity," when technological change happens so rapidly it literally "represents a rupture in the fabric of human history." This increase in both biological and non-biological intelligence will then expand out into the universe at light speed.

Singularity

In *The Singularity Is Near*, Kurzweil lists the many principles behind the Singularity, which include a number of factors that must be met. Among them:

∞ The rate of both paradigm shifts and the power of information will grow exponentially at a faster pace, now doubling every year.

∞ We will have the hardware to emulate human intelligence with supercomputers by the end of this decade, and effective software models of human intelligence by the mid-2020s.

∞ Once that happens, we will have passed the Turing Test, which indicates that computer intelligence has become indistinguishable from human intelligence. This is predicted to occur by the end of the 2020s.

∞ Nonbiological intelligence will eventually be able to download information, skills, and knowledge from other machines, and then eventually from humans.

∞ Nonbiological intelligence will continue to experience the double exponential growth of price-performance, speed, and capacity.

∞ Machines will be able to design and engineer technology just as humans do, but at far higher speeds and capacities.

∞ Machine intelligence will improve its abilities in a feedback cycle that humans will not be able to keep up with.

∞ Nanotech will enable the design of nanobots, which, when interacting with biological neurons, will extend human experience by creating virtual reality within the nervous system.

∞ Nanobots will assist the nonbiological portion of human intelligence and eventually predominate it.

∞ The Law of Accelerating Returns will continue until nonbiological intelligence comes close to "saturating" the matter and energy in our part of the universe with human-machine intelligence.

∞ Ultimately, the universe itself will become saturated with our intelligence, in what Kurzweil describes as "the destiny of the universe," leading eventually to the universe becoming intelligent and leading to Singularity.

Paradigms

Is this the next step on the evolutionary ladder, and could it possibly accelerate faster and happen sometime sooner, say around 2012? With the annual doubling rate of information and capacity, we may see the destiny of the universe play itself out in our own lifetimes.

Even Carl Sagan, the great astronomer, author, and philosopher, believed that our evolution is marked by "mastery of change," which in our time is quickening in pace. Kurzweil adds that technological evolution is an outgrowth of, and continuation of, biological evolution, and that it leads to increased paradigm shifts. "A half millennium ago, the product of a paradigm shift such as the printing press took about a century to be widely deployed. Today, the products of major paradigm shifts, such as cell phones and the World Wide Web, are widely adopted in only a few years' time."

These specific paradigms, he adds, create exponential growth until its potential is exhausted, which then leads to a shift that allows even more exponential growth to continue. In fact, the life cycle of a paradigm would be best described, Kurzweil states, as a three-stage process:

∞ **Stage 1:** slow growth—the early stage of exponential growth.

∞ **Stage 2:** rapid growth—the late, explosive phase of exponential growth.

∞ **Stage 3:** leveling off as the specific paradigm matures.

Robots

Whether or not the point of Singularity occurs in line with the predictions of a major transformation that will change all of humanity around 2012, we can already see signs of increasing progress with robotics. At the Laboratory of Intelligent Systems at the Swiss Federal Institute of Technology, a team led by Dario Floreano has succeeded in creating robots that communicate with, and even help, each other. Michael Abrams reported in the January 2008 issue of *Discover Magazine* that Floreano and his colleagues created generations of robots by programming their neural circuitry with "genes, or elements of software code that determine how they sense light and respond." The robots were placed in environments with glowing patches of "food sources," as well as "poison" that recharged or drained their batteries upon contact. The team then recombined genes of the robots that proved to be the fittest at detecting the food source from the poison and downloaded the new code into the robots.

But by the 50th generation of robots, something amazing happened. The robots had learned how to communicate with each other, even to the point of alerting each other when they located "food sources" and the "poison." Some of the robot colonies developed the ability to cheat, telling others that the "poison" was the food source, then rolling over and devouring the food source themselves.

Floreano's team also found that some robots acted heroically by signaling danger to other robots, and some even "died" to save their fellows from peril. Surely, if robots can develop compassion, maybe one day humans may as well (note strong sarcasm here). This might alleviate some of the fear surrounding AI, the fear that sometime soon machines will overtake us in every aspect of life, including heroics and altruism.

While some predict machines may become the new man, others, such as journalist Robert Frenay, believe machines may instead be inspired by living things in a more positive collaboration of technology and biology. Called "living systems," this growing trend emphasizes what nature can teach us about how systems and cycles work, and what dynamics drive evolution.

In his book *Pulse: The Coming Age of Systems and Machines Inspired By Living Things*, Frenay focuses on technological mimicry of living systems, which result in a much more environmentally friendly flow of progress that suggests devices, companies, and even economies perform better across the board when they behave similar to living organisms and ecosystems. Nature knows best, and that can be applied to advancements in the machine-age as well, affecting every area of invention and innovation. So although some propose that AI will one day outdo human evolution, Frenay sees a more human-driven approach that benefits everyone all the way around, creating a new kind of culture that closes the gap between those who respect nature and those who seek new advancements in technology around every corner. This kind of transformation can happen just as quickly, but keeps the power in the hands of "living things," rather than nonbiological machines.

By remembering that the cell is the basic life form, Frenay sees machines and even corporations evolving in much the same way nature uses cells as the foundation, adding the building blocks that lead to complete life forms. Even computers would take on a new sort of "cyberbiology," allowing scientists more glimpses into the inner workings of organic processes such as genetics and evolution. But, Frenay warns, even this new biology would require attention to environmental negatives, such as increased pollution and pesticide use, and a new kind of "green revolution" must accompany any kind of transformation of human endeavors. He does suggest, though, that perhaps industrial ecosystems could be created such that the waste products of one manufacturing process become the raw materials of another, closing the conflicts between the green movement and corporations seeking to improve their bottom line.

Nanotechnology

When nature meets robotics, the most amazing, and perhaps potentially chilling, advances throughout the next five years will involve the integration of nanotechnology into medicine, biotech, electronics, engineering, and just about every other arena one can think of.

Aside from the science fiction hype about nanotech, which usually involves some type of self-replicating nanomachines, tiny yet deadly, that swarm and destroy everything in their path, this brave new world actually does have the potential to completely alter the way we live. It could even usher in a new kind of technological and industrial era of stunning advancement and ingenuity that was unheard of 50 years ago.

Nanotechnology is described as the engineering of functional systems at the molecular scale. The original sense of the word described the ability to construct materials and devices from the "bottom up" with atomic precision, using molecular components that use molecular recognition to chemically assemble themselves. But there is also a "top down" approach to nanotech involving the construction of nanomachines from larger objects without the atomic-level control.

According to the Center for Responsible Nanotechnology, the word itself was popularized in the 1980s courtesy of K. Eric Drexler, who at the time was talking about building machines smaller than a cell, including robot arms, motors, and entire computers. Drexler spent the next decade working on his ideas, even as technology itself was catching up to his rather forward-thinking concepts. Now, the U.S. National Nanotechnology Initiative (USNNI) officially defines nanotech as anything smaller than 100 nanometers with novel properties.

Mihail Roco, also of the USNNI, describes nanotech as occurring in four generations:

∞ **First Generation:** Passive Nanostructures—materials designed to perform a single task.

∞ **Second Generation:** Active Nanostructures—able to multitask, as in actuators, drug delivery systems, and detectors and sensors.

∞ **Third Generation:** Systems of Nanosytems—guided assembling, 3-D networking, and nanosystems with thousands of interacting components.

∞ **Fourth Generation:** Molecular Nanosystems—the first integrated nanosystems, functioning like a mammalian cell with systems, emerging functions, and atomic design.

Interestingly, Rocco predicts that we will enter the Third Generation around the year 2010, moving into the Fourth Generation sometime between 2015 and 2020.

Right now, nanotech has really been applied commercially only in terms of the use of colloidal nanoparticles in "first generation" passive nanomaterials—things such as cosmetics, lotions, protective coatings, drug delivery, and even stain-resistant clothing, but advances are underway to bring medical imaging to the nano level, hopefully resulting in new and exciting ways to incorporate molecular imaging and therapy into treatments for cancer and other major killer diseases.

This book can in no way cover nanotech in one chapter; suffice it to say that the next five years will see an explosion of inventive new nanotech devices that allow us glimpses into the human body, and the ability to create everything from blood-cell-sized machines that deliver insulin to treat to DNA sequencing technology that will allow people to sequence their own genomes, and other advances in genomics and proteomics will offer potential cures for genetically based diseases.

Though nanomedicine is right now the most productive area of research for many in the field, we can look forward to the continued creation of new materials in other areas of technology as well, including carbon nanotubes, nanorods, and even components for quantum computers. Molecular

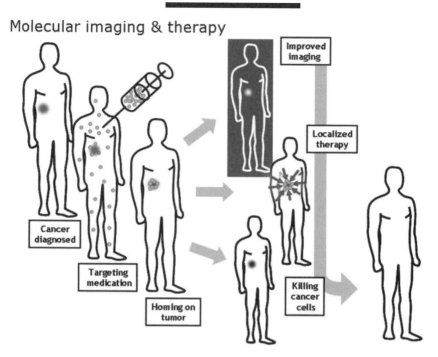

Molecular imaging & therapy

Figure 9.1: Molecular imaging opens new doorways in the treatment of cancer using nanotechnology. Image courtesy of the Open Source Handbook of Nanoscience and Nanotechnology.

electronics is a new field that seeks to develop molecules with electronic properties, and nanoionics is developing devices on the nano scale for conversion and storage of charge, energy, and information. We can also look for advances in nanorobotics, scanning probe microscopy, atomic microscopics, and even nanolithography.

In the December 2007 article "Scientific American Reports: The Rise of Nanotech," the popular magazine documents all of the cutting-edge research involving the control of molecules, including:

∞ tiny DNA computers that "speak" to living cells.

∞ invisibility cloaks using plasmonics to alter the electromagnetic field around an object, rendering it invisible.

∞ nanoscale valves and computer storage devices.

- ∞ electronic advances involving the use of random networks of tiny carbon tubes to create printable solar cells, electronic paper, and bendable touch screens.

- ∞ "molecular Lego" devices enabling the design and manufacture of nano-scale structures programmed to have any shape desired.

- ∞ the extension of nanotech based on DNA from two dimensions to three dimensions to design solid materials based upon a specific series of DNA sequences and then combining them.

- ∞ plasmonics that squeeze electromagnetic waves into nanostructures to create new superfast computer chips and ultrasensitive molecular detectors of single virus particles and pieces of DNA.

- ∞ real-world applications in biomedical research, therapy, and the diagnosis of disease, including tiny devices that can locate tumors (even those just a few cells in size) and infections, nanoparticles that can release drugs to specific sites at specific times, and artificial hips coated with nanoparticles for better bonding to surrounding bone.

In the issue's article, "Plenty of Room Indeed," Michael Roukes discusses the advances made in the field by Nobel laureate Richard Feynman, and states, "We've only just begun to take the first steps toward his grand vision of assembling complex machines and circuits atom by atom." But if we can expect the Law of Accelerating Returns to snowball the progress of technology, it will no doubt include nanotech, resulting in some mind-boggling announcements throughout the next five years, many of which will echo the science fiction stories once thought impossible and utterly unimaginable.

The Speed of Information

One of the most anticipated technological breakthroughs involves computing information at speeds that boggle the brain cells. Quantum computing will literally harness the power of atoms and molecules to perform memory and processing significantly faster than the silicon-based computers of today. Much progress has been made since physicist Paul Benioff at the Argonne National Laboratory first proposed quantum computing three decades ago.

Using distinct quantum mechanical phenomena, such as entanglement and superposition of states, these mind-blowing computers store information not as "bits," as in current computers, but as "qubits," or "quantum bits." Bits hold either a one or a zero bit of information memory. But a singe qubit can hold a one, a zero, and even a superposition of both that allows for an infinite number of states, thus increasing the amount of processing capability and memory capacity.

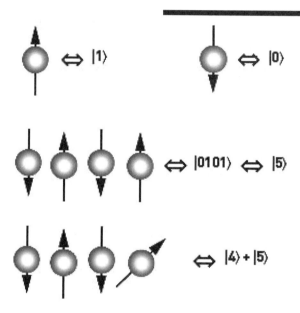

Figure 9.2: Qubits can be in a superposition of all the classically allowed states at one time, allowing quantum computing to work at amazing speeds and process amazing amounts of information. Image is courtesy of Wikimedia, adapted from *Nanocomputers and Swarm Intelligence,* by JB Waldner.

As of the writing of this book, experiments with quantum computers using a small number of qubits have been successful, but no practical applications are yet effective. Research is expanding rapidly—not just by commercial and university interests, but also by the military and defense agencies for purposes of improving national security.

Researchers point to many problems involving practicality and decoherence, which means that the slightest interaction of the quantum computer components with external objects could cause the entire system to decohere. Studies are currently underway to use "quantum error correction" to avoid decoherence, but again, we are years away from a practical quantum computer that we can apply to our day-to-day lives, unless you count those popularized in movies and novels such as Michael Crichton's *Timeline* or the 2007 *Transformers*, in which those nasty Decepticons utilized the power of quantum computers to crack the U.S. Army's data code.

Plants

While we humans may be years away from quantum computing, plants have been discovered to use a process similar to quantum computing to process water and carbon dioxide into simple carbohydrates. A team of researchers at the Lawrence Berkeley National Laboratory, led by Graham Fleming, reported that the photosynthesis process relies on superposition, such that a photon's energy can be in several different states at the same time. Just as a quantum computer would evaluate a number of states in superposition, then collapse and choose one state, photosynthesis also picks and chooses the best reaction path within the chlorophyll molecules, and the energy is transferred accordingly as the superposition collapses.

Information Chips

Technology isn't always intended to help the civilian populace work and live better. Sometimes, it has more sinister implications. For example, by the year 2035, a long way off indeed, we may have such things as "information chips" wired into the human brain; electromagnetic pulse weapons able to destroy communications systems in specific regions or even an entire city; neutron weapons that destroy living things, but spare structures; unmanned weapons that offer the explicit use of biological and chemical weapons; and death rays. Yes, death rays.

Research and Development

In the October 2007 issue of *Discover Magazine*, reporter Sharon Weinberger listed in her article "The Dark Side" some of the darker missions of the proposed 2008 trillion-dollar American defense budget. If you were wondering where much of your tax dollars were going, how about into projects currently under research and development that not only further improve existing projects (such as the Aurora, a top-secret hypersonic jet oft called the SR-72), but also into programs that could one day control the brains of soldiers on the battlefield.

Meanwhile, the Army is investing in solid-state lasers that will soon reach the minimum power necessary to become deployable, and DARPA, the Defense Advanced Research Projects Agency, is "exploiting neuroscience in pursuit of better battlefield technology." DARPA hopes to complete a project in the next few years involving the use of advanced optics with an EEG system that monitors the brain's activity in the prefrontal cortex. Dubbed "Luke's Binoculars," as a reference to *Star Wars*, this system is designed to alert a soldier's brain about imminent threats even before his own consciousness can perceive the threat.

This kind of futuristic science is at the forefront of the Pentagon's goals for the next decade or two, despite some skepticism from some of its own researchers, who have concerns that some of the projects are too bold, especially the "dream counterterrorism program," which national security analyst William M. Arkin said is seeking to create a "silver bullet" to solve terrorism; a poor replacement, he feels, for examining why terrorism occurs in the first place.

Outer Space

One final frontier with promises of major advances is outer space. We can be sure to see more and more private space races among the rich and powerful such as Virgin Galactic and SpaceX and the Bezo's Blue Origin, even as NASA struggles to overcome funding, reputation issues, and increased competition from the European Space Agency, China, and other rising "space powers." But without the common goal of space exploration once enjoyed in the 1960s, it will be hard to garner the enthusiasm needed for a return trip to the moon, or a first-time jaunt to Mars.

Sometime around the year 2020, NASA hopes to have a return voyage to the moon on board the *Orion*, a key component of NASA's multi-billion-dollar space transportation program called Constellation. Established in 2006, the Constellation program has been pushing forward with *Orion*, as well as various rocket launchers and service modules by working to make stays on board the International Space Station more comfortable and long-term effective. Along with Lockheed Martin, NASA hopes to be able to transport humans back and forth to the moon on board *Orion* vehicles, and eventually serve as the means to get to Mars.

Orion will also allow astrophysicists to place radio telescopes on the far side of the moon in order to study particle acceleration in supernovae and quasars; other scientists hope to use *Orion* to launch studies into the x-ray emissions between solar winds and the Earth's magnetic field. Meanwhile, other NASA programs hope to scan the skies for asteroids, such as the Large Synoptic Survey Telescope predicted to find 80 percent of moving objects sometime between 2014 and 2024 (and hopefully before these objects find us!). In addition, the National Research Council plans to send up 17 new satellites during the next 10 years to detect everything from gravitational distortions caused by water movement, to global warming impact, to measuring incoming solar radiation.

And in 2013, the European Space Agency will launch their ExoMars Rover with a chemistry lab on board and a drilling platform that can dig down 2 meters to see if organic material exists on the Red Planet. In 2011, NASA will launch the *Juno* orbiter to study Jupiter.

Perhaps on board one of those missions there will be a quantum computer able to process information at light speed, or a biomachine able to walk the surface of planets no human could step forth upon....

It will be a brave new world indeed.

10

Shift
Shapers

*One can resist the invasion of armies; one cannot
resist the invasion of ideas.*
—Victor Hugo, *Histoire d'un crime*

The years between now and that first morning of 2013 will be filled with shifts not just in technology, medicine, and science, but in the way we think and feel and live. Paradigm shifts don't just occur on a technological level, they occur in the collective psyche of peoples and nations, cultures and races, and humanity as a whole.

Those who look forward to the trends of tomorrow don't just pay attention to the movements of today, they intuit the needs of groups of people in the coming years, and find ideas and innovations that might fulfill those needs. Shifts, tipping points, memes, trends, and waves begin in the past. Our present.

Today.

Who, and what, will be the "shift shapers" of 2012?

The most obvious movement of the 21st century will no doubt increase in popularity, and downright necessity, as climate change, famine, economic hardship, disease, and shifts in geopolitical power shift the foundation below our feet. The earth, it seems, needs some attention, and without that attention, will whither and die, taking us all down with it.

The Importance of Sustainability

Sustainability is the key word of the next five years, as we move toward the end date of the Kyoto Protocol in December 2012, and nations battle for dwindling resources, including water, food, and fossil fuels. The growing trend toward "greening" may have begun with the spirit of the 1960s to the power of the flower, and then expanded in our consciousness every Earth Day, but this will go down as the decade when humanity either made its stand, or chose to turn its back against a planet crying out for a little love and care.

It no longer comes down just to what we as individuals can do—conserve water, use less pollutants, drive less, water lawns in the morning, install low-flow toilets, and so on. The problem of a taxed earth has reached a tipping point and now requires a greater call to action, one that is being met in some interesting ways.

Global warming, for instance, may be fought not just in carbon trading coupons and emission reduction deals, but with kangaroo farts. Yes, you read that right. Kangaroo farts.

We have all heard about how cattle and sheep passing gas contribute to rising levels of methane. As more rainforest is flattened to make room for more grazing lands for more cattle and sheep, the problem seems rather, well, explosive. But researchers with the Queensland, Australia, state government, led by senior scientist Athol Klieve, have discovered a clever way to offset those smelly emissions. Give cattle and sheep kangaroo stomachs. Or, stop raising so many cattle and sheep, and start eating kangaroo instead.

According to a December 8, 2007 *Agence France-Presse* article titled "Eco-friendly Kangaroo Farts Could Help Global Warming," the kangaroo has a special bacteria in its stomach, thus its gas contains no nasty methane. The idea is to somehow get that special bacteria into the stomachs of other grazing species to see if it does the same, but first scientists have to isolate the bacteria, a plan they say will take about three years.

Meanwhile, other scientists are looking to seaweed and algae as possible weapons against global warming. The oceans contain vast amounts of seaweed and sea grasses that can absorb carbon dioxide in what are called "carbon sinks," essential to controlling greenhouse gases. Some seaweed can absorb five times more carbon dioxide than any terrestrial plant, and researchers in South Korea, Japan, and Australia are rushing to utilize some of the 8 million tons of the slimy stuff cultivated each year.

Even private enterprise is showing some innovation in fighting climate change. A company called Skyonic is developing a system to turn the carbon dioxide from smokestack emissions into usable baking soda. The idea, called SkyMine, was developed by Skyonic CEO Joe David Jones, who got the brainstorm while watching a Discovery Channel show with his kids.

Conservation projects that will impact the next five to 10 years include attempts by loggers, conservation biologists, and indigenous peoples to protect biodiversity by creating models of land use that both benefit the local economy and allow for wildlife protection. One such project is the Planted Forests Project in Malaysia, which has allocated approximately 1,900 square miles as a planted forest zone that will include areas for logging, conservation, and living space for indigenous people.

Seed Vaults

At the North Pole, a giant "doomsday" vault is being constructed on an Arctic island that will house a collection of seeds that may one day feed humanity. The Svalbard Global Seed Vault, located in an archipelago 600 miles of Norway, will store more than 4.5 million seeds in its reinforced concrete walls, seeds destined to protect the diversity of crops. In the past 200 years, the United States alone has seen 75 percent of its plant variety disappear from crops. This trend toward less genetic diversity endangers the food supply, because in order to endure, plants need varied gene pools.

Interestingly, the notorious Abu Ghraib prison in Iraq was once that nation's seed bank. Once the U.S. invaded Iraq, the seed bank was destroyed and looted. In 2006, a typhoon destroyed the seed "gene" bank in the Philippines. The need for a massive vault, protected by its forbidding, icy location, is more obvious than ever, because many other countries only house specific seed types in their banks. Other seed banks are found in Mexico, which houses more than 20,000 maize seeds; India's Pearl Millet bank, the bean seed bank of Colombia; and Syria's seed bank, which stores 30,270 types of wheat.

Ecosystems

One of the biggest trends in conservation efforts involves combining the needs of the planet with the needs of the people. In the October 27, 2007 *Scientific American* article "Conservation for the People," reporters Peter Kareiva and Michelle Marvier examine how pitting nature against people makes no sense, and that human health and well-being can indeed go hand-in-hand with conservation.

One idea is to focus on protecting ecosystems specifically vital to peoples' health and material needs, as long as these ecosystems include forests, wetlands that maintain clean water, mangroves for storm protection, and reefs for fishing. This kind of win-win attitude creates more public, private, and government support for protecting wild places and species, because we humans come out on top, too. The authors write that "we and a growing number of conservationists argue that old ways of prioritizing conservation activities should be largely scrapped in favor of an approach that emphasizes saving ecosystems that have value to people."

This would also serve to lessen the reputation of the conservation movement as being "anti-people," because of forcing millions of people off their land to protect the habitats of wild creatures.

This new kind of "service paradigm" puts the focus on how natural capital results in products and services that benefit people, such as medicines, timber, water filtration, pollination processes, and any other "ecosystem service" that promotes economic increase can protect biodiversity. In 2000, the United Nations called for a major study of these "ecosystem services," and government and corporate interest is high in this new trend toward conservation strategies that help more than just plants and animals.

Ecovillages

The increasing popularity of the sustainability movement has led to the creation of "ecovillages," which are small local communities that "minimize ecological impact but maximize human wellbeing," according to Jonathan Dawson, executive secretary of GEN-Europe, the Global Ecovillage Network. Dawson is also the author of *Ecovillages: New Frontiers of Sustainability*, part of a series of booklets on key issues of our time called "The Schumacher Briefings," named after E.F. Schumacher, an internationally influential economist and educator.

Ecovillages are like living laboratories that seek to find the best and most effective balance between the needs of the Earth and the needs of the humans inhabiting it. The focus is on designing in conjunction with nature, using permaculture design, organic local food production, small-scale energy generation, waste management, community education and currency systems, and low-impact transportation systems. These communities foster a sense of unity, peace, and holistic well-being among those who live and work there, and many such communities, according to Dawson, are springing up in the United Kingdom, India, and even in the States. The next five years should see a greater migration towards sustainable communities, as more and more people flee the pressures of urban and suburban life, and desire to live closer to the earth.

Dawson writes that replication is a big problem that the ecovillage movement needs to address, because approximately 90 percent of ecovillage plans never get off the ground. Because there are so many factors involved, envisioned communities never get built. Dawson hopes that existing communities will act as pioneers to help others attain the same levels of success in a world that is becoming bigger in numbers, and smaller in resources, with each passing year.

Even as individuals move toward the creation of new communities that foster new ways of living together and alongside nature, this can only be achieved in conjunction with a shift in the paradigm of global economics. In a September 2005 issue of *Scientific American*, Herman E. Daly writes about "Economics in a Full World," stating that it has long been a popular belief that growing economies can ignore sustainability. That belief is now being challenged, and the new paradigm will call for a way to increase global progress while taking into account the finite biosphere in which we live and work.

Daly believes most contemporary economists ignore the issue of sustainability and believe instead that because we have already come so far with growth, we can keep on going "ad infinitum." Daly goes on to say that the finite resources at hand demand that any subsystem, such as the economy, must at some point stop growing, and therefore "adapt itself into a dynamic equilibrium, something like a steady state." This would mean that birth and death rates must be equal, and that production rates of commodities would be equal to depreciation rates.

A "sustainable economy" would require a tremendous amount of effort on all nations throughout the course of many years, and take the position of "ecological economists" that natural and man-made capital are more often complementary than substitutes for each other, and that national capital needs to be maintained on its own "because it has become the limiting factor" to further economic growth. Uneconomic growth occurs when a population reaches a "futility limit, the point at which it is not adding any utility with its increased consumption." Daly believes for many rich nations, the futility point is close to being reached, it if hasn't been reached already. He also warns us not to become dependent on new technologies to carry us out of the futility limit hole, pointing to how the ozone hole and global warming are two examples of consequences of new technologies.

The Shift in Global Economy

A shift away from global corporate power is also emerging as we move closer to the year 2012. In his book *End of the Line: The Rise and Coming Fall of the Global Corporation*, Barry C. Lynn writes about the damaging global system of today that upsets social balances and undermines healthy competition, thus damaging international relations. For the global economy to work, the corporate entities driving that economy must shift focus toward being a force for increased fairness, peace, and prosperity, and against the ideologies and politics that put workers at risk and create more poverty.

In the coming years, the global corporation may give way to a global "cultural and spiritual consciousness," according to David C. Korten, author of *The Great Turning: From Empire to Earth Community*. The idea, Korten writes, is to turn away from an empire, which features "organization by domination," and toward Earth Community, or "organization by partnership." The organizing model of Earth Community would nurture the expression of higher-order human capacities for responsible service, rather than the current narcissistic attitude by which humans are driven.

This "me to we" shift would emphasize win-win situations through "local living economies" that allow a higher quality of life for all involved, increasing the "generative power of the whole." Unlike empire-based economies, which focus on more money for less people, the local living economies favor both economic growth and prosperity, along with the rights of people and protection of community interests, all while maintaining fairness, equity, and responsibility to a greater good.

And what better way to build stronger family units than to give them communities that empower them, rather than disempower them? In this day and age of "family values," we certainly have not been placing too much emphasis on making life easier for families, let alone communities. A "me to we" shift in perspective promises to do just that, all the while protecting the planet and its resources. That shift must include actions toward promoting prosperity, progress, and power to the many, not the few, mirroring the goals of the United Nations' Millennium Development Goals, which focuses on eight specific goals and four important themes of poverty, health, education, and sustainability. The UN hopes to meet these goals on or before 2015.

The United Nations Millennium Development Goals

1. *Eradicate extreme poverty and hunger.*
2. *Achieve universal primary education.*
3. *Promote gender equality and empower women.*
4. *Reduce child morality.*
5. *Improve maternal healthcare.*
6. *Combat HIV/AIDS, malaria, and other major diseases.*
7. *Ensure environmental sustainability.*
8. *Create a global partnership for development.*

Visit www.un.org/millenniumgoals/ *for details.*

The Power of Women

One of those goals mirrors a major shift that will change the face of economics, politics, religion, and culture in the coming years. Gender equity and female empowerment have been big issues since the 1960s, but as we move toward the year 2012, the role of women in the world is going to be one of the biggest transformations on the horizon.

Gender imbalance is not just about women not getting paid as much as men. It's about access to real power in the world. In the past, women's roles placed them in a second-class position, where the home front bowed to the power of the workplace. But as more and more women entered the workforce, and began to climb the same corporate ladders as their male peers, the shift toward a more feminine dynamic gave women the newfound ability to negotiate their jobs, and their lives.

According to Population Connection, one of the key components of empowering women is to give them voluntary access to family planning resources, including contraceptives. By giving women the resources they need to make important decisions, women usually choose to have smaller families, which leads to greater investment in each child, as well as healthier mothers and children. It also allows women to participate in the workforce, adding prosperity to the family unit, and the community at large. Access to education also empowers women to become active participators in their communities and find economic opportunities to add to her family's well-being.

But until women reach some type of gender equity on a religious and cultural level, it will continue to be hard for them to make further inroads into the business or education world, and even to choose their own reproductive destiny.

In the coming five years, we will no doubt see more and more women flocking to religious traditions that honor the female, the yin. In many tribal cultures, women hold equal positions of power and status with men, and, as a result, their populations have a stability that the wealthier, imbalanced "civilized nations" lack. According to Thom Hartmann, noted author of *The Last Hours of Ancient Sunlight*, we must "re-empower" women and return the earth to the balance it needs to survive. Hartmann also points to the nations where women are treated relatively equal to men, and how these nations have achieved a sustainable population.

"In this regard, you could say that the women's rights movement is truly a human rights movement. So another solution to this mess we find ourselves in is to give power back to women in all realms, including the social, familial, religious, military and business worlds."

Until women's empowerment is accepted by the traditional Western religions, this balance may be difficult to achieve, which is why more women and men are turning to feminine and earth traditions that seek to place both yin and yang on equal footing; but change is in the air.

In *The Power of Yin*, editor Barbara Delaney interviewed three of the most celebrated and brilliant women in the human development arena: Hazel Henderson, futurist and revolutionary economist; Jean Huston, principal founder of the Human Potential Movement; and Barbara Marx Hubbard, president of the Foundation for Conscious Evolution. Their dialog predicts major shifts in the global community, many with women at the forefront of facing the coming challenges to our environment and its people.

Hubbard states, "The breakdown of current social systems and dominant patriarchal structure is more obvious. There is a desperate last-ditch stand of the old power structure to maintain itself. The flaws in the system are more apparent: the violence born of oppression, inequality and regressive memes are closer to the surface." Hubbard sees a turning away from the choice of war as a means for solving problems, and suggests that the time frame for change is shortening. "The 'macroshift' or bifurcation point where the system either breaks down or breaks through to a higher, more synergistic order is very close, many of us feel." This might explain the many women who are drawn to the more transformative elements surrounding the year 2012, as they have much to gain, and a greater role to play, in the outcome.

Jean Huston suggests that this "spiritual shift" coincides with the more physical shifts toward "cooperative consciousness," which first shows itself in the manifestation of more and more Americans moving toward sustainable ways of life. The objective action is the outer manifestation of the inner subjective return to a "Christic consciousness." She describes this as "any moment in which this frequency can begin to occur. It is a latent frequency that relates to the frequency of the Earth, and that ties you to the larger community, and to the community of the Earth itself." This sounds similar to the belief of the Maya that we would soon be leaving the Galactic Underworld and entering the transformative Universal Underworld.

Huston also makes an interesting comparison between coming transformational change and the excess of "maternal energy" that is a result of less reproduction. This maternal energy, she feels, will add about "35 percent more human energy than is now available to be invested in new tasks." Imagine what can be accomplished with this extra "nurturing" energy! Even Barbara Marx Hubbard agrees that "The energy that is going to be available, first of all by the release from the reproductive task, is coming along just when the planet needs creative action for the future. There is a strange concurrence here."

Yet perhaps to the Maya, that concurrence was "in the stars," so to speak, all along. The proactive energy to which these women refer is now on the loose in the world, shaping shifts, and setting the stage for a great new paradigm to rise out of the ashes of the old. Delaney, the book's editor, concludes with a very telling insight: "The influx of women into public places will most certainly infuse our political, social and even corporate structures with a more holistic sensitivity to life, a healthy dose of yin."

One has only to recall from Chapter 3 the Mayan belief that odd-numbered years of the Thirteen Heavens ushered in stages of progress and represented the "feminine" energy cycle. These were times of both novelty and activity, a stark contrast to the more aggressive even year cycles of "male" energy. Clearly, balance has always been the key.

Indigo Children

There could be no real transformation of consciousness without including women among those being transformed. But the same could be said of children, and one of the most persistent movements associated with 2012 is the concept of Indigo Children. The concept is used mainly with the more New Age/metaphysical movement to describe a generation of children with amazing paranormal and intuitive abilities. The first public reference to Indigo Children comes from a 1982 book by Nancy Ann Tappe, a psychic and "synesthete" who claimed she could see auras. In her book, *Understanding Your Life Through Color*, Tappe noticed that children born in the late 1970s had predominately "indigo" auras, and today Tappe estimates that 90 percent of children under the age of 10 do so, as well as 70 percent of those between 15 and 25 years of age.

The idea was further explored in the 1999 book *The Indigo Children: The New Kids Have Arrived*, by Lee Carroll and Jan Tober. Carroll claims his information comes from the channeled entity Kryon. Other writers have picked up on the concept, popularizing it in the public with novels, movies, and television shows about children with unusual abilities and intellects.

Many child behaviorists and psychologists claim there is absolutely nothing to the Indigo Child concept but for the desire of certain people to make money off of a movement based upon shoddy research. Many of the traits of the Indigo Child, such as a strong sense of self, great empathy for others, questioning of authority, trouble sleeping, and insatiable curiosity, are considered vague and could apply to almost everyone in that age group at one time or another. Certainly anyone familiar with the concept of accelerating information and knowledge, as described in an earlier chapter, can easily see the correlation between smarter, savvier children and the infiltration of high technology into their young lives. My own son could navigate a computer at the age of 4, even to the point of helping me solve file problems. He knew how to say "systems preferences" before he could say "chocolate milk," and can, at the age of 6, name all the extrasolar planets and planetoids that have been discovered in the last decade. Does this make him an Indigo Child or a real smart-ass?

Tappe also states that Indigo Children are easily recognizable by their large, clear eyes, and that they are bright, precocious children who serve as a sort of bridge to the future. These sensitive, gifted souls, she believes, will be at the forefront of changing the vibrations of our lives to create "one land, one globe and one species."

Indeed, there may be something to the entire concept of each generation of children being more spiritually, mentally, and intellectually advanced than those who came before. Again, if we look at how technology increases, doubling over certain time periods, we can easily see how our own brain capacity and capability surely increases along with it. Some observers feel that Indigo Children are nothing more than the results of influences by parents with metaphysical beliefs, as well as the abundance of TV shows and movies with magical and New Age elements.

Crystal Children

Other types of special children that may help usher in a new era of transformation are the Crystal Children, an even more evolved generation of children than the Indigos, and the Star Children, who claim both human and alien parents, and are to be the emissaries of goodwill and a new universal sense of belonging. It would not be a New World Order, but a New Cosmic Order. In her intriguing book *The Children of Now: Crystalline Children, Indigo Kids, Star Kids, Angels on Earth and the Phenomenon of Transitional Children*, author Meg Blackburn Losey explores the seemingly large number of children today with the gifts of telepathy and psychic abilities. Many of these kids, according to Losey, can even remember past lives in detail, and hold within them a wisdom far beyond that of most adults.

Losey, who works with actual Indigo/Children of Now and their families, also examines how the DNA of these special children differs from previous generations, and how many of these children display healing abilities and traits that should be encouraged and nurtured at home and at school. Many health professionals tend to diagnose these children with attention deficit disorder or hyperactivity, and often given Ritalin or other behavior-altering drugs to make them act more "normal" and suppress the very energy that makes them unique to being with.

Is society ready for a generation of children to lead us into the next decade? There is an old saying: When the student is ready, the teacher appears. Perhaps in the case of the Indigo Children, the student and teacher are one and the same.

Education

Turning to education, two of the most significant trends are: holding children back a year, and homeschooling. Many parents worry about kids keeping up with the test-oriented focus of the public school system, thanks in part to No Child Left Behind. The result is a rising number of kids being held back a year, to catch up to their more quick-minded peers. Sometimes this decision is based upon a child's age, size, and even emotional development, rather than their academic skill, and the trend seems to be spreading even into private schools, who can no doubt afford tutoring for those children "left behind."

In the last 25 years, many states have rolled back their cut-off age for starting kindergarten. Most kids under 5 years old now have to wait a year— far different from us Baby Boomers, who, myself included, started kindergarten at the ripe young age of 4. This cut-off age will allow kids to develop at more equal rates, or at least that is the hope. Some education experts feel that by postponing kindergarten, you also postpone every other developmental stage in the life of a child through the teenage years.

Homeschooling

Homeschooling, meanwhile, is rising in popularity all over the world, with more and more parents opting to teach their children at home, usually with the help of Internet class materials. Between 1999 and 2003 alone, the number of American kids being homeschooled jumped from 850,000 to more than 1.1 million, and this trend is continuing. The vast majority of homeschooled kids are Caucasian, and more than 40 percent live in the South.

Now legal in every state, homeschooling actually now claims more students than vouchers and charter schools combined, although public schools still reign supreme. But for parents who live in areas where public school performance is poor, crime is rampant, or their desire for religion is lacking from the educational system (although non-Christian homeschool programs are on the rise, too), keeping kids home for class time is the new option.

One has to wonder, though, about the effects of homeschooling on children and their ability to be out in the world, relate socially to others, and learn to solve problems as a unit, all of which kids in public and private schools learn to do on a daily basis. Still, if parents do worry about their kids losing valuable social engagement skills, they seem to think the trade-off is worth it, resulting in a growing industry focused entirely on homeschool supplies, especially those of a Christian bent. Perhaps we will only see the results of this trend as these children grow into adulthood and enter the open workplace, where social interaction is critical to getting ahead in life.

As these and other social and environmental challenges increase in intensity throughout the next five years, it will take entire shifts in perspective to deal effectively with those challenges. One hopeful trend is a return to "common sense," and as Marilyn Ferguson writes in *Aquarius Now*, which alone changed many a paradigm, "the very term implies a body of information that everyone knows, yet we ruefully agree that nothing is rarer than common sense." Without a move toward a collective sense of what is right and wrong, what works and what does not work, a society suffers a breakdown from the inside out. Often, during these dark times, the powerful elite takes advantage of the public, playing the fear card to inspire inaction, hopelessness, and resignation.

But Ferguson, being the futurist and visionary she is, sees viability in any society as a direct proportion to the number of people living their ideas and visions. "Cultural breakthroughs have always resulted from the insights and effort of individuals." No collective shift, positive or negative, can ever occur unless it first takes place in the hearts and minds of individuals. Then, as Ferguson concludes, "We need to scrap the idea of relying on our conventional methods. We need to emphasize connections rather than boundaries between areas of knowledge. Radical common sense is a universal skill."

As technology gets smaller and faster, the trends that will truly shape the quality of our lives on the first day of 2013 will involve a bigger, perhaps even slower way of being in the world—an expansive embracing of how we are all connected—not just to each other, but to the earth itself. If we slow down long enough to watch what we are doing, we can adjust our actions, individually and collectively, to create a sustainable economy, environment, and planet, that helps everyone meet their basic needs without losing the desire to go higher, faster, and smaller, which drives progress and makes us the exciting, innovative, and creative species we are.

We, then, become the paradigm we want to shift into shape.

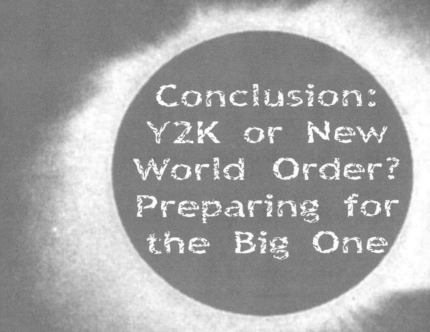

Conclusion: Y2K or New World Order? Preparing for the Big One

The year 2012 may be the human moment of truth; but it may not be the cosmic moment of truth, or even the moment of truth for life on this Earth.
—Rupert Sheldrake, *The Evolutionary Mind*

Prince Harry flies in space.
—Arthur C. Clarke's prediction for 2013

Do you mean now?
—Yogi Berra, when asked for the time

We are obsessed with numbers.

From the millennium and Y2K, 666 and the number of the beast (would that make 668 the neighbor of the beast?) to Orwell's *1984*, to a universe made up of "just six numbers," we ascribe powerful and profound influence and meaning to numbers.

A colleague of mine, Larry Flaxman of ARPAST (Arkansas Paranormal and Anomalous Studies Team), asked me what is probably the most important question I have had to consider in regard to the writing of this book. He asked me how anyone can possibly prepare for 2012.

Food for thought.

How does one prepare for the possible end of the world? If it truly is the end, why bother with preparations? Just go with the flow, and, as my dad always says, when that final flash, bang, or whimper comes, bend over and kiss your ass goodbye. It's all gonna be over anyway, so why fight it?

But if we are talking about a transformation of consciousness, and an ascension to newer heights of perception and experience, perhaps we can simply prepare by opening our minds, and our hearts, as we continue to try to do the right thing in our day-to-day lives *today.* I imagine people will suggest doing things such as praying more often, meditating more often, reaching out to be of service more often, and even practicing a personal spiritual path more often. Yet those are things we should be doing *anyway*, whether the year is 2010 or 2030.

As for the frightening earth changes we might face, preparing as best we can for any natural disaster only makes sense, but if we are looking at supervolcanism, comets striking the Earth, or even gamma-ray bursts, having three days' worth of food and water just won't cut it. So, we do the best we can, and instead of focusing on how we might survive such a catastrophic event (which, by they way, could happen as you are reading this book), perhaps instead we should focus on the things we CAN do—the things we have power and control over: war. Environmental degradation. Economic inequity. Gender imbalance. Decimation of species. Global climate change.

The truth is, we have more to say about what happens in the year following the events of 2011–2012 than we think, and more control than we like to admit.

We have the power to take a stand on issues that truly touch us, move us, anger us, and enrage us. We have the power to stop destroying the planet we call home, end violence against women and children, put the reins on governments that spend money like it's an endless supply of Skittles and send our young men and women off to die for their own greed and gain.

We have the power to first clean up our own act, and put our own house in order, because, as the popular song goes, "let there be peace on earth, and let it begin with me...." When individuals empower themselves, it snowballs. Families become empowered. Then communities. Cities. States. Countries. Soon, there is a global demand for justice, peace, and a return to the Golden Rule.

Too many of us instead choose to rely on what author Thom Hartmann calls "something will save us" solutions. When faced with problems we see as insurmountable, we look outside ourselves for saviors. In the context of 2012, I've heard everything from "the aliens will show up just in time," to "the Ascended Masters will do for us what we cannot do for ourselves," to the persistent cry of fundamentalist Christians convinced that Jesus himself will float on down upon a pillowy cloud and save the day.

This also applies to positive experiences. We look outside ourselves for everything good in our lives: to other people, to our jobs, to drugs and substances, sex, money, success—and even to the Maya and their calendrical systems—for the transformation we seek. Maybe, just maybe, nobody but ourselves will save us or uplift us or destroy us or even transform us, and what the Maya were trying to tell us is that we have the potential in 2012 to make a shift...if we so choose. The door will be opened, but we alone decide whether we will walk through it, or turn away in fear and resistance.

In a May 2007 article for *USA Today* titled "Does Maya Calendar Predict 2012 Apocalypse," Sandra Noble, the executive director of the Foundation for the Advancement of Mesoamerican Studies, states that the ancient Maya marked the end of a whole cycle as a time of celebration, and that to turn this into some doomsday prediction or moment of cosmic shifting is "a complete fabrication and a chance for a lot of people to cash in." Even senior religion editor for Publisher's Weekly, Lynn Garrett, chimed in by admitting that publishers "seem to be courting readers who believe humanity is creating its own ecological disasters and desperately needs ancient indigenous wisdom."

Perhaps 2012 is all a fabrication. But perhaps it is something else entirely: an opportunity to take that ancient indigenous wisdom, and apply it to the most pressing, in-your-face threats humanity has ever faced—threats of ecological, economical, and even spiritual catastrophes. What would be wrong in believing that maybe the Maya did know of our trials and tribulations, and that we would be in need of a little help from our friends—even if they did live thousands of years ago, speak a different language, and use a different means for measuring the passage of time.

Nothing is set in stone, because we ultimately hold the tool that sets the stone. The stone is fixed, but the words and images we etch upon it are ours and ours alone.

Destiny, and free will...combined.

In May 2012, some of the best and brightest minds on the planet will gather in New York City for the New Yorker Conference/2012. Artists, scientists, philosophers, politicians, engineers, financiers, and everyone in between will come together for one day and two nights to discuss new ideas, forward thinking, and eye-opening innovation that they believe will truly make a difference in the coming years. Conferences such as these will take place, no doubt, all over the world, as people come together to regroup and realign as we begin a new era of potentiality and transformation.

Other events we can plan on for 2012, unless we cease to exist, include presidential elections in the United States, France, and Mexico; Super Bowl XLVI; the 100th anniversary of the sinking of the RMS Titanic; The 2012 Summer Olympics in London; a total solar eclipse visible in the southern hemisphere; and the expiration of the Kyoto Protocol. China will launch the Kuafu spacecraft. NASA will launch *Orion*. The second-largest Near Earth Object, 433 Eros, will do a fly-by of our planet. Economists predict that within the next five years, China will introduce its own line of automobiles for purchase in the United States.

People will be born. People will marry and have children. People will die.

Meanwhile, alien-watchers and ufologists will be awaiting a stunning admission from a major government source of ongoing alien contact and cooperation, perhaps even from the United States itself. Many look to the recent release of classified UFO documents courtesy of the French government, and now the British Ministry of Defense, as proof that this announcement is forthcoming, possibly reserved for that special year of 2012. This, they say, will change everything. Others forecast the return of alien "caretakers" who they believe helped shape the first advanced human civilizations, and will return in 2012 to take us to the next level of achievement and progress. Others believe the aliens will visit, but with much more malignant intentions, including human enslavement.

The coming events of 2012, no matter what actual date or year they begin, will at the very least change us…and in some ways, drastically. But each of us can begin now to assure that we are as strong and resilient, as love-based and not fear-based, as courageous and bold as possible. By imagining the future the way we want it, we can create it. It's that simple, and yet it will be the hardest thing we ever do.

No matter what mysterious forces may or may not be at play, 2012 is right around the corner. What happens in the next few years may be for the good of all humanity, or it will bring humanity to the brink of survival.

Where will you be? Will you take a stand, or run for cover? As a Native American friend told me, it's time to go to the edge of the precipice, raise your head high, puff up your chest, and take a buffalo stance.

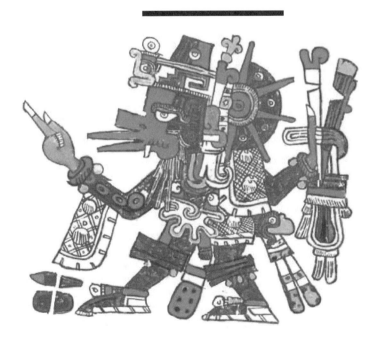

Figure C.1: Quetzalcoatl as depicted in the Codex Borgia, a prehispanic codex possibly of Mixtec origin. Image courtesy of Wikimedia Commons.

As I wrote this book, we moved from the Fifth Day in November 2007, to the Fifth Night of the Galactic Underworld. In November 2008, we will enter the Sixth Day. During this time, we are supposed to experience many changes as we move from the tense struggle of the growth stage ruled by Quetzalcoatl—a time of budding, into the time of Yohualticitl—to a time of flowering. A Renaissance. A time of coming into the full bloom that will end on Day 7 with Fruition and the beginning of the Universal Underworld. Budding, flowering, fruition—individually and collectively.

Yet even as we enter this new age, scientists at the Geological Societies of America and London have stated that the Earth is heading into a new geological epoch called the Anthropocene, an era of unprecedented global environmental change, most of which is not beneficial.

In my opinion, the greatest mystery of 2012 involves our own participation in the outcome of our individual and collective destinies. As a species. As a planet. As a member in the Galactic Union and the Universal Empire.

So, ultimately what will the world be like when we wake up on January 1, 2013? It just might end up being exactly what we intended it to be.

Visions of
2013:
Essays and
Opinions

Prophesy and the Next World
By David Carson and Nina Sammons

The gods and goddesses opened bundles containing cycles of time, and measure flooded the universe. Many generations of priest and priestess mathematicians and astronomers labored to understand the form and character of time. By careful observation these ancient scientists constructed brilliant calendars that have never again been equaled. These temporal constructs not only contained divinatory probabilities, but also deep psychological healing potential. The chronologies reconciled outward events with eternal truth, cognitive pathways one could use to find enlightenment and purpose.

Long before the people of 15th-century Europe landed their boats on this continent called Turtle Island, there were realized teachers walking this sacred land. Indeed, these teachers knew a depth of metaphysics more sophisticated than anywhere else on earth. Their teachings were unheeded by the colonizers. The knowledge was covered over and removed from historical records. Much of it was sent up in smoke. The great Venus-Sun Calendar of the ancient astronomers predicts with mathematical certainty that on December 21, 2012, a new ray of creation will stream into our planetary system. Our motherworld will be completely reborn and literally shifted into a new world.

Indigenous divinatory systems draw upon teachings from these empires of American mound-building cultures and the Mesoamerican temple builders. Temple and earth temple complexes stretched from northern Canada to Peru. Ancient seers knew that temples contained a double—the male temple in the sky and the female temple inside the earth. The temple in the earth circulated energy along gridlines. The male sky temple recorded cosmic history. The structure and form of these monuments corresponded to the entire universe. Sky temples manifested a numinous strand that linked with all other activated temples. The strands were not lines as we experience them, but interdimensional connections. Any point on the strand contained information on the symmetry of the entire temple complex. In other words, Spiro Mound in Oklahoma connected energetically to the spiritually charged Inca city of Qospo. The knowledge kept by these ancient temple priests and priestesses has been a mystery to modern people who share Western consensus beliefs. However, this is the time of revelation and the time of the return of the prophets.

Myths abound. A variety of enigmatic stories have been passed down encoding the creation of life and describing the forces that enliven this plane of existence. Cultures of the Americas and Mesoamerica left a legacy of cryptoprophetic information for us to ponder and study. They left accurate prophecies hidden in sacred mathematics and calenderical schemata. Most of the prophecies have already come to pass.

According to many indigenous legends, all life forms including humans emerged from under the earth. That world was dense, constricted, cold, and had limited possibilities while the new world offered a different sky, good food, comforts, and unlimited potential. This description is often used as analogy for the 2012 winter solstice transformation.

The coming world will be as different from our current one as day is from night. This world belongs to the black magicians who will destroy it—according to some prophetic scenarios—with greed, avarice, and a lust for power. Late in the year 2012, manufactured time will end. There will be a complete shattering of the dark mirrors of time's illusion, revealing dimensions that will sustain and nourish us. New light will be born and humanity will stand in this new light. We cannot predict the exact nature of the coming world, because it is beyond any known principles we can use as guides.

Edited and excerpted by authors David Carson and Nina Sammons from 2013 Oracle: Ancient Keys to the 2012 Awakening, *published by Council Oak Books. Carson is also the coauthor of* Medicine Cards: The Discovery of Power Through the Ways of Animals, *and has lectured worldwide and worked with Shamans from Siberia to Hawaii. Sammons is a writer and documentary filmmaker, and is associated with the sulha peacemaking movement in New Mexico.*

∞

2013: An Evolutionary Shift
By Larry Flaxman

According to traditional interpretations of the Mayan calendar, the world will end on December 21, 2012. Are we interpreting the "end" with literary creativity? Will there truly be an apocalyptic cataclysm of cosmic proportions, which will obliterate the human race? Will changes such as NASA's prediction of the reversal of the sun's magnetic poles cause substantive changes in our world, perhaps causing environmental instability?

Rather than embracing the popular "doom and gloom" predictions, I believe that 2012 will bring about evolutionary changes…but not in the manner that the classic tomes envisage. I believe that perhaps the "end" actually signifies a global transformative shift in mankind's consciousness and awareness. Much like a blind man unexpectedly gaining the gift of sight, I imagine that our newfound perceptions will likewise be as momentous.

Consider both Rupert Sheldrake's theory of "morphic resonance" and Dr. Carl Jung's model of "collective unconscious." Both posit strikingly similar concepts regarding a type of field that links all beings together. With the forecasted changes, is it outside of the realm of possibility to suppose that 2012 will unlock certain repressed neural pathways in a way that will allow universal access to this field?

For centuries we have been analyzing and considering the Mayan calendar ending as a possible link to our species' mortality. Rather than a literal end, will humankind finally reach the level of ascendancy that has been prophesized for thousands of years? Fortunately, we only have a few more years to find out.

A human being is part of a whole called by us "Universe," a part limited in space and time. He experiences himself, his thoughts and feelings, as something separate from the rest—a kind of optical delusion of his consciousness. This delusion is a kind of prison to us, restricting us to our personal desires and to affection for a few persons nearest to us. Our task must be to free ourselves from the prison by widening our circle of compassion to embrace all living creatures and the whole of nature in its beauty. We shall require a substantially new manner of thinking if mankind is to survive.

—Albert Einstein (1879–1955)

Larry Flaxman is the founder and president of ARPAST—the Arkansas Paranormal and Anomalous Studies Team, which is a member of the TAPS (The Atlantic Paranormal Society) family. He has been actively involved in paranormal research and investigation for more than 10 years, and melds his technical, scientific, and investigatory backgrounds together for no-nonsense, scientifically objective explanations regarding a variety of anomalous phenomena.

Larry is also the co-developer of ParaTracker—a revolutionary integrated case/member management system geared toward the paranormal community—and has appeared in numerous newspaper, magazine, radio, and television interviews. He has authored several published articles regarding science and the paranormal, and serves as technical advisor to several paranormal investigation groups throughout the country.

Larry is also coauthor with Marie D. Jones of 11:11: The Time Prompt Phenomenon—The Meaning Behind Mysterious Signs, Sequences, and Synchronicities *for New Page Books.*

∞

Quest for "Truth"
By Madaline Weber (www.mayanmajix.com)
This has been a mantra of mine for more than 50 years:
Being a Master Communicator brought me to this portion
of my life. Holding the light for the main stream of consciousness
is the gift I had been given. Using this gift wisely allows me to be
a "Way Shower"...*Love* is *my* foundation...Grace and Ease is *my* path.

Will cosmic and earthly chaos disrupt our lives with destructive sunspot cycles, volcanic super eruptions, monster storms, mass extinctions, and asteroid threats?" Grandfather Sun and Mother Earth know exactly what they're doing, everything on Mother Earth has been gifted to us, no ownership, what have we done to our gift? Grandfather Sun, Mother Earth have lost their patience...this statement "global warming" was made up so the "powers that be" could create more fear into the souls we call human beings.

Grandfather Sun is hotter then he's ever been in our life time, He's the one that is creating the movement that we're experiencing now...Mother is clearing land, moving people around where they "need" to rely on one another for comfort. When do people come to the rescue? When there's a need, a disaster. On Sept. 11 I heard a women say, "I've lived here for more than 20 years, this is the first time I've met my neighbors.

WHAT'S UP WITH THAT?

So, we have two new phrases: global warming, and multitasking. These phrases come with a condition when reading want ads, "multitasker wanted, etc." more stress, more drugs. I believe there will be millions if not billions of people leaving the planet. Ian Lungold (Mayan Majix) had said, "They wouldn't like where we're going anyway. Will this be the Evolution Revolution of human consciousness...or the Final Countdown that leads to Armageddon itself?"

For those who are awake to this reality, the one that is guiding us to remember who we are, and our choice to be here at this time, this is a once-in-a-lifetime experience...I for one wouldn't miss this no matter what. This Evolution of Consciousness is the grand pupa; this one is for all the marbles. I don't see an Armageddon—what I see is a world that works for all that are on the Ethical Train. You can't be ethical with some things and not with others. Ethics is your ticket into the New World. Remember who you are, knowing that you've chosen these times to be on this train, being a way-shower is the reason we're in this HERE AND NOW.

∞

2012 As I Foresee It
By Michael P. Byron

The year 2012 will be full of fundamental transformation due to the convergence of several factors, all being human-caused. As Shakespeare had Cassius say to Brutus in his play *Julius Caesar*: "The fault dear Brutus is not in our stars but in ourselves..."

The following trends will culminate in the epochal year 2012.

Worldwide production of oil will certainly have peaked. Since our planetary civilization runs on oil, desperate measures will be taken by powerful nations to ensure that the wheels keep turning. Wars and rumors of wars will fill the news headlines. Crash programs to produce energy using coal and nuclear power will be hastily implemented without environmental safeguards.

Global climate change will have become both undeniable and irreversible in this fateful year. Due to the peaking of oil production, coal will be increasingly ripped from the ground and burned, thus releasing more carbon dioxide more rapidly into our planet's increasingly unstable atmosphere. Flood, fire, drought, rising seas, crop failure, disease, and insect pestilence will be the result. Due to all of these factors, the global economy will contract dramatically.

Recession and then depression will ensue. Governments will fall as currencies plummet in value. As chaotic and disastrous as all of this will be, it will also be a unique opportunity to reform our values, our civilization, and ourselves. With profound crisis comes great opportunity. As our present civilizational structures disintegrate, we can transform and reintegrate ourselves from desire for short-term gain at the expense of others and the planetary biosphere, to a just, humane, and environmentally rational civilization, which can endure for ages to come. Two thousand and twelve will be the year that we act decisively to bring about this fundamental renewal of civilization.

Michael Byron is author of The Path Through Infinity's Rainbow: Your Guide to Personal Survival and Spiritual Transformation in a World Gone Mad, *and* Infinity's Rainbow: The Politics of Energy, Climate and Globalization.

∞

2012: Ascension or Apocalypse?
Dr. Rita Louise

Hopi Stone Tablets

There was the cycle of the mineral, the rock. There was the cycle of the plant. And now we are in the cycle of the animals coming to the end of that and beginning the cycle of the human being. When we get into the cycle of the human being, the highest and greatest powers that we have will be released to us.

It is believed by many that we are entering a time when the fulfillment of prophecies spoken throughout the ages is culminating. Each of these great prophesies talk of a major change to life on earth as we know it. These predictions often indicate one of two things: either death or destruction with an eventual renewal and rebirth, or the evolution of the conscious man, with the shift occurring without the need for hostility, bloodshed, or trauma. What will happen and which way our future will unfold is unknowable at this point in time, but it does seem as if we play a pivotal role in how things turn out.

One of the most talked-about ancient prophecy in recent days, with a date that is fast approaching, is the one associated with the end of the Mayan calendar, which occurs in December of 2012. The Maya were excellent time-keepers. Accordingly, 2012 marks the end of several large cycles, including the 26,000-year Mayan calendar cycle, the 78,000- and 26-million-year earth cycles, as well as the 225-million-year galactic year.

Much has been speculated as to the meaning or implications associated with the ending of these cycles. As this date draws near many ask, "What will happen to us, our planet?" From a dense, fear-based point of view, a number of theories have emerged. The best, or perhaps most widely accepted views is the one presented in the Bible, often referred to as the Rapture, the Apocalypse, Armageddon, or the end of days.

Discussed primarily in the New Testament in the last book of the Christian bible, the book of Revelation, it is foretold that the end of days will be foreshadowed by plagues, earthquakes, famine, fires, meteor storms, and much more. As these natural disasters plague the earth, the Antichrist will appear on the scene and assume world domination. Next, as the prophecy continues, comes the battle of Armageddon and the return of Jesus to the earth. Finally, the Antichrist and his armies are destroyed, and we will live in a golden age of peace and prosperity for 1,000 years.

Other theories that also fall under the category of gloom and doom include the appearance of Planet X, first contact with an alien race, the shifting of the magnetic pole from North to South, and the impact and subsequent devastation of a giant comet or asteroid that collides with the Earth. Scenarios that are can also be found in this category are environmental, social, or geological earth changes that interrupt life on earth.

Similar to the apocalyptic scenario, many of these prophecies promise a new life, a rebirth, and a period of harmony after the initial death and destruction.

Prophesies of the Hopi Indians describe the disruption, devastation, and ultimate renewal we will experience as part of a purification process. This period of purification is foretold by a number of "signs." It is believed that the time is now upon us, because all of the prophecies have been fulfilled. The prophecies go as follows:

The Fourth World shall end soon, and the Fifth World will begin. This the elders everywhere know. The Signs over many years have been fulfilled, and so few are left. These are the signs that great destruction is coming.

- ∞ *"This is the First Sign:* we are told of the coming of the white-skinned men, who took the land that was not theirs. And men who struck their enemies with thunder."

- ∞ *"This is the Second Sign:* our lands will see the coming of spinning wheels filled with voices."
  —the white men bringing their families in wagons across the prairies.

- ∞ *"This is the Third Sign:* a strange beast like a buffalo but with great long horns, will overrun the land in large numbers."

  —the coming of the white men's cattle.

- ∞ *"This is the Fourth Sign:* the land will be crossed by snakes of iron."

  —the coming of the train and train tracks across the country.

- ∞ *"This is the Fifth Sign:* the land shall be criss-crossed by a giant spider's web."

  —the coming of telephone and electric lines.

- ∞ *"This is the Sixth sign:* The land shall be criss-crossed with rivers of stone that make pictures in the sun."

  —the coming of roads, highways, and freeways across the country.

- ∞ *"This is the Seventh Sign:* You will hear of the sea turning black, and many living things dying because of it."

  —the spilling of crude oil offshore.

- ∞ *"This is the Eighth Sign:* You will see many youth, who wear their hair long like my people, come and join the tribal nations, to learn their ways and wisdom."

  —the 1960s flower power generation who sought truths outside of the church.

- ∞ *"And this is the Ninth and Last Sign:* You will hear of a dwelling-place in the heavens, above the earth, that shall fall with a great crash. It will appear as a blue star."

  —the crash of Skylab in 1979.

Very soon after this, the ceremonies of my people will cease.

It is after the fulfillment of the signs that the Hopi believed we will have the opportunity of cleansing ourselves and our psyche, through which we will be able to open the door to the fifth world and enter the cycle of Human Beings. They also let us know that how intense and how painful this transition will be is totally up to us.

As the Hopi indicate, there is another choice other than doom and gloom, death and destruction. In fact, there are a growing number of people who believe that we are in a period of planetary acceleration, which will lead to evolutionary changes of the human psyche. According to these proponents, we are in the process of ascending to a new level of being, so that by the year 2012, we will be ready to move into a new frequency, a new dimension of existence.

Is this what the Hopi meant when then talked about the age of the "human being"?

The thought of ascension is as old as the Bible itself, and is an undercurrent of Jewish thought and mysticism. The concept that we will be moving out of the density of our 3-D world echoes back to the story of Adam and Eve and their fall from grace. With the fall of man, symbolized by the eating of the apple, we descended into our 3-D world where we were no longer able to see, talk, and interact with God, the angels, and other beings that existed in the Garden of Eden. It is said that our place in the universe will be restored with the advent of the messianic age. Even in Jewish thought, there are conflicting views as to whether this shift will occur due to the birth and life of a savior, or if we as individuals will transcend our limited consciousness and usher in a new age of living or new way of being.

So what is this all about? What do ascensionists see as the outcome of the days to come? It is speculated that we are poised at a point in our evolutionary history where we can ascend—that is, we can drop our physical bodies and live either as energetic beings or as crystalline bodies of light. It is held by some that this occurs when we convert our make-up from being carbon-based to utilizing silicon as its primary building block. This conversion from carbon to silicon will make us invisible to those who inhabit the 3-D world. And like the biblical descriptions of the Rapture, we will have seemed to have just disappeared.

As we move toward this physical transformation, it is also believed that changes to our DNA, especially the strands that have traditionally lain dormant until now, are being activated. As they come online we will begin to experience new abilities, new awareness—the likes of which have never been seen before. As we move through this process, a variety of physical symptoms have been described as being associated with this genetic shift.

In their book *2012: You Have A Choice!* authors Sri Ram Kaa and Kira Raa list 22 symptoms of ascension. They are:

1. Headaches or non-localized pressure in the head.
2. Your vision may seem to be shifting or non-stable.
3. You may feel you require glasses one day and a different shift the next.
4. You may feel a deepening sense of the ability to "see."
5. Sleep pattern interruptions: feeling that you are going crazy, losing your mind, or an inability to focus.
6. Emotional tenderness, mood swings, and "mania."
7. Embracing unity consciousness.
8. Heightened sensitivity to smell, sound, and taste, or change in eating preferences.
9. Losing track of "time."
10. Physically dropping or bumping into things.
11. "Hearing" high-pitch tones, or a series of tones or pressure in one or both ears.
12. Spiritual death or brief suicidal thoughts.
13. A heightened sense of not being on the planet or a sense of detachment.
14. A general sense of "free flowing" energy, which can often manifest and be misinterpreted as anxiety without basis.
15. Jolts of energy that are felt physically and often will move the body.
16. Lack of focus and attention for any length of time.
17. Heightened/newfound discomfort with some public environments.
18. Sudden urge to make everything spacious, to release personal treasures, or remove old clutter from your environment.
19. Heartburn or chest pressure.
20. Attraction to new colors.
21. Change in priorities in your career/relationships.
22. Feeling of time "moving fast."

If you find yourself resonating with this list, you may be asking yourself "What can I do to support the changes going on in me?" To begin, first, make sure you are drinking plenty of water, getting lots of rest, eating good nutritious food, and most importantly, give to yourself. That's right; be sure to love and nurture yourself.

Ascension is a process. We ascend by releasing emotionally, that is, second chakra blockages, typically one layer or issue at a time. For many, this means accessing old, painful memories, identifying the limiting patterns of behavior that keeps it locked in place, and transforming the underlying fear to the vibration of love and compassion. It is only through recognizing, altering, and releasing our deep emotional wounds, hurts, and pain that we can learn to love ourselves and thus open ourselves and our hearts to others.

What will happen to us when we reach 2012 is anyone's guess. According to the Hopi we are being given a choice. The choice is: we can think with our heads or we can think with our hearts. According to their tradition, if we think with our heads, the path will lead to self-destruction. On the flip side, if we think with our hearts we will be allowed to move from the Age of the Animals into the Age of the Human Beings with relative ease and grace. In the end, the choice is ours—destruction or love and light. And akin to Neo in the movie *The Matrix*, we can choose the red pill or the blue pill. My hope is that we, as a society, chose correctly.

Founder of the Institute of Applied Energetics, Dr. Rita Louise is the host of Just Energy Radio and the author of the books Avoiding the Cosmic 2 × 4 *and the* Power Within. *A 20-year veteran in the Human Potential Field, it is her unique gift as a medical intuitive and clairvoyant that illuminates and enlivens her work. Her unique insights bridge the worlds of science, spirit, and culture, and are changing the way the world views physical, mental, and emotional health. Website: www.soulhealer.com.*

A Future Forecast: Destruction vs. Transformation
By Nick Redfern

The year 2012 is a date that, for some people, provokes dread, fear, and graphic imagery of planetary catastrophe and the end of all things. For others, it's a date to be embraced, and a period in humankind's development when the past and the present are radically replaced by a new world—hopefully, a more spiritually enlightened and compassionate one.

For me, I cautiously await the arrival of 2012 with deep interest and a degree of both trepidation and excitement. And I say that for one, key reason: prophecy and the alleged ability to forecast future events have long fascinated the Human Race. We only have to look at Nostradamus.

I recall, as the year 1999 closed in, how the world's media began to comment, sometimes ominously, on this prediction that in "...the year 1999, seventh month, from the sky will come a great King of Terror...." Of course, the world did not end, and today people continue to debate the nature of Nostradamus and his predictions.

However, in my life I have experienced several very vivid dreams that, for me, were quite clearly glimpses into my own future. They were not anything of a dramatic nature—indeed, they were just normal day-to-day things. But when the events came to pass, those same dreams were enough to convince me that our understanding of time—past, present, and future—is far from complete. For that reason, I do not dismiss the idea that ancient man may have had reason to believe, or forecast, that something of significance may occur in 2012.

Certainly, there is a rising awareness that all is not well in the world—in terms of the planet itself (such as with respect to global warming), the way in which our civil liberties are being ever more eroded, and the dramatic and disturbing changes in our weather. My own view is that if profound events do occur in 2012, they will likely revolve around a positive transformation of the Human Race—a transformation borne out of a realization that our world and our civilization teeter on the brink of collapse. As an optimist, I see a world where hopefully the old order of chaos, war, and global damage will be replaced by something far better: a world where control is taken out of the hands of powerful, ruthless men with sinister agendas, and who are driven by nothing more than greed and the need for complete and utter control. By definition, this may indeed mean that our present civilization—in its current form—may be nearing its end. But the Human Race will prevail. Overwhelming transformation may not mean overwhelming destruction.

Nick Redfern is the author of many books on unsolved mysteries and the paranormal, including Memoirs of a Monster Hunter, On the Trail of the Saucer Spies, Strange Secrets, *and* Celebrity Secrets. *He writes regularly for numerous publications, including* UFO Magazine *and* Fortean Times. *He can be contacted at his Website:* www.nickredfern.com.

∞

How the Snake Sheds Its Skin: A Tantric Path to Global Transformation
By Daniel Pinchbeck

That we could interrupt our current suicide march and institute a harmonic and peaceful planetary civilization within the next few years, embrace a non-dual realization of the universe, and institute practices of deep ecology and collective psychic ritual may seem far-fetched to some. The history of human thought, however, reveals an extraordinary tendency for ideas that at first seem radical, absurd, or beyond comprehension to quickly become commonplace, even truisms, leading to new conditions and transformed social structures. Before the 18th century, for example, people knew about lightening, but nobody had any idea that electricity could be shaped to human purposes and made into a transformative energy for the world. Once someone learned this trick, we engineered industrial civilization and changed the entire surface of the Earth in less than two centuries—not even a blink of evolutionary time. If we did it then, we could do it again, under different conditions, with different goals, on a far more concentrated time scale.

This is an unprecedented moment for humanity. The material progress of the last centuries has slammed against the limits of the biosphere, putting our immediate future in jeopardy. Equally surprising to the modern mind, many indigenous cultures around the world recognize this time through their prophecies and myths, and may possess insight into its deeper meaning. For these cultures, we are transitioning between World Ages; this shift not only involves changes in the physical body of the Earth, but also a transformation of human consciousness—a regenerative cycle of initiatory death and rebirth, leading to a higher level of manifestation.

Excerpted from The Mystery of 2012: Predictions, Prophecies and Possibilities, *Published by Sounds True, 2007.*

Daniel Pinchbeck is the author of 2012: The Return of Quetzalcoatl *and* Breaking Open the Head. *He has written for* New York Times Magazine, Village Voice, Esquire, Wired, *and many other publications.*

∞

A Brief Look
By Hilly Rose

"I can tell you that I join with others in seeing the end of 2012 as a new beginning, not an ending."

Hilly Rose has been an investigative reporter for more than 30 years and is a pioneer of the talk show radio format. He has hosted radio talk shows for KFI, KABC, KGO-FM, and done more than 500 shows for Siruis Satellite Radio focusing on the paranormal. Currently, he does the "Hilly Rose Show" for FATE Magazine, *and also occasionally hosts "Coast to Coast AM." He is one of the most widely known and respected voices in the paranormal field.*

∞

2012: A Deeper Meaning
By Edward F. Malkowski

The world will come to an end on December 21, 2012? Will there be some type of mass transformation of consciousness, and the world will enter a new age of enlightenment? Or, will nothing at all happen?

Of course, no one knows for sure whether either of these will occur until that day. However, the likelihood that there will be a sunrise on December 22 is, in my opinion, a sure thing for the betting man. Nonetheless, the two divergent opinions—that the world will end and a new age will begin—are not as ridiculous as critics believe.

Why they are not is that both prognostications reflect growing concerns within an increasingly integrated world civilization. A fear that the world will encounter some worldwide cataclysm, as it has before a number of times, is a valid concern. Likewise, the hope that we will overcome divisive and destructive cultural, political, and religious practices is the most noble of civilization's goals.

But there is a deeper meaning, I think, concerning 2012. The men who constructed the Mayan calendar were aware of the cyclical nature of the cosmos, and with the stars as their master they fashioned a way of accurately counting time. Why bother with such an endeavor? Perhaps they knew something that we are only now beginning to understand: Our existence is a direct result of certain precarious conditions that encompass the entire cosmos.

Earth's existence, and its ability to sustain life, is a result of its orbit around the sun, and that the state of the solar system is dependent upon its orbit of the Milky Way's galactic core, which in turn is dependent on the gravitational pull from other neighboring galaxies, which in turn is dependent upon mysterious events modern physics has no laws for. In our lives we take these facts for granted. But with these scientific particulars I have to ask myself the question "who are we, really, that we are endowed not only with the ability to perceive ourselves but are given the ability to perceive the intricacies of cosmic order?"

Science has also determined that our bodies contain elements that were created from the cosmic cycle of stellar birth and death. If so, it could be said that we are, in fact, the cosmos itself engaged in the process of self-perception. Could it be that the essence of humanity, of civilization, occurs in cycles dictated by the ecological ebb and flow of the planet?

Perhaps a deeper meaning for 2012 is that we are just beginning to realize that knowledge from ancient times is not only our past, but also our future.

Edward F. Malkowski is the author of Sons of God—Daughters of Men, Before The Pharaohs, *and* The Spiritual Technology of Ancient Egypt.

∞

My Thoughts on 2012 and Beyond

By Joshua P. Warren

As an active researcher, author, and radio host, I've heard much about 2012. So what does it all mean to me?

There are so many opinions, such a plethora of various thoughts, that I can't form a concrete idea. But here's what I'd like to think:

Everything seems to work in cycles. It's funny to realize humans existed for thousands of years without a telephone, yet an inventor named Elisha Gray applied for a telephone patent caveat the same day Alexander Graham Bell applied for a patent: February 14, 1876. Bell was number five and Gray was number 39 on the day's list. What are the chances two inventors would apply for rights on such a globe-changing device the same day?

Because no one is an island, and we apparently travel together on collective waves of thought and circumstance, it seems we may build toward realizations together. The year 2012 might be one of those critical points, when the crest of a wave finally reaches its climax, and suddenly, most of the world "gets it." But what are we getting? Maybe that our current course of actions has led to nothing but redundant warfare, greed, and selfish division, and nothing will change unless we change ourselves. If there's anything to astrology, and it seems there is, then perhaps the impending alignment will play a role. On the other hand, I have a more poetic idea of how things could work out. Indulge me.

Let's suppose word hits that a huge, grim asteroid is headed to Earth, and will destroy most life around December 2012. Knowing that information travels down a pyramid of authority before hitting the general public, we can presume the most important people in the world—the richest and most influential—would hear about it first. After all, we see that politicians and rich folks give their immediate family and friends the first advantages (it's just human nature, the idea of heirs to the throne). If those people learn that only a select few can be saved, they might want to hoard all the resources for themselves, without telling the general public and risking those resources being distributed to the herd.

Now in this hypothetical scenario, what if the only way to survive the asteroid is to go deep underground, and a subterranean chamber is being built that will only accommodate 10,000 people for a few years? All of the important people, with access to the big money, will have gradually moved themselves and their valuables into this mass bunker to seal themselves off tightly while the rest of us are vaporized, or worse. We can understand their position, but it's not very humanitarian, eh? So they all go down and seal themselves off, indelibly separating "them" from "us."

But incredibly, due to miscalculation or some other unseen force, the asteroid misses the Earth! The rest of us survive. However, when it comes time for them to open their lair and reemerge, there is a problem with the seal. They can't open it, panic, and slowly, eventually die. The "poetic" part comes from the fact they have selected themselves as the most greedy and self-centered, with no care for the mass public, and will therefore die from their elite knowledge, cleansing the earth, for now, of their kind.

Do I think such a scenario will occur? I don't know, but it would be a fitting end to our grandest problem. That is the problem of enabled, out-of-touch people, drunk with ego, spoiled for generations, controlling the herd with money, deceiving the masses through whatever means necessary, including spilling our blood—OUR blood—for their wars. If it all fell like a house of cards, it would be too easy, though. Therefore, I'm not counting on this one just yet. Thus where does that leave us in the end?

Most look at the Y2K computer bug as an example of global mass hysteria for nothing. But was it really? Maybe we avoided a genuine tragedy because we all knew of the potential and made changes in our lives to adjust for it or prevent it. It's important to understand we are not simply the product of external forces completely beyond our control, but can also use ourselves—our inner beings—to affect the world around us, and outcomes of problems, as well.

But 2012 is vaguer than Y2K. It's expected by many to be an odd time of change for the better. Yes, there may be death in some ways, but that is always necessary for rebirth. Regardless of background, everyone seems to realize this system we have, this civilization, is still broken and needs to be fixed. So hopefully enough people, around the world, want a change—not with guns and bombs—but with spiritual reawakening and open-mindedness, that we will *create* 2012 and beyond with our collective desires reaching that critical mass. And hopefully—hopefully—we will create something better. Then we must have the strength and clarity to keep it for a while.

Joshua P. Warren is a paranormal investigator, author of nine books (includ-ing How to Hunt Ghosts *and* Pet Ghosts*), host of a Clear Channel radio program called* Speaking of Strange, *producer of documentaries such as* Inside the Church of Satan, *and has appeared on TV shows on Discovery, History Channel, TLC, and Sci-Fi Channel. He and his research team, L.E.M.U.R., made the cover of the science journal* Electric Space Craft *in 2004 for their groundbreaking work on rare plasmas that manifest in nature. He is also a frequent guest on the Coast to Coast A.M. radio show. You may learn more about him and his work at: www.JoshuaPWarren.com*

∞

2012: Take Five

By Cate Montana

2012 take one: It's 1978, and the year 2012 means nothing to me be-yond the fact that in that year I will be 61 years old—an impossible age to envision when you're a 26-year-old hot-shot television editor feeling self-important while hopping around the world on planes (even the occasional Lear jet) between bowl games, golf tournaments, commercial shoots, and late-night editing sessions for HBO.

I know the Mayan Long Count calendar exists because I minored in archaeology in college. I know about the death and rebirth imagery that characterizes most Mayan mythological traditions, but any metaphysical notions about the calendar's and 2012's significance as a harbinger of great change—let alone a Revelations-type disaster scenario of biblical proportions—I dismiss as sensational nonsense.

Then, in 1981, I experience my first Saturn return, a divorce, a car acci-dent, and a complete disenchantment with chasing after material goods. I quit the networks, got a sedate job as a video engineer at an ABC affiliate in Atlanta, and fell into the bosom of the New Age. Consuming vast quantities of books about everything from Buddhism to quantum physics to alien encounters to conspiracy theories, it's inevitable that the year 2012 surfaces in my consciousness in a whole new way. This second-stage awareness can best be summed up as:

2012 take two: Wow. Isn't it cool that modern interpretations of the Vedic Yuga doctrine place the end of the descending Kali Yuga in 2012, and that Michel de Nostredame, the great seer of the French Renaissance, predicted great changes around this time? And wow, the end of the Mayan Long Count ends in 2012 at the same time that the winter solstice sun crosses the galactic equator of the Milky Way. I wonder if all this means something?

2012 take three: It's 1991 and I'm really scared. I think it's much too horribly coincidental that all this stuff is pointing toward the year 2012. My guru says 2012 marks the End of Time. I don't really know what he means. Although I haven't been to church since my first wedding, I keep thinking about it in terms of the End Days the Bible talks about. And that means only one thing: death and disaster; fire raining from blood-red skies like the Hopi legends speak of; the end of life as we know it.

Part of me thinks this is not such a bad thing. The world is going to hell. Consumerism is epidemic, epidemics are epidemic, teen suicides are skyrocketing, the ecology of the planet is disintegrating, terrorism is making its debut, and worst of all—far too few people seem to care. Even fewer seem willing to take action. I'm one of them, because I simply don't know what to do to help.

Taking the advice of my guru, I stockpile vast quantities of food. The local Mormon Church is very helpful in that regard. I put up everything from beef to cocoa to popcorn in metal cans. The ladies at the Mormon canning facilities don't seem to mind that I'm not a member of their church. It's enough that I mirror back to them an earnest desire for preparedness and survival.

For that's what 2012 means to them and to me: survival at its most ugly, rudimentary level. I move to an isolated spot in the Pacific Northwest. I buy guns. Thank heavens I was raised on a farm and my father taught me how to shoot and to hunt. The automatic shotgun is for birds—and more terrifyingly—crowd control at close quarters when the desperate and terrified hordes evacuate the cities and storm the countryside looking for food. The rifle is for larger game and longer-distance crowd control. I quite fancy assault rifles and buy an AR15 at a gun show. It looks cool slung across my shoulder along with a couple bandoleros—I look like Jane Fonda in *Cat Ballou* or *Barbarella*. The image almost keeps me from remembering what I'm buying all this firepower for.

Almost.

I never stop meditating on what 2012 and the End of Time really mean. I have to understand what I'm facing. I've evolved enough to know that consciousness has various levels, and that fear and survival lie on the bottom rung. My meditations bring me moments of being beyond fear, moments of deep love, glimmers of the Divine, all-encompassing and whole. But I can't hold on to these states for more than a few precious heartbeats.

In the face of what seems to be coming, this is not much defense. All the same, I'm beginning to "get" that I am not a physical being. And if I am not a physical being, what does it matter if 2012 comes and goes and my body dies along with it? Surely it is more important that I focus on my spiritual essence and let the rest go?

2012 take four: Breakthrough. It's 1996. I now understand that the End of Time is nothing to be afraid of. I experience it every day in my meditation. It is a state of consciousness that bridges beyond any sense of personal self or linear time flow. I call it "being present" or "being the Is." In eight years Eckhart Tolle will write a book called the *Power of Now*, exactly describing this state.

I sell my guns.

I leave my guru.

I keep my food storage because deep contemplations are showing me that humanity cannot continue to exude such appalling psychic negativity and downright destructiveness without reaping psychic and physical consequences. From internal experience, I realize that in higher states of consciousness there is no cause and effect. There is only Is. Ongoing, imperturbable, eternal, infinite Being. Oneness. Life lived in this state of consciousness is the height of peacefulness, joy, and harmony.

But this is not the state of mind humanity on planet Earth exudes. Here, cause and effect, resulting from the illusion of separation of self from the Divine Mind; the separation of self from everything—other people, the world, animals, spirit—is in full swing.

Despite my progress, I am forced to include myself in this picture. I still can't manage to maintain a state of expansiveness with my eyes open, let alone at work writing newspaper articles about humanity's ills. On the way to town I flip the bird at irritating drivers. My lover can still drive me up the wall. And even though I now know better, I'm still afraid of death.

Sometimes I cast my gaze ahead to 2012 and assess my evolution. It is clear humanity is coming to a decision point. A schism of some sort seems inevitable. The sheer weight of the difference in consciousness between the spiritual New Thought community and the frightened robber baron focus of the ego that has predominated in most Earth cultures for so long has to have consequences. Will there be a splitting-off of worlds, of which the Rapture images of the fundamentalist Christian Right are a caricature? If I'm still worrying about money and stupid inconsequentials like my weight, on which side of the fence will I find myself when the time comes?

Or will 2012 prove more gracious? Does its significance indicate a tipping point in consciousness, where a growing world community emanating love and life values provides a quantum leap in consciousness for the whole of humanity? I pray for the second option, for I am still uncertain whether my breakthroughs will be enough to carry me through the perils of Rapture.

2012 take five: It's 2008. Y2K has come and gone. Sept. 11 has come and gone. All my family is gone. I've sat at a friend's bedside and watched her die of cancer. I am astonished at the body's tenacity—its sheer capacity for life despite terrifying punishment.

Is this what the Earth is doing? Holding on despite the brutal onslaught of greed, need, pollution, despair, fear, and rising chaos? We spin faster and faster, absorbing meaningless information and messages that overwhelm us in an unstoppable tide. Iraq, Iran, Hurricane Katrina, climate change, Bird Flu, recession, depression, obsession, and yet…

I have spent three years working with the filmmakers of the film *What the Bleep Do We Know!?,* editing and publishing their online newsletter. I've started the *Global Intelligencer.* I've talked with thousands of people who are doing amazing transformational work in all areas of human endeavor. The spiritual isolation I once experienced vanishes as a river of change evidences itself everywhere I turn—in the arts, education, business, economics, architecture, health, and social institutions. I interview people such as astronaut Edgar Mitchell, Deepak Chopra, and Barbara Marx Hubbard, who talk about the upward spiral of human evolution. I interview men and women working in every capacity, from global regeneration projects, to green businesses, to developing alternative currencies. These people exude hope, for they are awake, they are responsible, and they are marrying higher consciousness with action.

I see the whole world changing around me—just as I see myself changing. My own shifts in consciousness are bringing me a simple joy that is easier and easier to maintain. I just don't seem to worry much. I have recognized that the ego called "Cate"—the person who wanted to know about 2012, the identity that worried about it, planned for it and feared it, is truly not the real me. She is a self-created mental construct, a thought form with no more reality than a dream in the night.

And yet, there is still an identity that calls itself Cate that is embracing community and sustainability as a way of life. That "I" is making choices that no longer reflect the fears of the ego, which struggles so hard to maintain its pitiful sense of superiority and being in control of things. This new "I" feels aligned with Nature, with the life force that supports the body and all things of and beyond this world. This "I" is being called to the Amazon forests of Peru. What awaits, I have no clue.

What will the year 2012 bring? I don't know. According to my astrological chart, I'll still be here in 2013—although what "I" and "here" mean are both open to interpretation. Looking back on the last 30 years, my takes on 2012 have shifted and grown in proportion to my capacity to expand my awareness about absolutely everything. And "I" really haven't seemed to have much choice in the matter. As part of the universal whole, I've been drawn, magnetized, pushed, pulled, and pummeled—forced to expand in consciousness and apply it to life.

Whatever else it may be, 2012 is a force of dynamic change that can no more be limited to a point in space/time or a date circled on a calendar than the feathered serpent Quetzalcoatl himself can be. The year 2012 is movement, a process that is already amongst us, propelling us toward new horizons. Or, perhaps it is simply guiding us back home.

Ms. Montana's lifelong career focus has been communications. She is currently changing from being the publisher of The Global Intelligencer, *www.globalintelligencer.com, and a freelance nonfiction writer specializing in the fields of metaphysics, quantum mechanics, and biophysics, into…?*

∞

2013—Humans in Healing

By Jay Allen

I believe 2013 represents an exciting time in human evolution, as there are great world changes in the wind as well as many predictions, mostly with a focus on catastrophic events. Ultimately, however, I believe our future is in our own hands as we are all cocreators in the game of life, not only for our own futures, but the future of the world.

What we are witnessing is a radical shift in consciousness taking place, as more and more people are questioning their basic beliefs and examining their life patterns. We see this as an increasing desire to escape from reality as people from every race and country, and from all walks of life are disenchanted with life as they presently live it, seeking someone or something outside of themselves to create a sense of joy and well-being within. Fear and uncertainty are rampant as a great number of people fear that the best of times are past and the future looks bleak and uncertain. It is normal to resist change or be uncomfortable with dramatic changes, especially when people feel they are not in charge and in control of their future.

In order for us to make this transition into the age of expanded awareness with a minimum of stress and strain, we need an awakening among the masses to the realization that there must be changes in behavior within the collective consciousness. In other words, it is time to reclaim our spiritual power and to consciously step into our roles as active instigators of change. As spiritual and creative beings, our purpose is spiritual growth, to learn to live as conscious cocreators. As cocreators of the future, we must script our new reality and be very clear as to what we wish to experience in the future.

Fortunately for us, everything we need to create peace, harmony, and safety we already have; as all the components are in place, we must simply take the correct action and learn how to use what has already been created within. Each person must take responsibility to clean up old business, take inventory, and try to discover what lessons are to be learned from each situation.

Life is prodding everyone in an effort to get each soul's attention, and to begin the process of self-discovery and self-improvement. We either grow and ascend in consciousness or sink deeper, so it is more important than ever to "know thyself" and to rediscover the true meaning of life as we become the conscious directors of our own future. There must be an inner evaluation and clearing process as each person must lay a strong foundation to help create peace and harmony around them. We can heal the past through forgiveness, consciously cocreate, and script our future through intention and participation, and accomplish this while learning to live in the present.

World Peace Through Inner Peace

We must learn to use the universal laws of manifestation in order to clearly outline and manifest the future we desire with the understanding that transition begins within and gradually radiates out into the world. In other words, there is inner work to be done first before we can manifest harmony and balance in our outer world. As more and more people achieve inner peace and begin to fulfill their roles in life, all of humanity benefits as we get "on purpose." Under the universal laws of cause and effect, all our thoughts, intentions, and actions are stored within our auric field and chakra system, and we radiate these vibrational patterns. As we take responsibility for our own energy or "vibes," we can all contribute and play an important role in healing our planet. It is important to understand that life is a perfect feedback mechanism and will only give back to us what we have created in our own lives. There is no use trying to fool anyone or get away with anything, as it only delays our progress.

This healing process begins within with the forgiveness of Self, which facilitates a forgiveness of all others. This is an integral step in the healing process, as forgiveness is a very personal act and it must come from the heart. When we forgive from the heart, it changes the energy dynamics between ourselves and others. It does not matter if others forgive us or not, and we must allow others to change in their own time and way. As we make a concerted effort to return to harmony and balance within our own being and take responsibility for our own spiritual growth, our loving energy speaks for itself and can create miracles. Forgiveness is the key to living and experiencing a "soul-focused" and "heart-centered" relationship with ourselves, others, and with God knowing it is all one and the same.

Attuning to the earth and her well-being is also a vital part of the transformation process now in progress. In order to facilitate the healing and balancing of the earth via the forces of nature, we will likely experience extreme weather patterns and other violent acts of nature, which will bring into the consciousness of humanity what needs to be rectified. The emphasis on attuning to nature will grow, and "save the earth" ecology will continue to grow in popularity.

We will also see this in the business world, as businesses based on integrity that benefit all will thrive as people become more attuned to the vibrational patterns of harmony and discord, and will not do business with those who are not. Every person we interact with is a mirror for how we see ourselves, and every situation that is presented to us each day contains a lesson to be learned. We must endeavor to see the best in everyone, and consciously seek to make an attitude adjustment.

We are indeed living in a critical time in human evolution, and it is the global will of humanity that will ultimately decide our fate. All possibilities are available to us at any moment, and they include visions of turmoil and visions of peace, visions of terror and visions of joy. Probability is determined by our will, by our desires, and by the conscious intentions we project out into the Universe at any moment.

World conditions today demand that if we are to overcome the obstacles facing our society, we must work together in a spirit of cooperation as teammates in life, members of one race—the human race. Humanitarianism is the vital component, the invisible force underlying all the other sectors, and it is through compassion that we can awaken the global conscience as we awaken our individual conscience. We must begin to ask ourselves how much pain and adversity we are willing to endure on both an individual and global level before we surrender to the Law of Life. The Law of Life is to refine the nature of humankind until we are a complete and perfect expression of life itself. In other words, regardless of race, religion, or nation, we are all "in training" to evolve to God/Christ consciousness. As citizens of the world we will discover that we have more in common with each other than we could ever have in difference.

Adversity always brings people together and forces us to look within ourselves for answers to life's fundamental questions. As we direct our attention inward through prayer and meditation we begin to exercise and experience the power of God within our own being. This is how we enter the age of expanded awareness. Just as lessons in life are repeated until learned, history repeats itself until we learn the lesson. The time is NOW…the need for change is greater and more urgent than ever. Global healing and world peace begin within the individual, one Soul at a time through a greater understanding of ourselves and the world we live in.

Jay D. Allen is the author of Humans in Training *and founder of The Science of Whole-Being Conditioning. Jay is a former athlete turned spiritual teacher who was given 15 months to live 20 years ago. Jay has keynoted and trained thousands of people all over the world with his unique and thought-provoking approach.* www.humansintraining.com.

∞

My Leap of Faith
By Peter A. Gersten, Esq.

On the winter solstice of 2012 at exactly 11:11 UT a Trans-Dimensional Event (TDE) will open a cosmic portal in Sedona, Arizona, and a leap of faith—from the top of Bell Rock—will propel me through its opening.

But let me start at the beginning.

Prophesy, the bible code, ancient calendars, channeled information, as well as the Time Wave-Novelty (TW-N) theory each direct our attention to a particular point in time and space—which I refer to as the cosmic coordinate: 11 11 21 12 2012—referencing the exact second, minute, day, month, and year of the TDE. Among the aforementioned signposts, two in particular deserve mention. Terrence McKenna's TW-N theory holds that the structure of time collapses into a state of infinite novelty in 2012, and further that an unknown trans-dimensional event will occur on December 21st of that year—as the center of the galaxy rises to meet the solstice sun. But when it comes to heralding the importance of the winter solstice of 2012 the legacy of the Maya—their cosmology and in particular their calendar—are at the forefront.

According to John Major Jenkins—the leading expert on Mayan cosmology and the author of *Comogenises*—a part of our sun will be aligning with the Dark Rift located at the center of our galaxy on all winter solstices between 1980 and 2016. He states:

The Galactic Alignment involves the shifting points of the equinoxes and solstices, with the precession of the equinoxes. During this 26,000-year cycle of precession, the December solstice point will align with the galaxy (where it crosses the zodiac in early Sagittarius) in the years around 2012. That is where the Dark Rift is located.

I find it intriguing that the Maya believed that the Dark Rift is a cosmic portal leading to the place of their creation.

At the very center of our galaxy, strange things are occurring. Besides the popular black hole/neutron star theory, astronomers have discovered a loop-like structure some 20 light-years across along the galactic plane. The loop may produce subatomic particles with a thousand times more energy than those in man-made accelerators. And the team that found it believes the vast, bizarre structure could be some form of cosmic particle accelerator. Further, eight new sources of very high-energy gamma rays have recently been found also along the galactic plane, including two dark sources that have never been seen before at other wavelengths. And lastly, astronomers have detected an unusual, powerful burst of intermittent radio waves emanating from the direction of the center of our galaxy. One can speculate—with a slight degree of cosmic intuition—that some type of *TDE* will be triggered by an energy source emanating from the Galactic Center—affecting the galactic plane—during the Galactic Alignment. But when during this 36-year period will it occur?

I believe that physical reality is an illusion—part of an intelligently designed cosmic computer program manifested by digital codes. Sacred geometry, frequency, and vibration define our existence. Our genetic memory is triggered by these digital codes at specific points in our lives. They awaken the mind to the change and evolution of consciousness. 11:11 is such a code and a metaphor for the various cycles that manifest and re-manifest physical reality as if following a cosmic blueprint. The mystical 11:11 is also renowned for its symbolism—one aspect involving a cosmic portal. Most synchronistic is the fact that 11:11 is the exact time of the 2012 winter solstice. Could 21 12 2012 be a cosmic computer file with 11:11 being the cosmic equivalent of .exe?

On 11-11-1998 after several weeks of observing the enigmatic 11:11 in various places in increasing frequency, I had my 11:11 experience. Thus, even if there was no other evidence suggesting that the Winter Solstice of 2012 will be a very special day for humanity—its partnership with 11:11 is my signal that something very extraordinary will be happening then, at least for me. But of course my personal attachment to the *cosmic coordinate* is not in a vacuum. There is overwhelming evidence that ancient civilizations knew that a specific spectacular celestial event occurs at various points in time and space, and it was important enough to encode into their calendars, legends, and mythology—as a message for future generations. I believe it is also encoded into my genetic memory.

Popular Bell Rock—besides being one of those special magical places common to Sedona, Arizona—is also one of its many vortices. But most enlightening is its mythology, which refers to it as a cosmic portal. Oddly I discovered this last piece of information in 1998—during my experience with the 11:11 phenomenon—while I was investigating a signal that was allegedly coming from the direction of EQ Pegasi.

I am sure that you have embraced—at one time or another—certain beliefs, ideas, concepts, and theories that have resonated with you. I believe it is all part of our programming. The leap of faith metaphor has—in the past— captured my imagination and I believe—in the future—it will become my destiny. My favorite illustration of this metaphor is contained within the movie version of Ray Bradbury's *Martian Chronicles*. There is a scene in which one of the astronauts—believing that there is an unseen intelligence existing on Mars—jumps off a cliff to test his theory. What a strange way to prove a point, huh? But his leap of faith is rewarded when the Martians surround him with a protective bubble before both he and his belief strike the hard surface of the red planet. Coincidentally, an article on my Website discussing the Mayan calendar end-date states that: There is no reason not to take a leap of faith imagining what may be in store. So by now you must have an idea of what I plan to do on the winter solstice of 2012 at exactly 11:11 while on the top of Bell Rock—a place only a few miles from my home.

Most of you will think that I am delusional and that my insane act will certainly result in my death. Death is inevitable—at least nowadays—and 100 years from now it won't matter whether I died in 2012 or 2013 or even 2020. But I believe that some type of cosmic portal will be opening at that time and place and that an opportunity will present itself. I fully expect that it will lead to the next level of this cosmic program, freedom from an imprisoning time-loop, a magical martian-like bubble, or something equally as exotic.

In March 2012 I will reach 70 years of age, and nine months later we arrive at the cosmic coordinate. I think it will then be time for me to move on—in one form or another. I'd like to see what else our cosmic computer has to offer.

Peter was admitted to practice law in the states of New York and Arizona. He was formerly engaged in the practice of criminal law in New York City for more than 20 years both as a prosecutor and criminal defense trial attorney. He was chief trial counsel in more than 100 major felony cases.

Peter was formerly the executive director and chief counsel for citizens against UFO Secrecy (CAUS), an organization that utilizes the federal courts to obtain classified UFO-related documents pursuant to the Freedom of Information Act (FOIA). He is the author of The Ultimate Secret *and editor of the PAG E-NEWS (*www.pagenews.info*). He presently resides in Sedona, Arizona, and is employed as a deputy public defender in Navajo County, Arizona.*

∞

2012: An Interview With Jim Marrs

What role will human intention play in the events that manifest that year and beyond?

As we all are part of the universal energy grid (á la Einstein's Unified Field), I feel that human intention will play a large role in determining what we will experience in the year 2012 and beyond. While there may be events occurring outside our control, we nevertheless can control our reactions to them. Intention is critical in any activity as well-meaning intention, even if wrong-headed, releases only positive energy while any evil intent releases the opposite. It is really quite amazing that despite the fact that the vast majority of humans have the best of intentions and desires, we continually allow the few persons with evil or immoral intentions to rule over us. In every great disaster, human courage and the willingness to help others rise to the surface. Such deep and positive human attributes should be encouraged and lauded. After all, we're all in this together.

What do you feel is the one most critical issue we must deal with as the human race in the coming five years?

I feel the most critical issue facing humankind is coming to the understanding that we are all part of the universal energy of life, and we must learn to think for ourselves rather than allow any "leader" or "expert" to think for us. In the past, we have continually given away our individual power to those who seek it, whether they are politicians, civil servants, or religious authorities. Some of these people have worked for the betterment of the human race, but most have only sought wealth and power for themselves. When such leaders fall to bickering with each other, we find ourselves in war. The educated and thoughtful in the more developed countries must begin to teach their fellow humans how to learn and think for themselves…and be prepared to relinquish some of the power that has been taken from others in the name of paternalism.

Do you personally give more credence to prophecies based upon the Mayan calendar, religious texts, etc…or actual earth changes, geopolitical shifts, and technological breakthroughs in determining how the year 2012 might look?

If the predictions regarding 2012 came only from the Mayan calendar, it would be easy enough to disregard this as merely some Indians who had been smoking too much plant material. But when the Mayan prophecy is connected to the prophecies of Edgar Cayce, Nostradamus, Mother Shipton, as well as the legends of the Hopis, Egyptians, Cabbalists, Essenes, the Qero elders of Peru, Navajos, Cherokees, Apaches, Iroquois, the Dogon Tribe in Africa, and Aborigines in Australia, perhaps it is time we pay attention. There's an old saying that whenever everyone says you don't look well, you ought to lie down. Especially because science is adding considerable weight to these ancient prophecies by noting solar-system-wide changes, as well as the alignment of the Earth to the center of our galaxy slated for December 2012. Adding to this confluence of predictions and galactic alignment is the oddity of radio signals emanating from the center of the Milky Way. In 2005, astronomers began detecting strong and unusual radio waves emanating from the center of our galaxy, about 26,000 light-years from Earth. Editors at *National Geographic* wondered if these signals were the last "burping" of energy from a dying star, or if they represented something "completely new to science." The normally conventional publication even ventured to state that "the transmission's intriguing characteristics beg the question: might that source be intelligent?" All of this, along with the now-obvious climatic and environmental changes taking place on planet Earth, should underscore the validity of the Mayan contention that we are entering a "new age" in Earth's history. It is also necessary to understand that all past prophecies were made based on the consciousness level and understanding of those making the predictions. Any increase in knowledge, awareness, and understanding can negate or radically alter such prophecy. In other words, it's not over until it's over. The real question is whether or not humankind is prepared to move forward in a geopolitical and spiritual sense.

Do you believe that a mass transformation of human consciousness will be behind the events of 2012? If so, do you see it as a positive transformation, or a negative one?

A mass transformation of human consciousness is already well underway. Peoples all over the planet are awakening to the power they can exert if they only can gain the will to do so. But the forces of repression are formidable. In the Western world almost all forms of mass communication are under the control of five international corporations, the owners of which are not inclined to share their power and secrets. The rise of the Internet has provided a tremendous new opportunity for the sharing of information. But this tool only benefits those who make use of it. Simply chatting or looking at sports scores and recipes is not enough. Neither is looking only at sites with which one agrees. One must actively seek new information, especially in the areas omitted or clouded by the corporate mass media. In this way lies knowledge and thus, wisdom. This obviously can be a positive learning experience. But merely accepting as truth what is presented in the media or being lulled and distracted by meaningless media babble, is quite stultifying and can only lead to a new Dark Age of control and tyranny.

What, if anything, do you think we as individuals and as a collective society can do to assure that 2012 is not the end, but a new beginning?

As individuals, we must seek alternative sources of information and learn to think for ourselves. Only in this manner can we come to more truthful understandings of the universe and our place in it. Even if dramatic earth changes take place, disrupting what we have come to accept as everyday life, the person with understanding will do much better than the person who becomes fearful and disorientated by change. Some people believe that stockpiling food and arms will prepare them for life after 2012. But there are no guarantees, and the person who is prepared psychologically may do just as well as those already in survival mode. One thing seems fairly certain—by mid-2013 many people will agree that they are not living in the same world as they did in 2008, just as in 2008, most people agreed that they were not living in the same world as they did in the year 2000.

Jim Marrs is an award-winning Texas journalist and author. A graduate of the University of North Texas, he gained experience as a newspaper reporter and editor, a teacher at the University of Texas at Arlington for 30 years, and an executive with several public relations firms. He has produced several videos and is a much-requested guest at national conventions and major radio programs. Marrs is the author of two New York Times best-selling books: Crossfire: The Plot That Killed Kennedy *(1989) and* Rule by Secrecy *(2000). Other works include* Alien Agenda, *the world's top-selling nonfiction book on UFOs (1997);* The Terror Conspiracy: Deception, 9/11, and the Loss of Liberty *(2006); and* Psi Spies: The True Story of America's Psychic Warfare Program (2007).

∞

2013: After the Apocalypse
By Robert R. Hieronimus, PhD

When asked to contribute to this book, I knew immediately where I would focus. More than 40 years ago, in late 1965, I began to be plagued by horrifying dreams and visions of future calamities on this planet, and I found that the only way I could master them was to express them in my artwork.

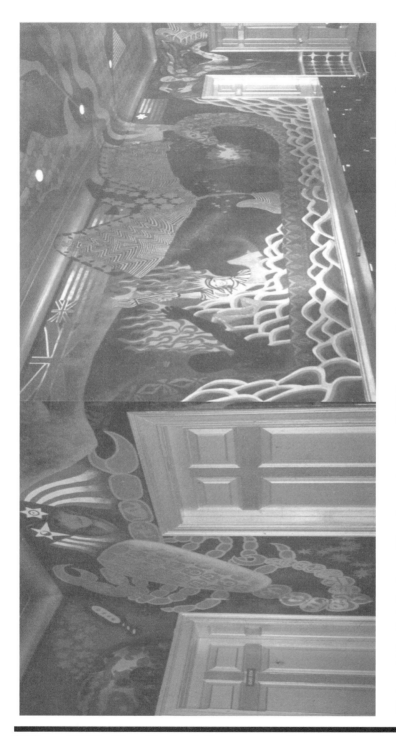

Figure E.1: Details from *The Apocalypse*, a 2,700-square-foot mural painted by Dr. Bob Hieronimus in 1968, still on view today at the Johns Hopkins University in Baltimore, Maryland. Image courtesy of Dr. Bob Hieronimus.

My magnum opus along these lines was the 2,700-square-foot mural I completed at the Johns Hopkins University student union building in 1969. Still extant today, it covers an entire room—four walls, ceiling, and stairwell—with the overarching theme that history is cyclical and not linear. Civilizations have repeatedly risen and died through cosmic, natural, and man-made cataclysms. I called this mural *The Apocalypse.*

My interpretation of Apocalypse, however, is not the end of the world, as many assume by its title or by misinterpreting its symbolism. What I attempted to depict was the evolution of our physical world through scores of symbols and mythologies. The main wall shown here is focused on America. Similar to much of my work during this time period, it was hailed by art critics (who called it "a work of genius," "prophetic," and me "one of the country's best muralists"), while at the same time it was verbally abused and even physically attacked by some members of the establishment and many of the fundamentalist Christian sects. It was partially destroyed when near completion in December of 1968 by a disturbed student, who, ironically, did not disagree with its message. As a Christian fundamentalist he believed a type of world-wide destruction was prophesied in the Bible, but he feared the message was too strong for most of his fellow Americans to see, and that it should be kept secret for the few. I spent the next two months repairing the damage.

I also went to court to testify in defense of this student and even agreed to help supervise him in order to keep him from being institutionalized. No stranger to confusing emotions over world-shattering visions, I could empathize with his rage, and after getting to know him realized we shared a lot more commonalities than differences. I was also quite used to my artwork inspiring this kind of defensive reaction in the public, particularly among people who have vested interests in the status quo. My dreams were showing me the death of America, and I was wrenched night after night with the sight of millions of bodies floating lifelessly in rivers of mud, some face up, some face down. It was not until I began to express my concerns in a series of paintings and constructions that I was able to control these visions.

The first creation resulting from these visions was a 12-foot-long sculpture of the American eagle lying in a coffin on wheels. I called this piece "The American Express." Covering the American flag that draped the coffin were

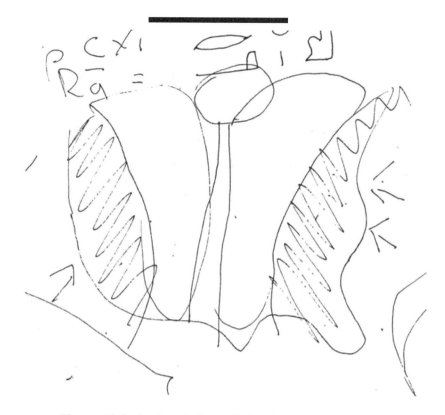

Figure E.2: A sketch from Bob Hieronimus's journal from October 1968 where he swiftly documented the vision he had of the future United States. It shows extreme flooding on both the Atlantic and Pacific coasts as well as up and down the Mississippi River.

medals and logos of corporate giants such as Coca-Cola, General Motors, Chiquita Banana, and play money. Always intensely patriotic and a lover of America's symbols, I didn't like the message portrayed by this construction, but I was being pushed to awaken others to the realization that America had lost its way, and even its very reason for being. Whenever it was shown on display at Johns Hopkins or other universities and galleries in the spring of 1967, it followed a familiar pattern of inspiring rave reviews from the art world, along with threats and abuse from the administration. This time even the Maryland Attorney General's office was involved, and there was some talk of locking me up for desecrating American symbols. Forty years later, America has changed a great deal. We are no longer respected around the world as the dominant world leader or power, a position we forfeited most recently with the invasion of Iraq. Despite this loss of our reputation worldwide, the number of fundamentalist-conspiratorialists in this country continues to grow, and these are the people who are insulted by any interpretation of American symbolism that differs from their own. In the past several decades, we have also voted in leaders who have allowed the corporations to control our media. This status has led to an ever-stronger worship of materialism and the military industrial complex. Meanwhile, the giant that is China rises.

Fortunately, we continue to evolve. As we speed toward the apocalypse predicted by the Mayan calendar in 2012, the New Age sciences have begun to provide a new basis for the science of spiritual transformation. The notion that 2012 marks the end of a cycle also means that the year 2013 marks the beginning of a new one. In the future, universal consciousness will bring enlightenment, and all humans will share the secrets of clairvoyance, telepathy, remote viewing, interspecies communication with extraterrestrials, and spiritual and non-physical beings. The knowledge and understanding of life after death will lead to a huge awakening and an openness to unconditional love and universal spirituality. A return to balance with the feminine side of consciousness where intuition is the guide will lead us to planetary transformations, the development of free energy systems, and a host of achievements that will lead to sustainability of the planet. We will realize that we are all Earth people and cocreators of our future, and will begin this process by visualizing and engaging in healing activities in every sphere of our being.

Many new paradigm thinkers have given us great hope regarding the huge shifts predicted for 2012. Though I personally believe we cannot escape widespread planetary weather crises that will result in great loss of life, we can diminish the impact by increasing the number of people who are conscious of their roles as cocreators of our future. Other writers have emphasized that the 2012 time period presages great shifts leading to a new phase of galactic evolution and its relationship with the UFO phenomenon (Jose Arguelles);

the global dawning of the wisdom age (Peter Russell); becoming a world-wide family and possibly part of a greater family in the cosmos (Gregg Braden); learning to use our breathing as a spiritual link to our Divine selves (John Major Jenkins); projecting new images into space to bring about healing and develop a coherent idea for an effective transition to the new world (John L. Peterson); huge surges in remote viewing, telepathy, clairvoyance, and interspecies communication leading to universal spirituality (Karl Maret); and a reminder that those who fear Armageddon may create their own private doomsday (Gill Edwards).

Understanding that great shifts are part of humanity's history on this planet can help us transform the fear for the future into hope. That's where I was at the end of August 1968 after spending a summer in New York City meeting backstage to discuss these ideas with Elektra Records recording artists. I had decided to decline the invitation to design album covers for the likes of Hendrix, Joplin, and Buckley (the proffered salary was abysmal, but I also felt urgently that I was wasting my time), and instead accept the commission from the Chaplain's office to paint the mural for Johns Hopkins University. Dr. Chester Wickwire had long been a supporter of my work and vision, defending me through the "American Express" brouhaha, and he wanted to give me complete freedom to express myself with the new mural. The design encompassed humankind's evolution from a hermaphrodite in the lost continents of Lemuria and Atlantis, through the advanced civilizations of ancient India, Egypt, and the Middle East, and continuing on to the rising landmasses in the Atlantic, Pacific, and Indian Oceans. It also included extraterrestrial craft overseeing our planet's evolution from the beginning.

The main wall seen here, which focuses on the United States, is the most relevant to the years around 2012. Measuring 32×9 (288 square feet), it reflects only about 10 percent of the entire mural. The story on this wall begins with the astrological sign Scorpio being monitored by a UFO mothership and three of its disc craft. A key to Scorpio is "desire," and it is used here to symbolize our soul's struggle to make itself known in the physical and desire worlds, which will lead to rebirth and regeneration. This is symbolized by Scorpio's three-tiered image: the scorpion, the serpent, and the eagle reflecting physical, psychic, and spiritual regeneration. The stage is set for America to become the seed for planetary evolution.

At the opposite end of the wall is the winged being Aquarius pouring from its urn the energies of altruism and brotherhood, giving birth to planetary consciousness and harmony. Aquarius is also overseen by a fleet of seven UFOs in a V formation monitoring our planet's evolution toward one people, one planet. The drama that unfolds between these two figures is the struggle from unconsciousness, to consciousness, to superconsciousness, and America is key to this struggle. This is shown along the top of the wall through a series of flags evolving from Great Britain's flag, to America's first flag of 1776, to America's 13-star flag, to the Confederate flag, to the 50-star flag (the last three mostly blocked by the eagle), followed by the flag of the Soviet Union (to show how the two former enemies could work together), and finally a new "nation" flag made up of the 13 red and white stripes with a canton containing the ancient symbol of the hex-alpha, a six-pointed star with a circle and point in the center. This represents a flag of planetary consciousness.

Beneath these banners we see the American eagle is sinking in the flood tides, being weighed down by corrupting forces of the corporate, fascistic, and oligargical powers bent on speedy profits at the cost of American liberties and the planet's very life force. Some of those forces are identified on the body of the sinking eagle, though a black and white reproduction of this detail makes them virtually invisible. We have General Motors standing for the petroleum-based energy systems, Coca-Cola representing the reduction of food to a non-nutritional diet and agribusiness, Chiquita or the United Fruit Company epitomizing the sale of other nations' illegal drugs to fund America's black budget operations, and the dollar sign to symbolize America's 70-trillion-dollar debt leading to our enslavement. In this picture, the American eagle is rent asunder because it has worshipped the material world and ignored the spiritual dimension. It is surrounded by natural cataclysms expedited by its domination of nature for profit. Geological and weather changes are shown with fire and water engulfing the Statue of Liberty and the Golden Gate Bridge (barely discernable in this photo, in front of Lady Liberty). Also engulfed in these radical transformations is the Russian bear in front of the eagle, predicting the dissolution of the Soviet Union. Both the Russian bear and American eagle are confronted by a long green dragon-serpent representing China. As the potential threat to both superpowers, the dragon of China is composed of inverted (hidden destiny) five-pointed-stars, the symbol for

Saturn (karma), and the number 666 (considered numerologically 6 + 6 + 6 = 18 = 1 + 8 = 9, the number of initiation).

Above the dying eagle there rises a transformed eagle in purple with silver and gold vibrations. This rebirth continues onto the ceiling where the transformation is completed in the form of the legendary phoenix that regenerates itself from its own ashes. On the ceiling we also see Poseidon/Neptune holding in his right hand a lost spiritual temple of Atlantis, which has been regained to preserve the spiritual sciences and assist the rebirth of our planet.

As one cycle is completed, a new cycle begins on the spiral of evolution. The outcome of these massive political, economic, geologic, and geographical changes is devastating to individual nations, but will serve to unite the planetary republic and pave the way for a more lasting peace. Human beings will realize we are not just physical beings, and that we all contain an immortal component that can lead us to universal wisdom, the oneness of beings, the oneness of all living things. The Apocalypse means a rebirth of spirit eventuating in planetary beings.

Robert R. Hieronimus, PhD, is a historian, visual artist, author, and radio host. His Johns Hopkins murals, including The Apocalypse *and* The Lord's Prayer, *were documented by Maryland Public Television in a program called "The Artist of Savitria," which received repeated national airplay on PBS beginning in 1971. His weekly program, 21st Century Radio with Dr. Bob Hieronimus, is now celebrating its 20th anniversary on the air broadcasting New Paradigm topics across the United States. He drives the only bio-diesel-fueled Artcar in the state of Maryland, a Mercedes sedan he painted with symbols of the Native Americans' influence on our form of government. He calls his car "The Founding Fathers." More about his most recent book,* United Symbolism of America: Deciphering Hidden Meanings in America's Most Familiar Art, Architecture, and Logos, *published by New Page Books in 2008, can be found at* www.UnitedSymbolismofAmerica.com.

2013

By Nancy Lee

We are at the beginning of the golden age of light. Angels dance on the earth, working side by side with mankind, singing praises to those who reside in the frequency of light. This is the end of the great cycle and brings transformation to Earth as she is ascending out of the density, into the lighter frequencies, taking with her the inhabitants and designers of higher consciousness.

All will seek their level. We find ourselves in the reflective pool of our intentions, reaping the rewards of the seeds we have planted, and recognize ourselves in the eyes of those looking back at us. Cosmic and earthly chaos will disrupt lives, as the earth continues her evolution back into the light. The clearing will continue even as the human body rids itself of waste, so too, the earth. There is greater discrepancy between the lower and the higher frequencies, moving into alignment with the Earth's ascension into unification back into her dedicated place in the universe

There will be great discoveries in the West that will turn the world on its ear. The world voice will rise up and sound its truth from ancient texts long sealed, now revealed. It will change the way the world views religion, government, and history. It will speak to the one mind of God and will dispel the myths that have been perpetrated for enslavement, and will free men's souls. The tablets of the ethereal city will be discovered in the holy city in the Rocky Mountains. There will be a new declaration of spiritual independence, combined with the frequency of the holy cross of the earth. As foretold by Saint Germaine on July 4, 1932, the cities of Chicago and Denver will unite the forces of communication of ancient knowledge with the discovery of the origins of the universe.

The return to a nurturing, compassionate, loving expression of God's world has come. The earth will have gone through painful periods of cleansing and chaos, mass exits through disaster and disease, now seeking balance. We will be at the right place and time for all things manifesting the destiny of each soul's blueprint. It is a time of rebuilding that which has broken down.

"As above so below," or rather, as you resonate, so will you attract—instantaneously. Knowing self has been the directive. The mandate is to forgive all and to love all; to "send light into the heart of darkness, love into the face of fear."

New technologies in medicine, bio-fuels, and transportation will emerge seemingly spontaneously. Huge leaps in technology occur; computers perform higher function than the human brain. The bionic human will be on the playing field, but healing will be more accomplished through self-realization and mastery. The projection of perfection for Self and others will manifest vitality as we claim our creatorship.

In the time preceding 2013, you were asked to sign up for the cause of your life, to make a statement to the world and to your own heart of who you are. To the eternal question "Who am I?" The answer will be clear and the living of one's evolutionary destiny from that place of cosmic design will flow quite naturally. All of these aspects will be telepathically revealed. We will know each other as the spirits in the heavens know one another.

The wars for fuel, water, and the earth's resources will continue until the last vestiges of scarcity and greed have vanished. Structures that are not held together by universal law and truth will crumble from the inside out. Those things no longer serving a purpose will dissolve back into the ethers.

Those who have manipulated through intimidation and fear will find their place back at the lower rungs of consciousness, while innocence and love shall fly freely into the halls of universal creation.

Blessings of eternal love to all beings!

Nancy Lee is a member the Colorado Association of Psychotherapists, a spiritual intuitive clairvoyant with the American Assn. of Psychics; the author of Awakening the Mystic, Adventures in Living From the Heart, *and* Voices of Light, Conversations on the New Spirituality. *She is a spiritual teacher, counselor, and speaker, and is the host and producer of "Lights On! with Nancy Lee" inspirational talk radio since 1997, heard on* www.healthylife.net. *Nancy is the president of S.P.R.E., the Society for Psi Research and Education,* www.spre.org. *Reach Nancy through her Website at* www.nancylee.net.

∞

Sustainability, a 21st-Century Enigma
By Edgar Mitchell, ScD

The population explosion that became noticeable in the 20th century is the result of advances in healthcare, education, affluence, and technological innovation beginning largely in the late 19th century. It is the engine driving the post-modern era into unsustainable exponential growth in each and every measure of human endeavor. World population more than tripled in the century between 1900 and 2000 for the first time in recorded history, from under 2 billion to more than 6.5 billion. Although population is projected to stabilize near 9 billion by mid-21st century, and even perhaps decline, the effect on our planetary ecosystem has become devastating. Climate change with increased greenhouse gases, drought spreading to previously lush areas, glacier melt at the north and south poles, deforestation, and defoliation which diminish Earth's oxygen supply, are established facts of 21st-century existence, though hotly disputed by some as being significantly influenced by human activity.

The scientific and technological genius unleashed in the 20th century has had magnificent benefits, but also a major down side. Discovery of how to harness nuclear energy both for peaceful uses and in warfare has added new threats to contemporary living. Even though electric power generation with nuclear processes offers great benefits when properly implemented with safety provisions, the safe disposal of spent residue from this process is problematic. The deliberate use of nuclear weaponry in warfare is a major threat to civilization as a whole, as any usage will invite retaliation and escalation from adversaries, as violence only breeds more violence and uses of technologies of more massive destructiveness. In other words, all life forms on earth are at risk, unless nuclear warfare is avoided by concerted and well-policed international treaties, and acceptable forms of waste disposal are employed for beneficial uses.

Although cultural myths and belief systems still drive much of the thinking of our global civilization, science in its 21st-century manifestation is moving surprisingly fast to uncover new facets of cosmic reality. Major new telescopes both on Earth and in space have opened new vistas into the cosmos. Not the least of the new discoveries is evidence suggesting habitable planets in many solar systems, an idea that had been largely disparaged, even in science until very late in the 20th century. In addition, since the year 2000, a few military and political leaders in several nations have acknowledged their countries' records of extraterrestrial visitation, although the United States has curiously refused to acknowledge the same. There is no evidence to suggest that there is any threat to Earth civilization if these admissions are validated.

The disaster that destroyed the world of the dinosaurs, presumably a large meteor strike, still exists, and is an ever-present danger. However, it is a danger that observation, vigilance, and foresight coupled with modern technology is able to overcome. There has been discussion of this danger since the onset of spaceflight, but only limited preparation for the eventuality.

The greatest immediate threat to our civilization and way of life is one of our own making. It is the awesome power of modern technologies coupled with consummate greed in amassing wealth and power. Control of the global marketplace and the assets represented is relentlessly being concentrated into fewer and fewer hands. The notion of selfless service to the greater good of society, and to thereby contribute to the well-being and sustainability of civilization as a whole is losing acceptance. The economic middle class, who traditionally represents those who make a culture function, is being squeezed into poverty. The contest for dominance between communism and capitalism, which consumed much of the late 20th century, though won through collapse of the Soviet Union, is subjecting the world to an economy dominated by the greed of the world's most wealthy. With this focus on economic betterment being dominated by money markets and corporate acquisitions worldwide, the consumption of nonrenewable resources is alarming, and damage to the sustainability of global ecology is critical. The global system is imploding from its own excess. Only through enlightened economic management by the world's democracies, and concerted action by those in positions of power, can global civilization be restored to where there is the promise of human rights and sustenance for the burgeoning human population.

In the long run, provided we humans can resolve our immediate problem of learning to live sustainably on this planet, it is likely that our technology will allow us to begin exploration beyond our solar system by the end of the 21st century. As surely as the ancient Phoenicians began exploration of the Mediterranean Sea in their time, and the South Sea Islanders explored the vast Pacific in their dug-out canoes, we began exploring the air and space above us in our time; going beyond our solar system is our destiny. In fact, leaving this planet must be our eventual journey as our sun is now about halfway through its projected 5-billion-year life cycle.

Dr. Edgar D. Mitchell, ScD, is a former U.S. Navy captain and Apollo XIV *astronaut. He was the sixth man to walk on the moon. He is the founder of the Institute of Noetic Sciences, cofounder of the Association of Space Explorers, and a revered speaker and lecturer. Author of two best-selling books,* Psychic Exploration: A Challenge for Science *and* The Way of the Explorer, *Dr. Mitchell has received several honors and awards, including the Presidential Medal of Freedom, the USN Distinguished Service Medal, the NASA Distinguished Service Medal, and the NASA Group Achievement Award (three times). He was a 2005 nominee for the Nobel Peace Prize. He was inducted in to the Astronaut's Hall of Fame in 1995. He lectures widely today on cosmology, human potential, and the future of humanity on planet Earth.*

Bibliography

Abraham, Ralph, Terence McKenna and Rupert Sheldrake. *The Evolutionary Mind: Conversations on Science, Imagination and Spirit.* Rhinebeck, N.Y.: Monkfish Book Publishing Company, 2005.

Braden, Greg, et al. *The Mystery of 2012: Predictions, Prophecies and Possibilities.* Boulder, Colo.: Sounds True, 2007.

Byron, Michael P. *Infinity's Rainbow: The Politics of Energy, Climate and Globalization.* New York: Algora Publishing, 2006.

———. *The Path Through Infinity's Rainbow: Crisis and Renewal in Interesting Times.* Lincoln, Nebr.: iUniverse, 2008.

Calleman, Carl Johan, PhD. *The Mayan Calendar and the Transformation of Consciousness.* Rochester, Vt.: Bear & Company, 2004.

Clippinger, John Henry. *A Crowd of One: The Future of Individual Identity.* New York: BBS Public Affairs, 2007.

Clow, Barbara Hand. *The Mayan Code: Time Acceleration and Awakening the World Mind.* Rochester, Vt.: Bear & Company, 2007.

Dawson, Jonathan. *Ecovillages: New Frontiers for Sustainability.* White River Junction, Vt.: Chelsea Green Publishing, 2006.

Deffeyes, Kenneth S. *Beyond Oil: The View From Hubbert's Peak.* New York: Hill and Wang, 2007

Ferguson, Marilyn. *Aquarius Now: Radical Common Sense and Reclaiming Our Personal Sovereignty.* Boston, Mass.: Red Wheel/Weiser, 2005.

Firestone, Richard, Allen West, and Simon Warwick-Smith. *The Cycle of Cosmic Catastrophes: Flood, Fire and Famine in the History of Civilization.* Rochester, Vt.: Bear & Co., 2006

Frenay, Robert. *Pulse: The Coming Age of Systems and Machines Inspired By Living Things.* New York: FSG, 2006.

Hartmann, Thom. *The Last Hours of Ancient Sunlight: The Fate of the World and What We Can Do Before It's Too Late.* New York: Three Rivers Press, 2004.

Hawkins, David R. *Power Vs. Force: The Hidden Determinants of Human Behavior.* Carlsbad, Calif.: Hay House, 2002.

Jenkins, John Major. *Galactic Alignment: The Transformation of Consciousness According to Mayan, Egyptian, and Vedic Traditions.* Rochester, Vt.: Bear & Company, 2002.

Johnson, Chalmers. *Blowback: The Costs and Consequences of American Empire.* New York: Henry Holt and Co., 2000.

Joseph, Lawrence E. *Apocalypse 2012: A Scientific Investigation Into Civilization's End.* New York: Morgan Road Books, 2007.

Kenyon, J. Douglas, et al. *Forbidden History: Prehistoric Technologies, Extraterrestrial Intervention, and the Suppressed Origins of Civilization.* Rochester, Vt.: Bear & Co., 2005.

————. "Forbidden Religion: Suppressed Heresies of the West." Rochester, Vt.: Bear & Co., 2006.

Kielburger, Craig and Marc Kielburger. *Me To We: Finding Meaning in a Material World.* New York: Fireside Books, 2004.

Kurzweil, Ray. *The Singularity Is Near.* New York: Penguin Group, 2005.

Kynge, James. *China Shakes the World: A Titan's Rise and Troubled Future and the Challenge for America.* New York: Houghton Mifflin Company, 2006.

Malkowski, Edward F. *The Spiritual Technology of Ancient Egypt: Sacred Science and the Mystery of Consciousness*. Rochester, Vt.: Inner Traditions, 2007.

McDonald, Libby. *The Toxic Sandbox: The Truth About Environmental Toxins and Our Children's Health*. New York: Perigree Books, 2007.

McQuaid, John and Mark Schleifstein. *Path of Destruction: The Devastation of New Orleans and the Coming Age of Superstorms*. New York: Little Brown, 2006.

Miller, Alan S. and Satoshi Kanazawa. *Why Beautiful People Have More Daughters*. New York: Perigree Books, 2007.

Penn, Mark J and E. Kinney Zalesne. *Microtrends: The Small Forces Behind Tomorrow's Big Changes*. New York: 12/Hatchett Books, 2007.

Pinchbeck, Daniel. *2012: The Return of Quetzalcoatl*. New York: Jeremy Tarcher, 2007

Scranton, Laird. *The Science of the Dogon: Decoding the African Mystery Tradition*. Rochester, Vt.: Inner Traditions, 2002.

Sitchin, Zecharia. *The End Of Days: Armageddon and Prophecies of the Return*. New York: William Morrow Books, 2007.

Index

About the Author

Marie D. Jones is the author of *Supervolcano: The Catastrophic Event That Changed the Course of Human History*, written with her father, geophysicist Dr. John M. Savino, and of *PSIence: How New Discoveries In Quantum Physics and New Science May Explain the Existence of Paranormal Phenomena*. Marie is also a New Thought/metaphysics minister and spiritual counselor with a background in metaphysical studies. She worked as a field investigator for MUFON (Mutual UFO Network) in Los Angeles and San Diego in the 1980s and 1990s. She currently serves as a consultant for the Arkansas Paranormal and Anomalous Studies Team (ARPAST).

Marie is a widely published author with hundreds of credits. Her book, *Looking For God in All the Wrong Places*, was chosen as the *Best Spiritual/Religious Book of 2003* by the popular book review Website RebeccasReads.com, and the book made the "Top Ten of 2003" list at MyShelf.com. Marie has also coauthored more than three dozen inspirational books for Publications International/New Seasons, including *100 Most Fascinating People in the Bible, Life Changing Prayers,* and *God's Answers to*

Tough Questions, and her essays, articles, and stories have appeared in *Chicken Soup for the Working Woman's Soul, Chicken Soup to Inspire a Woman, If Women Ruled the World, God Allows U-Turns, UFO Magazine,*

The Book of Thoth, Paranormal Magazine, Light Connection Magazine, Alternate Realities, Unity Magazine, Whole Life Times, Science of Mind Magazine, and many others. She is also a popular book reviewer for such Websites as BookIdeas.com and CurledUp.com. She has been interviewed on more than 100 radio talk shows all over the world, and has been featured in dozens of newspapers, print, and online magazines and podcasts.

She lives in San Marcos, California, with her son, Max, and can be reached via her Website at *www.mariedjones.com.*

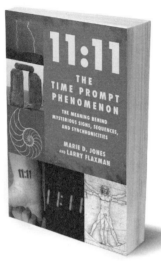